OECD and CCET *Economic Surveys* 1997
Electronic Books

The OECD *Economic Surveys*, both for the Member countries and for countries of Central and Eastern Europe covered by the Organisation's Centre for Co-operation with Economies in Transition, are also published as electronic books – incorporating the text, tables and figures of the printed version. The information will appear on screen in an identical format, including the use of colour in graphs.

The electronic book, which retains the quality and readability of the printed version throughout, will enable readers to take advantage of the new tools that the ACROBAT software (included with the diskette) provides by offering the following benefits:

❏ User-friendly and intuitive interface
❏ Comprehensive index for rapid text retrieval, including a table of contents, as well as a list of numbered tables and figures
❏ Rapid browse and search facilities
❏ Zoom facility for magnifying graphics or for increasing page size for easy readability
❏ Cut and paste capabilities
❏ Printing facility
❏ Reduced volume for easy filing/portability

Working environment: DOS, Windows or Macintosh

Subscription 97: FF 1 800   US$317   £230   DM 550

Complete 1995 series on CD-ROM:
FF 2 000   US$365   £255   DM 600

Complete 1996 series on CD-ROM (to be issued early 1997):
FF 2 000   US$365   £255   DM 600

Please send your order to OECD Publications 2, rue André-Pascal 75775 PARIS CEDEX 16 France or, preferably, to the Centre or bookshop with whom you placed your initial order for this Economic Survey.

OECD
ECONOMIC
SURVEYS

1996-1997

GERMANY

ORGANISATION FOR ECONOMIC CO-OPERATION AND DEVELOPMENT

ORGANISATION FOR ECONOMIC CO-OPERATION AND DEVELOPMENT

Pursuant to Article 1 of the Convention signed in Paris on 14th December 1960, and which came into force on 30th September 1961, the Organisation for Economic Co-operation and Development (OECD) shall promote policies designed:

- to achieve the highest sustainable economic growth and employment and a rising standard of living in Member countries, while maintaining financial stability, and thus to contribute to the development of the world economy;
- to contribute to sound economic expansion in Member as well as non-member countries in the process of economic development; and
- to contribute to the expansion of world trade on a multilateral, non-discriminatory basis in accordance with international obligations.

The original Member countries of the OECD are Austria, Belgium, Canada, Denmark, France, Germany, Greece, Iceland, Ireland, Italy, Luxembourg, the Netherlands, Norway, Portugal, Spain, Sweden, Switzerland, Turkey, the United Kingdom and the United States. The following countries became Members subsequently through accession at the dates indicated hereafter: Japan (28th April 1964), Finland (28th January 1969), Australia (7th June 1971), New Zealand (29th May 1973), Mexico (18th May 1994), the Czech Republic (21st December 1995), Hungary (7th May 1996), Poland (22nd November 1996) and the Republic of Korea (12th December 1996). The Commission of the European Communities takes part in the work of the OECD (Article 13 of the OECD Convention).

Publié également en français.

Table of contents

Boxes

Tables

Figures

BASIC STATISTICS OF GERMANY

THE LAND

Area (thousand sq. km)	357.0	Major cities, June 1994 (thousand inhabitants)	
Agricultural area (thousand sq. km)	195.3	Berlin	3 478
Forests (thousand sq. km)	104.2	Hamburg	1 704
		Munich	1 251
		Cologne	963
		Frankfurt	656
		Essen	620
		Dortmund	602
		Stuttgart	592
		Düsseldorf	573
		Bremen	551

THE PEOPLE

Population (thousands), end 1994	81 539	Labour force (thousands), 1996	38 386
Number of inhabitants per sq. km	228	Employment (thousands), 1996	34 465
Net natural increase in population		*of which:*	
(thousands), 1994	−115	Agriculture, forestry, fishing	965
Net migration (thousands) 1994	329	Industry (including construction)	11 938
		Private services	14 351

PRODUCTION

GDP, 1996 (billions of DM)	3 541	Origin of GDP, 1996 (per cent)	
GDP per head, 1996 (US$)	27 618	Agriculture, forestry, fishing	1.0
Gross fixed investment 1996:		Industry (including construction)	32.3
Per cent of GDP	21.0	Services	66.7
Per head (US$)	6 059		

THE GOVERNMENT

Public consumption, 1996, (per cent of GDP)	19.6	Composition of Parliament:	Seats
General government current revenue, 1996		Social Democratic Party (SPD)	252
(per cent of GDP)	45.2	Christian Democratic Party (CDU)	244
Public debt, end 1996 (ratio to general		Christian Social Union (CSU)	50
government current revenue)	143.4	Greens	49
		Free Democratic Party (FDP)	47
		PSD	30
		Last general election: October 1994	
		Next general election: 1998	

FOREIGN TRADE

Exports of goods and services, 1996		Imports of goods and services, 1996	
(per cent of GDP)	24.3	(per cent of GDP)	23.0
Main exports, 1996		Main imports, 1996	
(per cent of total merchandise exports):		(per cent of total merchandise imports):	
Products of agriculture, forestry		Food	9.9
and fishing	1.1	Raw materials and semi-finished goods	14.3
Basic materials and semi-finished goods	22.4	Finished goods	68.2
Manufactured foods and tobacco	4.3	*of which:*	
Other consumer goods	10.9	Primary products	11.4
Investment goods	56.8	End products	56.8
Other exports	4.5	Other imports	7.7
Total	100.0	Total	100.0

THE CURRENCY

Monetary unit: Deutschemark		Currency units per US$, average	
		of daily figures:	
		Year 1996	1.505
		June 1997	1.726

Note: An international comparison of certain basic statistics is given in an Annex table.

This Survey is based on the Secretariat's study prepared for the annual review of Germany by the Economic and Development Review Committee on 10 June 1997.

•

After revisions in the light of discussions during the review, final approval of the Survey for publication was given by the Committee on 8 July 1997.

•

The previous Survey of Germany was issued in September 1996.

Assessment and recommendations

*Overview of
current policy
issues*

The German economy was last reviewed in July 1996, when there were signs that output growth was about to pick up again following a rather poor economic performance in the preceding eighteen months. This view has been broadly confirmed, as has the expected dependence of the expansion on the strength of the export sector: continued weak labour market developments – the recovery has so far been associated with falling employment – mean that economic growth is not being underpinned by domestic demand. At the same time, the macroeconomic policy environment has been increasingly shaped by the pursuit of the entry requirements for the European Monetary Union, and the first two chapters of this year's *Survey* examine recent trends and short-term prospects for the economy against this fiscal and monetary background. For Germany, as for other prospective members, the longer-run economic benefits of monetary union will depend upon the progress made towards a structurally-sound and economically-adaptive economy. Among the most urgent policy requirements for achieving these attributes, the *Survey* discusses the progress made towards more flexible labour and product markets, the final chapter containing a follow-up on the recommendations made for Germany under the OECD *Jobs Strategy* in the 1996 *Economic Survey*. The causes of high unemployment are complex, but are linked, in part, to the burden of social security charges. Crucial to reducing these is further progress in health reform, both to control costs and to improve efficiency, and this subject is reviewed in the special chapter.

Growth has showed signs of recovery since the second half of 1996

The upturn thus far has been characterised by initial rapid output growth, followed by a protracted slowdown and a weak jobs market from early 1995. GDP grew by 1½ per cent in 1996, the slowest rate of growth since the recession year of 1993. Employment declined and the unemployment rate rose by almost a percentage point, to an annual average of 10.3 per cent. Output expanded more rapidly in the second half and the business climate began to improve. Driving the rebound was stronger export demand from outside western Europe and a marked improvement in German competitiveness, due to on-going productivity increases, a lower exchange rate and moderate wage developments. From the end of 1996 there were also signs from orders data that business investment could be finally starting to pick up after a long period of weakness, and inventory correction appeared to be complete. Manufacturing activity strengthened further in the opening months of 1997, capacity utilisation increasing and export orders being especially strong. Growth was, nevertheless, significantly retarded by weak internal demand and depressed construction activity. Private consumption was adversely affected both by the continuing rise in unemployment, which has held back labour income growth and eroded household confidence, and the fiscal squeeze on real disposable income. The most positive influence on personal spending has been the reduction of the inflation rate to well below 2 per cent.

... but is not sufficiently based on internal demand

From the second quarter onwards overall activity should accelerate, as strong export orders in the early months come through in increased output. Buoyant exports and strengthening business investment are being underpinned by improved competitiveness and profitability, with wage developments projected to remain moderate over the projection period. On balance, GDP is projected to expand by some 2¼ per cent in 1997, accelerating to 2¾ per cent in 1998 so that the output gap will close relatively slowly. Employment is not, however, expected to recover significantly in 1997, so that the labour market will continue to hold back the growth of private consumption. In this respect, growth will remain unbalanced, with an excessive dependence on exports. With consumer confidence already fragile, any weakening in foreign markets could have an important negative impact. As far as other risks are concerned, shifts in expectations about the ability of countries to meet the Maastricht criteria and therefore prospects for a timely start to European Monetary Union could have unpredictable confidence effects, impacting on bond yields and exchange rates. Prospects for appreciably faster growth than expected would be based on a smooth path to monetary union, which is underpinned by continuing sound fiscal and monetary policies and structural reforms, including the implementation of the proposed tax reforms in 1998. A self-sustaining strengthening of the growth process will depend on stronger investment and a recovery of private consumption.

Present monetary conditions should support faster growth

Monetary conditions have eased substantially since the last review. Against the background of low and stable inflation, the Bundesbank lowered the repurchase rate in August 1996, at a time when the Deutschemark was temporarily appreciating and activity was sluggish. There has been no subsequent cut, but in keeping rates stable the Bundesbank has sought to counter market expectations that the end of the interest rate cycle may have been reached. Money growth has been quite rapid, and an overshooting of the monetary target was allowed during 1996. Underpinned by market expectations of persisting low inflation, there has been a marked fall in market-determined rates. In real terms, short-term rates of interest are at a twenty-year low. Long-term rates, although volatile, have come down significantly in relation to the dollar rates, and this has been associated with a substantial depreciation of the Deutschemark against the dollar since mid-1995. This exchange-rate adjustment has been the most important factor contributing to financial conditions which appear favourable to business growth. With forward rates in the money market showing little sign of any expected tightening of policy and inflation well under control, there is currently neither the expectation nor justification for a tightening of stance. A case for further easing would arise if output grew more slowly than projected; indeed, such a response would be built into a strategy based on matching monetary expansion with potential output growth, insofar as money growth fell below target. Although the Bundesbank does not follow an exchange rate target, any substantial shift in the value of the Deutschemark would also affect the assessment of monetary conditions.

... and the case for maintaining a stability-oriented approach remains strong

Most importantly, monetary policy currently faces the challenges of preserving the benefits of a stability-oriented strategy, which has anchored inflation expectations and allowed long-term rates to come down, and achieving a successful transition to monetary union. The most valuable contribution that monetary policy can make to solving the problem of unemployment, which is for the most part structural in nature, is to nurture a wage-setting and investment environment based on stable and realistic expectations. Progress has been made insofar as wage behaviour appears to have become more flexible and forward-looking. But long-term rates may still be seen as discounting the risk of a reversion to past patterns of wage behaviour as the economy recovers. There is also the operational consideration that the framework for evaluating monetary policy questions is changing with the run up to European Monetary Union, making monetary management and appraisal more difficult. Monetary conditions in Germany will increasingly reflect expectations about the prospective monetary stance for the area as a whole. Long-term rates may already be discounting increasing substitutability between currencies and the prospect that interest rates will converge with the approach of EMU. Anchoring market expectations in this environment will be more difficult. By already specifying a monetary target for 1998 the Bundesbank has sent a signal in favour of continuity, and against any destabilising action, which should help safeguard the economy against any volatility or deterioration in inflation expectations which could otherwise emerge in the run up to monetary union.

In the short-term, fiscal policy is focused on meeting Maastricht deficit criterion

Medium-term fiscal objectives are based on a reduction in the budget deficit to 1½ per cent of GDP, while lowering the government spending-to-GDP ratio to pre-unification levels and also reducing the tax ratio. In the short term, the focus has been on the need to meet the Maastricht budget deficit criterion, and fiscal policy has been characterised by a succession of measures in pursuit of this objective. In 1996 intervention was needed to partially offset the operation of automatic stabilisers in order to contain the deficit. But at 3.8 per cent of GDP the budget deficit still exceeded plan. Fiscal policy in 1997 is scheduled to tighten by about ¾ percentage points of GDP. Tax receipts are coming in lower than expected, in part because of high levels of unemployment, which have increased social transfers and reduced contribution revenues. According to OECD projections the general government deficit is likely to be around 3¼ per cent of GDP in 1997 in the absence of new measures. The difference from 3 per cent is well within the range of normal statistical revision so at this deficit level the criterion could be effectively regarded as being met.

However, if growth does not accelerate as projected, a strategy based on meeting the 3 per cent deficit target precisely would introduce the risk of pro-cyclical fiscal action. A key policy question is whether it would be possible, or even desirable, in the case of deteriorating growth and employment prospects and associated further budget slippage, to tighten fiscal policy in the course of the year. If revenue shortfalls were to make further tightening necessary, the authorities would have limited leeway: tightening expenditure controls would have little effect at this stage, since further cuts in investment have already been ruled out and government departments are already required to lower discretionary expenditures significantly as part of the 1997 budget. One alternative would appear to be to raise excise taxes. But the likely negative impact of piecemeal tax increases on confidence, as well as on longer-term economic goals, would have to be weighed against the potential costs of budget slippage. In particular, backing away from declared fiscal objectives could have adverse effects on bond markets and the exchange rate, as market expectations about future medium-term consolidation deteriorate. Any measures taken should be consistent with the general aims of tax and structural reform. These could, in principle, include accelerated privatisation receipts which could have a major impact on the government debt ratio.

... but an equally important challenge is to re-establish progress toward medium term fiscal goals.

In purely economic terms, the fiscal objectives laid down by the Maastricht Treaty for 1997 should serve only as milestones on the way to a sound medium-term fiscal position. The acceptability of the 1997 budget outcome should be judged on the basis of whether the underlying fiscal position is sustainable in 1998 and beyond – not just in terms of the debt and deficit commitments of the Stability and Growth Pact, but also in terms of tax and expenditure goals. On these issues the evidence for Germany is mixed. OECD projections for 1998 show the deficit coming in at under 3 per cent of GDP, so that there has not been a reliance on one-off measures. The debt ratio is above the 60 per cent threshold, and is likely to remain just above this through 1998, but unification has played a role here. However, some of the ways in which the deficit has been contained – such as the rise of social security charges – have run contrary to the attainment of other longer-run fiscal objectives on which future economic performance, and the credibility of fiscal policy, depend. Reconciling the objectives of fiscal policy has proved particularly difficult with respect to the promised cut in the Solidarity tax surcharge and the abolition of the business capital tax, both of which have been deferred until 1998. In formulating the budget for 1998 the authorities will need to re-establish the medium term consolidation path which shares expenditure cuts between lower deficits and tax reductions. In particular, the government needs to proceed with the long-promised reduction of the Solidarity tax surcharge, while a consensus needs to be reached with the Bundesrat on the abolition of the business capital tax.

Tax reform is a priority for higher growth and employment

Particularly difficult decisions need to be taken about reform measures in the area of taxation, which will require the development of political consensus. Last year's *Economic Survey* noted that there was a pressing need to simplify personal taxes and overhaul the company tax system. Among the problems noted were high marginal income tax rates, which may discourage work and entrepreneurial activity, and a narrow tax base due to extensive tax expenditures. The government has now put forward the elements of a comprehensive tax reform which would result in lower income tax rates at both ends of the income scale and in a cutting-back of special tax allowances both for households and enterprises. In total, including a reduction in the Solidarity surcharge, tax cuts could amount to around DM 87 billion, to be financed by reductions in tax expenditures and an increase in indirect taxes, leaving a net reduction of the tax burden of DM 20 to 30 billion (0.5 to 0.8 per cent of GDP), mainly accruing to households. The programme – in combination with already accomplished changes in wealth and inheritance taxes – would represent an important step forward. But a political consensus needs to be established, since agreement must be reached with the Länder on proposals affecting them financially. As with all tax reforms, the effects on income distribution need to be taken into account, packages based on improving incentives generally involving a reduction in tax progression; but in this case both the inequalities caused by long-term unemployment and the possibilities of life-time mobility through the income scale should be considered. With respect to timing, the tax reform is due to be implemented in 1999, but proposals to bring forward the introduction of revenue-neutral features relating to company taxation into 1998 are constructive.

The pension system needs to adjust to demographic changes

Further cuts in public spending are needed if the medium-term aim of lowering expenditures to the pre-unification level of 46 per cent of GDP by the year 2000 are to be achieved. As stressed in previous *Economic Surveys,* this will require determined policy action over a wide range of entitlement programmes, including public pensions, health and labour-market related spending. The government has now tabled the draft legislation for pension reform. This does not differ greatly from the recommendations of the government's expert panel, which proposed maintaining the present pay-as-you-go system linked to the development of net wages, but rejected suggestions to move to a

8

system of funding, either partial or full. Pressures arising from demographic change are to be dealt with by amending the indexation formulae, such that the average replacement rate would decline from 70 per cent at present to around 64 per cent in 2030. The proposed reform would allow contribution rates to decline by about a 1½ percentage points from 2000 to 2010. However, budget subsidies would continue at a high level and contributions are projected to rise steeply from the second decade onwards. In view of the need to make decisions now for the long term, the option to develop additional private provisions needs to be looked at more closely, as does a gradual increase in the funding component.

Although a start has been made in health reform, cost-effectiveness needs to improve

As in most OECD countries, health expenditures have shown a long term underlying tendency to increase in relation to GDP and, since Germany depends on compulsory wage-based contributions for finance, this has put pressure on non-wage labour costs. Health expenditures in relation to GDP surged in the 1990s with the incorporation of the new Länder into the health system, and in the future population ageing and technological progress should continue to exert pressure on costs. Health reforms introduced since the early 1990s have aimed to stabilise contribution rates, while preserving universal access and a high quality of health service. Contribution rates initially declined but have since increased, partly because of the weak growth of the contribution base. Most indicators of health outcomes are close to the OECD average, even though health expenditures are relatively high, pointing to a potential for improving efficiency. This judgement is supported by detailed studies of hospitals, doctors and prescription practices which point to considerable room for cutting costs while preserving high-quality health care. Inefficient resource use can be traced to the pattern of incentives implicit in the institutional structure. Health care financing (via the health funds) has been passive, leading to significant supply-induced demand for medical services. There has been little co-ordination between the hospital and ambulatory sectors to ensure that health services are integrated in either a medically or economically efficient manner; or between investment decisions (in the hands of the Länder) and current spending. And remuneration provisions have often, perversely, given incentive to over-provision. Budget ceilings have been introduced and can be effective in the short run, but if prolonged they exacerbate allocative inefficiencies by preventing adaptation to new priorities. There is thus the need for a set of incentives which encourages health suppliers to reduce costs in a sustainable manner; for a system which strengthens the integration of the health system between the ambulatory and stationary sectors; for decision-making about investment to be related to responsibilities for current financing; and for households to be given incentives to use health care services economically. To meet these objectives will require further changes in the way health funds operate and in the institutional structure of the health system more generally. From this perspective, reform measures which have come into effect in 1997 are ambitious. Consumers have been given greater rights to move between health funds, and financial disciplines on the latter have been strengthened. Moreover, health care institutions have started to show some flexibility by experimenting with new ways of delivering cost-effective health care. However, the ability of the health funds to compete on the basis of cost efficiency in providing health care remains restricted and they still have limited possibilities for dealing with health suppliers directly.

Greater competition between health funds should lower costs...

The logic of the current reform process, and of international experience, suggests that the health system should move away from the present system of passive financing, towards active purchasers of health care which would be concerned with improving the efficiency of health suppliers – and indeed this is already taking place to a small extent. In principle this could be achieved via one universal health fund or through a system comprising independent and competing health funds. The authorities have opted for the latter course and the decision not to specify a minimum health care package – something which is exceedingly difficult to do in an economically efficient and medically justified manner – clears the way for competition between funds by removing the concern that universal access to high-quality health services would suffer. However, the development of a solidarity-financed system of competing statutory health funds is likely to raise competition issues with the risk-based system of private health insurance which is available to persons with income above a threshold level. Steps might have to be taken to level the playing field between the two systems, for instance, by financing a greater proportion of social benefits from general taxation. This would also lower the economic costs associated with a system financed on the basis of wage-based charges.

... but further initiatives are required to increase the scope for new contractual relations

The ultimate objective of competition between the health funds is to lower the costs of health care. To this end, the contractual possibilities for dealing with health suppliers will need to be widened, as the current institutional setting of health suppliers fits poorly with the aim of more cost-effective provision of health services. A provision in the current law permits experimentation with new institutional forms and the development of some new contractual relations which is starting to occur. But the scope for innovation is likely to be too restrictive to form a basis for policy since it requires the agreement of those institutions whose future role could be questioned. Although greater integration in the supply of health services is likely to occur further policy measures will be required. To support recent improvements in the economic incentives facing hospitals, they will need to be placed on a more business like footing by their owners – predominantly state and local government – and the provision of investment funding improved; the barriers, legal and otherwise, separating ambulatory and stationary care will need to be further reduced. Finally, given the close medical complementarity between normal health care on the one hand, and rehabilitation and nursing care on the other, consideration will have to be given about how the two separately-financed systems could be more closely related so as to reduce total costs and improve the package of health supply for patients.

Persistently high unemployment calls for continued emphasis on labour market reform

Unemployment has reached record levels, while employment has fallen. Service sector employment has been growing for some time, but not enough to compensate for the fact that manufacturing employment has been declining rapidly. At the same time, there has been a tendency towards higher-qualified employment. These tendencies are expected to continue, so that the challenge for economic policy will be to facilitate both the restructuring of employment and the re-absorption of the unemployed. To this end the government has introduced an impressive range of legislation affecting labour-cost, work-time and employment flexibility, which goes broadly in the direction of the recommendations of the OECD *Jobs Study*. However, some of the measures, such as the reduction of legally-required sick pay, represent changes in the framework for bargaining by the social partners. Implementing the programme has not been easy, and generous "grandfathering" provisions mean that it will take some time for the effects of several of the policy changes to become apparent (*e.g.* the increase in the early retirement age, loosened dismissal protection). With respect to wage costs in general, the improvement in aggregate flexibility seen in 1996 and 1997 still needs to be reinforced by greater exploitation of existing possibilities for plant-level bargaining. A higher degree of flexibility would require that opening clauses could be exercised by agreement at the company level without the need to refer back to the tariff partners. To this end the authorities need to maintain their support for more flexible wage bargains.

... as well as in product markets   As far as product-market competition is concerned, the government's resolve in the difficult area of subsidies has been weakened by the agreement to continue coalmining subsidies at high, though declining, levels for some years. By contrast, the benefits of reduced state intervention are already becoming evident with respect to the partial liberalisation of shop hours, which appears to have had a beneficial effect on employment. Remaining regulations are nevertheless restrictive in comparison with other OECD countries and should be liberalised further, giving market forces more scope to determine the actual shop opening hours. In general, apart from improving the tax system, the principal requirement for encouraging an entrepreneurial climate remains that of cutting excessive regulation, which needs to be pursued in both goods and financial markets. Proposals by the government to open financial markets both with respect to the provision of greater risk capital and more transparent corporate governance procedures are welcome in this respect. Important progress has been made in the liberalisation of air transport and the telecommunications sectors. But it is important that the parliamentary decision-making process on the draft energy law should not allow locally-owned utilities to continue monopolisation of the energy supply. Communities have the powers to force

local utilities to become more competitive, and need to utilise them. The deregulation of the electricity sector should not be frustrated by protection of local commercial interests. More generally, further efforts need to be made to open up the provision of public services at the local government level. There has been little progress in this area thus far, market access remaining restricted by regulatory barriers and discriminating tax provisions, while effective privatisation has been limited. Progress is required in these areas but will need broad political compromise.

... while in the new Länder subsidies remain high and need to be curtailed

In the new Länder, draft legislation has been put forward restructuring the support programme, by concentrating support on industry and simplifying the system in favour of investment allowances. The programme maintains high support levels for six years, declining from 2002 on. The need is to ensure both that subsidisation does not preserve, or create, enterprises which would not be able to survive in a market environment, and that the labour market will adapt. The original approach, which sought to compensate for deficient legal and physical infrastructure, has been highly successful in achieving its original objective of increasing investment since reunification, but overall unit labour costs are still well above the western German level and the gap between the east and west has declined only gradually, preventing the emergence of self-sustaining growth. While overall productivity in eastern Germany has increased and there are significant differences among sectors, it has improved to only just above a half of that in the west. Enterprises consider cost competitiveness narrowly defined as their greatest problem, rather than more general weaknesses, such as inadequate infrastructure. This is followed by concern about increasing competitive pressure and the financial conditions of the enterprises. In these circumstances, further subsidisation should be conditioned on an articulated strategy to achieve real competitiveness and prevent the development of a dependency culture. For this the number of programmes needs to be rationalised and curtailed and bureaucratic co-ordination improved.

Summing up   The challenges facing Germany are particularly complex, structural problems in the social security system, taxation and the labour market coinciding with a still-slow economic recovery and the run up to European Monetary Union. The Maastricht budget requirements have provided a valuable focus for framing longer-term fiscal goals, but the precedence ascribed to achieving the Treaty's short-term objectives has raised pressures for short-term expedients which sometimes run contrary to longer-run needs, and which need to be resisted. Considerable headway has been made towards structural reform. However, to achieve durable gains in the reduction of unemployment will require greater progress than has been achieved to date in the areas of labour and product market reform. The process of reform has been made more difficult by the fact that effective consensus-based decisions have proved elusive. The policy debate has remained focused on static income-distribution issues, rather than on the need for a dynamic response to a changing global and European economy and on the overwhelming requirement to create the conditions for employment growth. Considerable pressures have arisen to reverse appropriate policy positions, which should be resisted. The German economy has, in several respects, shown remarkable powers of resilience: companies are in the midst of a major restructuring to maintain competitiveness and this has been bolstered by realistic wage setting, which indicates that the labour market may be gradually adjusting to new conditions. So far restructuring has concentrated on reducing manpower, but the combination of improved competitiveness and favourable monetary conditions should provide the basis for both output and employment to grow moderately this year and next. It nevertheless remains for policy to create an institutional framework where the full benefits of European and global integration can be realised and unemployment durably and markedly lowered. Major policy decisions will need to be taken in the current and coming year, particularly with respect to the tax and social security systems, and these could set the stage for a return to a more optimistic view of the future.

I. Recent trends and prospects

The expansion in perspective

The present upturn dates from the second quarter of 1993, but has yet to become self-sustaining. Rapid growth during 1994 was followed by a continuous slowing of the economy during 1995 and early 1996 as, contrary to previous recoveries, investment failed to pick up and exports slowed. From mid 1996, activity strengthened again, but incipient weakness in consumption and construction has underlined its dependence on the external sector, on which business sentiment seems closely to depend. With export markets strengthening and the real exchange rate having depreciated substantially, the prospects are for moderate growth to continue into 1997 and 1998. Inflation remains low, at under 2 per cent for consumer prices. However, high unemployment and fiscal consolidation are likely to continue to weigh heavily on household confidence, so that a broadening of demand to include a strengthening of consumption is by no means assured.

Signs of resumed growth

GDP grew by 1.4 per cent in 1996, the slowest rate since the recession year of 1993 (Figure 1). The deceleration affected the new Länder in particular, where GDP growth fell from 5.3 per cent in 1995 to 2 per cent in 1996. However, in the course of the year, the downward trend in business expectations reversed, with the business climate improving since mid-1996 (Figure 2). GDP expanded by 3.1 per cent (seasonally-adjusted annualised rates) in the second half (Table 1). A further pause occurred during the last quarter of 1996, when public and private consumption declined and construction activity fell sharply.

Strengthening activity in the second half of 1996 was the outcome of two conflicting tendencies. Exports surged by 12 per cent (seasonally-adjusted annu-

17

Figure 1. **MACROECONOMIC PERFORMANCE**[1]

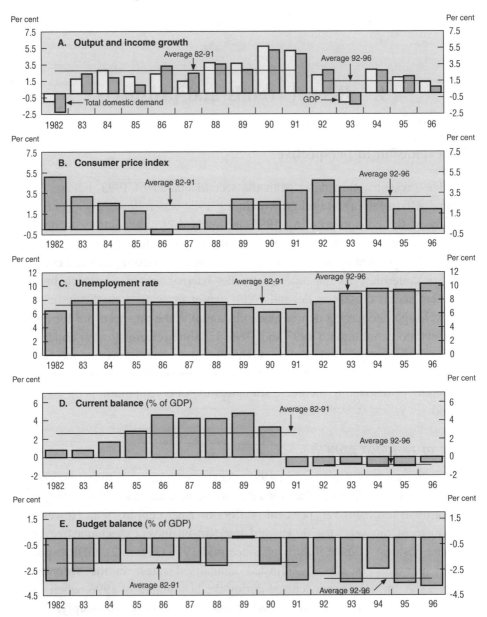

1. Western Germany up to 1991.
Source: OECD.

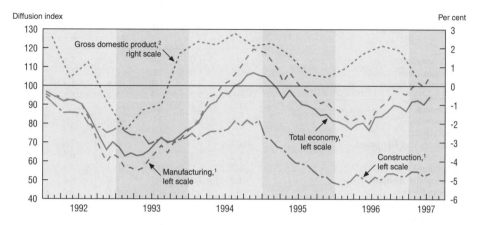

Figure 2. **THE BUSINESS CLIMATE**
In western Germany

1. Weighted average of present and future (6 months ahead) business situation. A level of 100 corresponds to "normality".
2. In 1991 prices. Percentage change over 4 quarters.
Source: IFO; Deutsche Bundesbank.

alised rates) and with imports temporarily lagging, net exports made a significant contribution to growth (Table 1). At the same time, investment expanded by some 8.6 per cent; although a great deal of this apparent strength was due to a recovery of construction from a very weak first half,[1] investment in plant and machinery also picked up strongly. Consumption, on the other hand, weakened significantly, with private consumption growing by only 0.6 per cent. Government consumption also weakened, reflecting ongoing measures to control expenditures, as well as a deceleration in the rate of growth of health expenditures.

Following strong growth in the third quarter, GDP stagnated in the fourth quarter largely due to a marked decline in both private and public consumption, while construction expenditures fell by about 5 per cent (s.a.a.r.). The weakness in construction was not due to adverse weather conditions to any great extent, but to an ongoing contraction in the industry, in part caused by a fall in public sector investment. This decline has affected the new Länder in particular. Indeed, weakness is likely to intensify because the termination of special tax allowances

19

Table 1. **Demand and output**

Percentage change from previous period, 1991 prices

	1993	1994	1995	1996	1996[1]	
					I	II
Private consumption	0.3	1.0	1.8	1.3	1.8	0.6
Government consumption	–0.0	1.3	2.0	2.4	2.2	1.7
Total fixed investment	–5.6	4.2	1.5	–0.8	–4.4	8.6
Construction	0.9	7.7	1.2	–2.7	–8.8	11.5
Business	–1.8	2.6	1.2	–4.5	–9.5	6.5
Residential	3.8	12.4	3.0	–0.3	–3.0	7.6
Government	–2.1	4.0	–4.4	–6.8	–10.8	6.0
Machinery and equipment	–14.1	–1.2	2.0	2.4	2.9	4.4
Final domestic demand	–1.2	1.8	1.8	1.1	0.5	2.6
Stockbuilding[2]	–0.2	1.0	0.3	–0.3	0.1	–1.2
Total domestic demand	**–1.3**	**2.8**	**2.1**	**0.8**	**0.6**	**1.3**
Net exports[2]	0.2	0.1	–0.1	0.6	0.4	1.7
Exports of goods and services	–4.9	8.0	5.9	4.9	1.6	12.0
Imports of goods and services	–5.7	7.6	6.4	2.6	0.2	5.1
GDP at market prices	**–1.1**	**2.9**	**1.9**	**1.4**	**1.0**	**3.1**
Memorandum items:						
Total employment	–1.7	–0.7	–0.3	–1.2	–1.5	–1.1
Household savings rate	12.2	11.7	11.6	11.6	11.9	11.3
Relative ULC in manufacturing	6.7	–0.2	5.2	–12.5	–18.2	–12.5
Export market growth in manufacturing	1.6	10.2	10.7	6.1	6.2	6.1

1. Annualised rate on previous semester, deseasonalised.
2. Contributions to changes in GDP (as a percentage of real GDP in the previous period).
Source: Statistisches Bundesamt; OECD.

for new apartments in the eastern Länder, as of January 1997, temporarily boosted construction activity in 1996 as many projects were moved forward. Manufacturing output also slowed, as did incoming orders, giving rise to questions at the time as to whether the economy was in fact entering a more marked slowdown rather than simply experiencing a pause. Services (excluding trade and transport) continued to grow at the brisk pace which has characterised this sector since 1992.

... which have continued into 1997

GDP is estimated to have grown by 2 per cent (s.a.a.r.) in the first half of 1997, underpinned by a strong external sector and in the second quarter by temporarily strong construction activity as the sector recovered from poor weather conditions at the start of the year. GDP grew by 1.8 per cent in the first quarter, driven by an 8.8 per cent increase of exports. Investment in plant and machinery also expanded and, with stocks no longer judged excessive, inventory accumulation picked up. Forward indicators have pointed to continued growth during the second quarter, both foreign and domestic orders expanding. The IFO indicator of business expectations continued to rise throughout the first half of the year, and export expectations reached their highest ever level. On the other hand, increased social contributions effective from the beginning of 1997 are further reducing household disposable income, which is already weak on account of falling employment. As a result, private consumption stagnated in the first quarter and is estimated to have remained sluggish in the second quarter. The seasonally-adjusted unemployment rate stood at 11.2 per cent in the first quarter of 1997, in comparison with 10.1 per cent a year earlier. The increase was particularly pronounced in the new Länder where the first quarter unemployment rate was 17.2 per cent, compared with 15.8 per cent one year earlier. Contrary to expecta-tions, the seasonally-adjusted rate of unemployment continued to rise up to May.

Consumer prices increased by some 1.5 per cent in 1996 (Figure 1) but accelerated somewhat at the end of 1996 and into 1997 as import prices rose due to the depreciation of the currency and higher energy prices. By the end of the first quarter they had returned to about the same slow rate of increase suggesting that, under conditions of weak demand, the pass-through of higher import prices will be limited. Producer prices also benefited from renewed declines in energy prices.

Improving international competitiveness

Overall export strength

The marked improvement in exports has been induced by stronger demand in several of Germany's main trading partners and underpinned by an improve-ment in the international competitiveness of German enterprises, which has led to a slower rate of loss in export market share. Strong export growth to the United States was supported by a marked depreciation of the DM with respect to the dollar. Exports to central and eastern European countries, which grew at double-digit rates in 1994 and 1995, accelerated, and the growth rate of exports to Japan more than doubled. Macroeconomic conditions in the EU, which accounts for some three-fifths of German exports, were less favourable, so that export growth to this market remained weak. Export growth to the dynamic Asian economies also slowed, in line with balance of payments adjustment in the region (Table 2). As in 1995, German exports benefited from the fact that foreign demand was largely investment driven. Exports of capital goods grew by some 4.5 per cent, mainly on account of mechanical and engineering products and road vehicles. Exports of consumer goods nevertheless also picked up in the second half of 1996 (Table 3).

The real effective exchange rate, as measured by relative export prices of manufactures, has depreciated by some 3½ per cent since 1995 and broader measures based on goods prices indicate a similar improvement (Figure 3). The

Table 2. **Trade by region**

Percentage change from previous year

	1992	1993	1994	1995	1996	Share 1996 (per cent)
Exports to [1]						
EU	1.1	−13.4	8.9	8.8	2.8	57.1
EFTA	−4.1	−5.7	10.4	7.3	−2.7	5.8
Central and Eastern Europe			12.7	14.6	17.3	8.9
North America [2]	0.4	8.1	15.5	0.3	9.6	8.2
Japan	−10.9	7.3	13.6	5.2	12.5	2.7
Asia [3]	4.3	15.4	23.2	13.0	5.3	5.6
Central and South America	6.3	6.5	11.2	10.9	2.3	2.4
Other	8.6	10.8	1.7	2.0	5.4	9.1
Total	0.8	−5.8	9.9	7.9	4.6	100.0
Imports from [1]						
EU	−0.7	−16.5	8.1	9.2	2.6	56.1
EFTA	2.2	−3.5	11.1	6.2	5.3	6.1
Central and Eastern Europe			22.7	17.3	6.6	9.0
North America [2]	−0.9	−4.9	10.6	3.3	6.5	7.9
Japan	−4.1	−10.3	0.1	3.7	−3.7	5.0
Asia [3]	−6.0	4.3	8.1	8.0	−1.4	5.2
Central and South America	−7.2	−14.8	14.7	4.5	−6.7	2.0
Other	−0.6	2.6	7.9	−6.5	3.6	15.9
Total	−1.0	−10.3	8.9	6.6	3.2	100.0

1.   F.o.b., including adjustment.
2.   United States and Canada.
3.   Dynamic Asian economies.
Source: Deutsche Bundesbank, *Zahlungsbilanzstatistik.*

Table 3. **Trade by commodity**

Percentage change from corresponding period in previous year

	Exports					Imports				
	1995		1996		Share of total in 1996, per cent	1995		1996		Share of total in 1996, per cent
	I	II	I	II		I	II	I	II	
Energy[1]	-14.1	-5.6	0.0	68.0	1.3	-3.5	-7.7	15.2	42.5	7.8
Basic and producer goods	13.6	4.8	-4.1	1.2	22.0	19.1	5.0	-9.4	-5.1	20.8
of which: Chemical products	10.7	1.6	-1.3	5.1	12.9	14.1	6.0	-3.9	-1.3	9.0
Capital goods	9.0	7.2	2.9	6.0	55.9	6.4	5.9	4.9	0.7	39.4
of which:										
Mechanical engineering products	7.9	12.1	8.8	4.4	15.4	8.2	7.4	4.8	-1.7	5.7
Road vehicles	12.4	1.5	1.4	13.2	17.3	13.7	9.7	8.3	9.8	10.8
Electrical engineering products	9.9	10.7	4.7	2.3	12.9	8.2	7.4	3.4	-4.5	11.3
Consumer goods	4.1	3.5	-1.8	3.3	10.8	-1.9	-0.1	-0.5	0.1	15.3
Food and drink[2]	-0.3	5.7	2.2	3.5	5.3	5.5	0.2	-1.3	-0.7	10.4

1. Computation by the Deutsche Bundesbank, based on the foreign trade statistics of the Federal Statistical Office.
2. Food and tobacco, including agricultural products.
Source: Deutsche Bundesbank.

Figure 3. **MEASURES OF THE REAL EFFECTIVE EXCHANGE RATE**

1975 = 100[1]

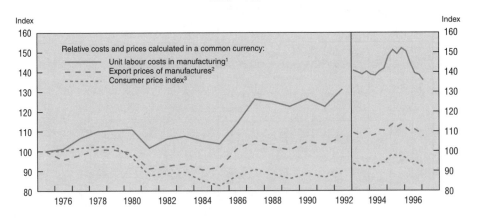

1. Until 1992 annual averages; from 1993 quarterly averages. Data for 1997 are OECD estimates.
2. Weighted real external value of the DM against currencies of 24 industrial countries (OECD).
3. Weighted real external value of the DM against currencies of 18 industrial countries (Bundesbank).
Source: Deutsche Bundesbank; OECD.

nominal effective exchange rate depreciated between January 1996 and April 1997 by 5.6 per cent, the depreciation accelerating at the end of 1996 and in the opening months of 1997. The process was even more pronounced with respect to the dollar, the DM depreciating by 14.6 per cent over the same period (Figure 4).

The improvement in international competitiveness is even greater in terms of relative unit labour costs in manufacturing, which declined by some 10 per cent between the first quarters of 1996 and 1997. This has been driven by a substantial increase in labour productivity in industry of 8½ per cent between January 1996 and February 1997, and by wage settlements, which were much more moderate in 1996 than in the year before. In western Germany, tariff wages (monthly basis) increased by 1.9 per cent, and in eastern Germany, by 4.8 per cent, after 3.7 per cent and 7.7 per cent, respectively, in 1995. In addition, in return for unchanged sick-pay entitlements, negotiations agreed to some cuts in bonuses. Increases in social insurance contributions at the start of 1997 have only partially offset the effects of this wage moderation. The improvement in competitiveness has been

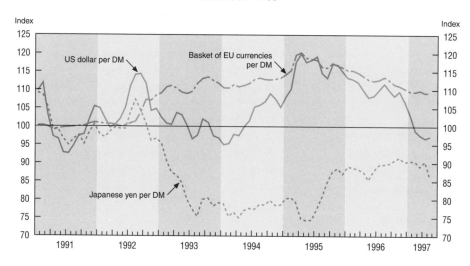

Figure 4. **DEUTSCHEMARK EXCHANGE RATE AGAINST SELECTED CURRENCIES**
Index 1991 = 100

Source: Deutsche Bundesbank.

associated with substantial restructuring at the enterprise level, marked by a pronounced employment shakeout in manufacturing.

The balance of merchandise trade improved throughout 1996, and for the year as a whole the surplus on a f.o.b. basis increased to DM 110.6 billion (3.1 per cent of GDP) (Table 4). The underlying position is probably even more robust, since the German balance of trade normally deteriorates for several quarters following an exchange rate depreciation.[2] In addition to rapidly rising exports, the balance of trade benefited from a low level of imports. Import growth was sluggish for most of 1996, before surging in the fourth quarter. The pick-up was not matched by a proportionate increase in domestic demand, so that it was probably related to the provision of intermediate products for the export sector and to some restocking of inventories: according to the IFO survey, the level of inventories fell to more normal levels during the course of the year. The current account also improved, though not to the same extent, the deficit declining from DM 34 billion in 1995 to DM 21 billion. The smaller improvement is attributable to both a widening deficit in the balance of services, mainly due to outward

Table 4. **The current account of the balance of payments**

DM billion

	1991	1992	1993	1994	1995	1996
Goods	32.4	44.4	69.1	83.8	95.0	110.6
Exports (f.o.b.)[1]	667.1	671.0	632.3	696.0	749.5	783.1
Imports (f.o.b.)[1]	634.7	626.7	563.3	612.2	654.5	672.5
Services	−35.2	−47.3	−54.4	−65.2	−66.4	−68.1
of which: Tourism	−34.4	−39.5	−42.8	−49.2	−49.0	−50.1
Factor income	34.3	26.8	20.4	10.0	−3.7	−8.5
of which: Investment income	32.2	26.3	21.1	11.1	−1.0	−5.8
Transfers	−61.4	−54.2	−58.5	−62.8	−58.7	−54.8
of which:						
Net contribution to the EU	−21.9	−25.3	−27.3	−31.7	−30.0	−27.5
Other public transfers	−26.8	−13.9	−15.5	−14.7	−12.1	−10.2
Current account	−29.9	−30.2	−23.4	−34.2	−33.8	−20.9
(Per cent of GDP)	−1.0	−1.0	−0.7	−1.0	−1.0	−0.6

1. Special trade, according to the foreign trade statistics, including supplementary imports excluding freight and maritime transport insurance costs, which are included under Services.
Source: Deutsche Bundesbank, *Zahlungsbilanzstatistik.*

tourism, and a larger deficit in the balance for property income, due to a rapid growth of payments abroad (Table 4). Increased debt service costs are to some extent related to borrowing abroad in connection with unification, but there are grounds for supposing that the deficit is over-stated due to statistical difficulties.

Weakness in the new Länder

Competitiveness problems in the new Länder are reflected not only in a low export base – exports account for only 12 per cent of GDP compared with 31 per cent in western Germany – but also in the difficulty of meeting domestic demand from local production. Although in some sectors the situation has improved during the course of 1996 – and exports have started to grow rapidly in some cases – overall, competitiveness remains unsatisfactory. A comparison of unit labour costs between the new and the old Länder can serve as a rough indicator of competitiveness. Although in the first two years following reunification unit labour costs in the new Länder improved substantially in relation to those in western Germany, over the last four years they have remained about 30 per cent greater than in the west.[3] The situation varies considerably across sectors.

Figure 5. **WAGES, PRODUCTIVITY AND UNIT LABOUR COSTS IN EASTERN GERMANY**
Western Germany = 100

──────── Percentage by which unit labour costs in the new Länder exceed those in the old Länder
(nominal).
─ ─ ─ ─ Compensation per employee in the new Länder as a percentage of compensation per employee in the old Länder
(nominal).
─ ─ ─ ─ ─ ─ Productivity per employee in the new Länder as a percentage of productivity per employee in the old Länder
(nominal).

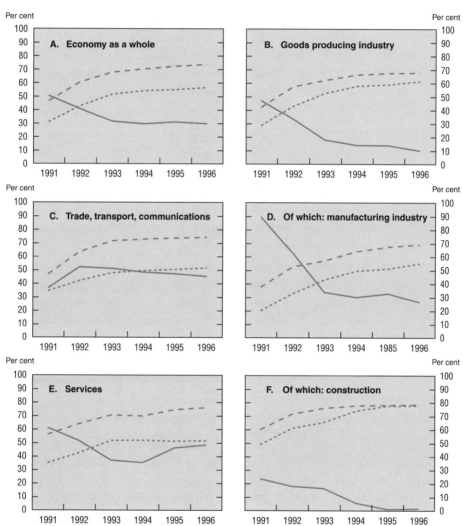

Source: Statistisches Bundesamt; OECD.

27

Figure 6. **SERIOUS PROBLEMS FACED BY EASTERN GERMAN INDUSTRIAL ENTERPRISES**[1]
In autumn 1996

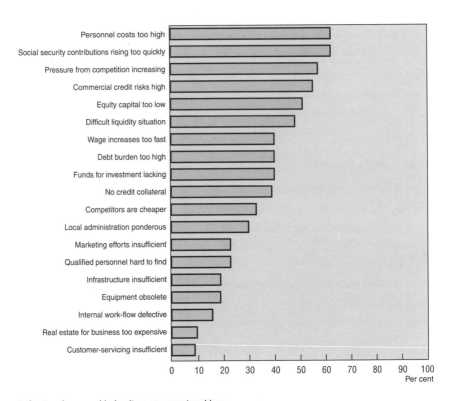

1. Per cent of enterprises considering item as a great problem.
Source : Gesamtwirtschaftliche und unternehmerische Anpassungsfortschritte in Ostdeutschland, Fünfzehnter Bericht, Institut für Wirtschaftsforschung, Halle, Forschungsreihe, 2/1997.

Measured in current prices, in manufacturing, which is most exposed to international competition, unit labour costs relative to those in western Germany declined from 189 per cent in 1991 to 126 per cent in 1996. Between 1995 and 1996, the decline was 6 percentage points. This decline was induced by a large reduction in employment. A significant improvement also occurred in construction, where labour costs are now roughly equal to those in western Germany, but the improvement has been less pronounced in the service sector (Figure 5).

Enterprises in eastern Germany consider cost competitiveness narrowly-defined as their greatest problem, rather than more general weaknesses, such as inadequate infrastructure. The two most severe problems mentioned in business surveys are that costs for personnel are too high, and social security contributions are rising too quickly. This is followed by concern about increasing competitive pressure and the financial conditions of the enterprises (Figure 6). Although deficiencies remain, infrastructure and legal conditions have continued to improve at a rapid pace. A more detailed analysis of companies' complaints about public administration reveals that delays in approval procedures are considered a primary reason of concern, although approval procedures are more flexible in eastern Germany than in the west. Concern about over-bureaucratic approval procedures also applies to western Germany, and has recently led to a reform of approval laws.

A weak pick-up in investment

Although investment in plant and machinery started to pick-up during the course of 1996, business investment has, in general, not supported activity to the same extent as in the past upturns. Figure 7 compares the current recovery with the two preceding cycles, the trough in real GDP serving as the reference point. In comparison with the past, both construction activity and public investment have been relatively supportive until recently, but this has been more than offset by comparatively weak investment in plant and machinery. Investment in 1996 continued to be primarily motivated by the desire to rationalise production in order to reduce production costs. According to surveys conducted by the German Chamber of Commerce, the share of west German enterprises stating a lowering of production costs as the main motive for investment peaked at 43 per cent during the recession in 1993 and has continuously declined since. For 1997 the progress made by companies in this respect is reflected in the fact that cost-reduction has been overtaken by capital replacement as the expressed primary motive for investment. Capacity-widening, however, continues to be far less important and the slow recovery represents an important impediment to raising potential growth. The pattern of responses is similar for enterprises in eastern Germany (Figure 8).

Figure 7. **RECOVERY PERIODS COMPARED**

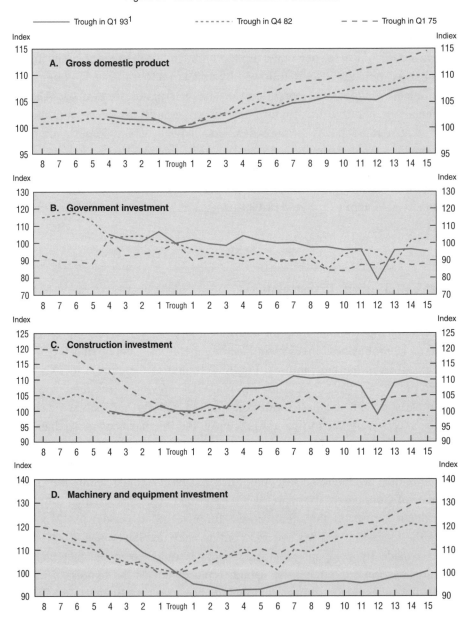

——— Trough in Q1 93[1]   - - - - - - - Trough in Q4 82   — — — Trough in Q1 75

A. Gross domestic product

B. Government investment

C. Construction investment

D. Machinery and equipment investment

1. Unified Germany.
Source: OECD.

30

Figure 8. **MAIN MOTIVES OF ENTERPRISES FOR DOMESTIC INVESTMENT**
Per cent

A. **Enterprises in western Germany**

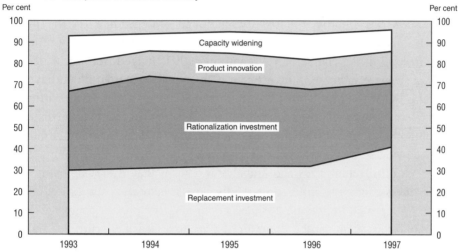

B. **Enterprises in eastern Germany**

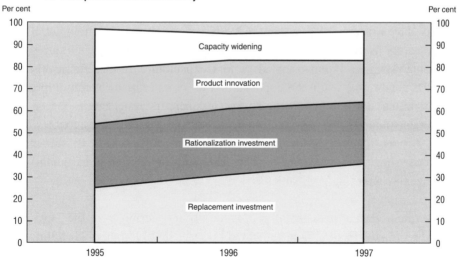

1.   Motive for investment in the reference year according to surveys conducted in autumn of previous year.
Source: Deutscher Industrie und Handelstag.

Low levels of business investment activity have been linked in past *Surveys* to low profitability. However, declining unit labour costs, the real depreciation of the DM, and falling interest rates combined to lead to a recovery in profits in 1996, while the fall in capital market interest rates has made investment in real capital more attractive than investment in financial assets. The average yield of fixed assets has improved markedly, although – depending on the method applied – the 1991 level may only now have been restored.[4] Capacity utilisation also increased in the course of 1996 and into 1997. Judged from these developments, a stronger increase in investment than actually occurred might have been expected. But while profitability has improved at the aggregate level, particularly in the internationally-exposed sectors, some indicators suggest that the dispersion of profitability across different types of enterprises and sectors may be high.[5] A survey conducted by the Chamber of Commerce in February 1997 among 25 000 enterprises of different sizes and branches, confirms that at the beginning of the year business conditions differed markedly across sectors.[6] While export-oriented enterprises reported improving business conditions and profits, companies which were more dependent on the domestic market assessed their current conditions less positively or weakly. This was particularly true for construction, but it also holds for producers of consumption goods, which are subject to weak domestic demand, and for domestic trade. The record high rate of bankruptcies, which increased by a further 14.3 per cent in 1996, was led by construction, but affected other sectors as well. Business expectations for 1997 follow a similar pattern, with enterprises in export-oriented sectors expecting a further improvement in business conditions, while the opposite is true for enterprises operating predominantly in the domestic market. This assessment is reflected in the sampled investment plans of the companies. While the proportion of companies which report further planned reductions in investment still exceeds those reporting increases, a turn-around is apparent in manufacturing, which is particularly pronounced for exporting companies.

While domestic investment is only slowly recovering from the 1993 recession, direct investment abroad remained buoyant in 1996, although falling short of the exceptionally high level reached in 1995.[7] (Figure 9). Studies indicate that the bulk of German direct investment abroad appears to be motivated by the desire to secure foreign markets and to support German exports.[8] But a recent poll conducted among some 7 000 enterprises, mainly from industry, also identi-

Figure 9. **FOREIGN DIRECT INVESTMENT**
DM billion

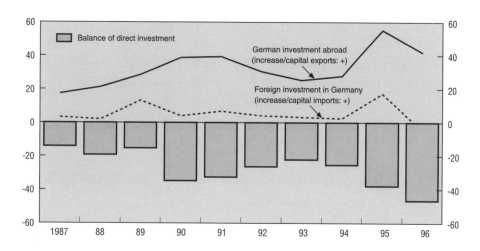

Source: Deutsche Bundesbank.

fied motives for shifting production abroad;[9] 28 per cent of the companies sampled plan to invest abroad for the purpose of taking up or expanding production within the next three years. Within this group 62 per cent of industrial companies identified high domestic labour costs as their main motive, followed by the tax and contribution burden (21 per cent). Other factors, such as exchange rate risks and administrative impediments, were of relatively minor importance.

Employment continues to decline

With GDP growth modest, investment relatively weak, and enterprises (particularly in manufacturing) focusing on cost reduction and rationalisation, employment continued to decline in 1996. Indeed, the decline has been longer and more pronounced than in previous periods of cyclical recovery (Figure 10). In western Germany, employment fell by 1.3 per cent between the fourth quarter of 1995 and the fourth quarter of 1996, which was almost twice the decline that occurred in 1995 (Figure 11). The increase in employment in the eastern Länder

Figure 10. **EMPLOYMENT GROWTH IN DIFFERENT RECOVERIES**

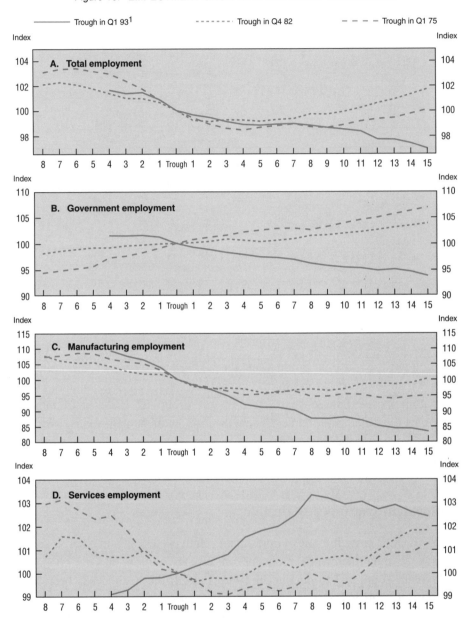

———— Trough in Q1 93[1]   - - - - - - - Trough in Q4 82   – – – – Trough in Q1 75

A. Total employment

B. Government employment

C. Manufacturing employment

D. Services employment

1. Unified Germany.
Source: OECD.

34

Figure 11. **EMPLOYMENT AND UNEMPLOYMENT RATES**

Quarterly seasonally adjusted figures

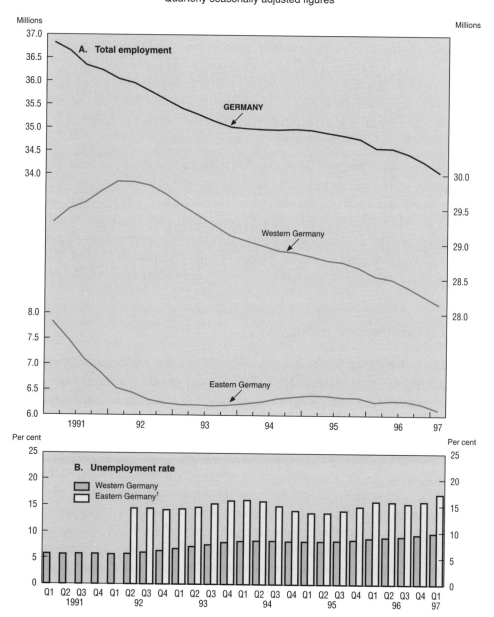

1. Before Q2 1992 data are not available for eastern Germany.
Source: Deutsche Bundesbank.

which started in 1994 ceased in 1996. Employment in eastern Germany was 2 per cent lower in the fourth quarter of 1996 than a year earlier, due only in part to a further decline in the participation of employees in active labour market measures and training programmes.[10] The deterioration in the overall labour market continued in the first months of 1997. In Germany as a whole, employment reduction was most pronounced in construction, but also affected manufacturing, trade and transport. Significant increases in employment, both in the old and the new Länder, occurred in private services. However, they were not sufficient to compensate for the adverse development in other sectors.

In response to the poor labour market situation, the trend has been for wage agreements to incorporate more flexible working-time arrangements, often associated with strengthened responsibilities at the company level.[11] Such opening clauses are still restricted in scope and in cases other than working time still need to be referred back to the social partners. Although the arrangements are associated with commitments to secure existing employment, to the extent that they lead to lower overall labour costs total employment should eventually increase.

Short-term economic prospects

The momentum given by exports should ensure the continuation of a moderate upswing during 1997 and 1998. The marked effective depreciation of the currency up to June 1997 – which is assumed to continue to obtain over the projection period – should allow Germany's exports to at least match market growth, in contrast to recent losses. Higher export growth is projected to stimulate a recovery in investment in machinery and equipment. This process should be underpinned by an increased rate of return on investment induced by past efforts of enterprises to rationalise, more moderate wage agreements, which are likely to extend into 1998, stable monetary conditions, and relatively low interest rates. Inventory decumulation is expected to come to a halt. On the other hand, construction expenditure is expected to remain stagnant, partly as a correction to the high growth rates in recent years. Consumption will expand only modestly in 1997, restrained by cuts in benefit programmes and an increase in social security charges, as well as a lack of confidence in view of adverse labour market conditions. Fiscal policy is programmed to tighten over the projection period, but with the output gap narrowing only gradually and inflation low and stable, monetary policy is expected to remain supportive to growth. Overall, GDP growth could reach 2¼ per cent in 1997 and rise to 2¾ per cent in 1998 (Table 5). With orders improving, positive growth impulses in eastern Germany are expected from manufacturing. But in comparison with high growth rates in the first years after reunification, growth in the new Länder is expected to remain relatively modest exceeding west German levels only marginally.

Firms are expected to continue restructuring – in part via reduced employment – in order to remain competitive, and with wages projected to increase less than 2 per cent, unit labour costs are expected to decrease further in 1997. However, with the recovery maturing and employment increasing somewhat, unit labour costs should stabilise in 1998. Although service sector employment will continue to expand, unemployment is expected to remain high over the projection period, the structural reforms implemented so far being insufficient to offset the negative effects of high non-wage labour costs and a regulatory environment still

Table 5. **Economic projections**

Seasonally adjusted at annual rates, 1991 prices

	1996	1997	1998	1996		1997		1998	
				I	II	I	II	I	II
Private consumption	1.3	1.0	2.0	1.8	0.6	1.0	1.5	2.1	2.4
Government consumption	2.4	1.1	1.1	2.2	1.7	0.9	0.9	1.2	1.3
Total fixed investment	−0.8	1.6	4.2	−4.4	8.6	−1.1	0.5	4.6	7.1
Construction	−2.7	−0.5	0.7	−8.8	11.5	−4.2	−3.9	1.1	4.8
Machinery and equipment	2.4	4.9	9.3	2.9	4.4	3.8	7.4	9.8	10.3
Stockbuilding [1]	−0.3	0.1	0.1	0.1	−1.2	0.5	0.5	0.0	0.0
Total domestic demand	0.8	1.3	2.5	0.6	1.3	1.0	1.6	2.5	3.2
Net exports [1]	0.6	1.0	0.3	0.4	1.7	1.0	0.2	0.5	0.1
Exports of goods and services	4.9	8.4	7.5	1.6	12.0	7.5	6.6	8.3	6.9
Imports of goods and services	2.6	4.8	6.6	0.2	5.1	4.0	6.2	6.7	6.8
GDP at market prices	1.4	2.2	2.8	1.0	3.1	2.0	1.8	3.0	3.2
Memorandum items:									
GDP deflator	1.0	1.2	1.1	1.1	0.0	1.8	1.3	1.1	1.0
Private consumption deflator	1.9	1.7	1.8	1.8	2.0	1.5	1.6	1.8	1.8
Unemployment (in millions)	4.0	4.3	4.2	3.9	4.0	4.3	4.2	4.2	4.2
Unemployment (per cent of labour force)	10.3	11.1	10.9	10.1	10.5	11.2	11.0	10.9	10.8

1. Contributions to changes in GDP (as a per cent of real GDP in the previous period).
Source: Statistisches Bundesamt; OECD projections.

unfavourable to employment. Surveys taken at the start of 1997 indicate that one third of employers plan to reduce employment in 1997, while only 10 per cent plan to expand employment. This is only a slight improvement compared with similar surveys taken one year ago. Employment is projected to decline in 1997 by almost a percentage point, with a stabilisation only occurring in the second half of the year. For 1998 a modest increase in employment by 0.4 per cent is projected. Consequently, the unemployment rate is projected to rise by another 0.8 percentage points in 1997 to 11.1 per cent. For 1998, a slight drop in the unemployment rate to around 10.9 per cent is projected.

As far as risks are concerned, growth is strongly dependent on exports, so that any weakening in foreign markets could have an important negative impact. In addition, expectations about the ability of countries to meet the Maastricht criteria by the end of the year could have unpredictable confidence and financial market effects. Prospects for appreciably faster growth than expected seem to depend on consumer confidence returning and on a recovery in inventory accumulation. Agreement on the first phase of a tax reform to start in 1998 could have benefits in 1997, stimulating investment.

II. Monetary and fiscal policies

The background to macroeconomic policies has remained complex. While the monetary authorities have adopted a rather steady stance in the face of significant financial market volatility, fiscal policy has been complicated by weak economic growth and higher unemployment. The consolidation of public finances and the objective of meeting the Maastricht budget deficit criterion have called for action to minimise the slippage caused by weaker economic activity, but some of the measures taken have unavoidably run contrary to the attainment of other longer-run fiscal objectives – such as the stabilisation of social security charges – on which future labour-market performance depends. Proposals to introduce the first phase of a wide-ranging tax reform in 1998 would recover lost ground in structural reform, but many key aspects remain to be negotiated and, in general, uncertainties about implementation have weakened the credibility of fiscal policy. Monetary and financial conditions have become more expansionary since the previous *Survey*, the exchange rate weakening against the dollar and long-term rates falling in response to low inflation. The Bundesbank has allowed relatively rapid money growth, and made a further cut in policy-controlled interest rates in August 1996 in pursuit of its "stability-oriented" strategy. In the run-up to European Monetary Union the framework for implementing such a strategy is likely to become more complex. This chapter discusses the background to these broad policy issues.

Fiscal policy

The 1996 budget outcome

Weak economic activity and lower employment resulted in the general government deficit increasing to 3.8 per cent of GDP in 1996 (Table 6). This

Table 6. **Public sector financial balances**

DM billion

	1992	1993	1994	1995[1]	1996[2]	1997[3]	1998[3]
General government	**−86.8**	**−109.7**	**−80.6**	**−122.9**	**−134.0**	**−118.3**	**−101.6**
(Per cent of GDP)	(-2.8)	(-3.5)	(-2.4)	(-3.6)	(-3.8)	(-3.2)	(-2.7)
of which:							
Territorial authorities	**−115.9**	**−137.8**	**−116.3**	**−109.7**	**−120.0**	**−114.0**	**−100.0**
Federal government	−39.3	−66.9	−50.5	−50.5	−78.5	−76.0	−66.0
State government west[4]	−15.9	−22.5	−24.7	−30.0	−31.8	−26.0	−25.0
Local government west	−9.4	−8.9	−5.9	−12.4	−4.0	−4.0	−4.0
State government east[4]	−15.1	−19.9	−19.9	−16.9	−15.3	−13.5	−13.0
Local government east	−7.5	−4.4	−4.8	−0.8	−2.5	−2.0	−2.0
German unity fund	−22.4	−13.5	−3.0	2.3	2.7	2.5	3.5
Other funds[5]	−6.2	−1.7	−7.5	−1.8	9.5	5.0	6.5
National accounts adjustments[6]	**31.3**	**20.7**	**30.3**	**−2.6**	**−0.8**	**−2.3**	**−2.6**
Social security	−2.2	7.4	5.4	−10.6	−13.1	−2.0	1.0
Memorandum items:							
Treuhandanstalt[7]	−29.7	−38.1	−34.4	..	..	..	..
Public enterprises[8]	−25.7	−20.5	−20.2	..	..	..	..
Extended public sector	**−142.2**	**−168.3**	**−135.2**	**−122.9**	**−134.0**	**−118.3**	**−101.6**
(Per cent of GDP)	(-4.6)	(-5.3)	(-4.1)	(-3.6)	(-3.8)	(-3.2)	(-2.7)
(Cyclically-adjusted, per cent of GDP)	(-6.1)	(-4.8)	(-3.7)	(-3.1)	(-3.1)	(-2.6)	(-2.3)

1. 1995 figures do not include (as a capital transfer item) the takeover by the federal government of debits of the Treuhand (DM 204.6 billion) and of the East German Housing Fund (DM 30 billion). Inclusion of these items would imply a general government deficit in 1995 of the order of 9 to 10 per cent of GDP.
2. Provisional.
3. OECD projections.
4. West without Berlin; east including Berlin.
5. Credit Fund, Economic Recovery Programme Fund, Financial Equalisation Fund, Compensation Fund, Railway Fund, Coal Fund and Inherited Debt Fund.
6. Including lending operations, privatisation receipts, timing adjustments, and, until 1995, profits paid by the Bundesbank into a debt sinking fund.
7. Wound up at the end of 1994. The successor organisation is financed directly from the federal budget.
8. Until 1995 included Post/Telecom and railway companies in the west and in the east; Post and Telecoms were incorporated in 1995 pending privatisation while subsidies are now paid directly to the railways by both the state and federal governments.
Source: BMF *Finanzbericht;* Deutsche Bundesbank, *Monthly report;* submission from the Ministry of Finance; OECD projections.

compared with an original fiscal plan to stabilise the deficit at 3.5 per cent, with spending restraint meant to reduce the impact of significant income tax reductions (a rise in the basic income tax allowance and in child allowances) and the abolition of a surcharge for the subsidisation of coal mining (*Kohlepfennig*), which became effective in 1996.[12] The slippage can be attributed to a drop in tax revenues and to a sharp increase in social spending, affecting the federal budget and the social security funds. Despite efforts to contain the fiscal slippage, the federal deficit was some DM 18½ billion over budget (Table 7), while the social funds ended the year with a combined deficit of DM 13.1 billion (Table 6). On the other hand, the local government deficit was smaller than expected.

On a financial basis, the federal budget deficit increased by DM 28 billion to DM 78.5 billion (Table 7). More than one-third of the increase was intended, in order to cover the income tax reductions called for by the Constitutional Court, while three-quarters of the slippage was due to unexpected shortfalls in tax revenues. GDP growth was 1 percentage point lower than expected and inflation was also lower. VAT revenues were even weaker than would have been expected from the development of demand or its concentration on (VAT-refundable) exports. In addition, the financing position of the budget was made worse by the

Table 7. **The Federal budget**

DM billion

	1994 Outcome	1995 Outcome	1996		1997 Budget
			Budget	Outcome	
Expenditure	**471.2**	**464.7**	**451.3**	**455.6**	**439.9**
(Per cent of GDP)	(14.2)	(13.4)	(12.7)	(12.9)	(12.0)[1]
of which:					
Consumption	90.6	91.5	93.1	91.6	91.7
Interest payments	53.1	49.7	53.4	50.9	54.4
Investment	12.0	12.3	12.4	12.1	13.0
Transfers and lending	315.5	311.2	292.6	301.0	282.9
of which:					
To other administrations	96.4	89.6	93.7	92.3	85.9
Others	219.2	221.6	198.9	208.7	197.0
Revenues	**420.6**	**414.1**	**391.2**	**377.0**	**386.5**
(Per cent of GDP)	(12.7)	(12.0)	(11.1)	(10.6)	(10.5)[1]
of which:					
Taxes	379.0	366.1	351.2[2]	338.6	345.7
Other	41.6	48.0	40.0	38.5	40.8
Financial balance	**–50.6**	**–50.5**	**–60.1**	**–78.5**	**–53.4**
(Per cent of GDP)	(-1.5)	(-1.5)	(-1.7)	(-2.2)	(-1.4)[1]

1. OECD estimates.
2. Includes a reduction of DM 21.2 billion due to the treatment of child benefits from 1996 as reduced tax revenues rather than social expenditures.
Source: Ministry of Finance; OECD.

delay to some privatisation projects; receipts from privatisation fell some DM 7 billion short of those budgeted.[13] On the expenditure side, the authorities sought to offset the increase in entitlement spending, mainly on account of high unemployment, by tight expenditure controls elsewhere, and were partly successful in this. Nevertheless, spending overshot the level set in the budget by 1 per cent. Federal government transfers to the labour office to cover its commitments for, among other things, unemployment benefits, totalled some DM 14 billion, exceeding the budget plan by DM 9.5 billion, while direct payments for unemployment assistance were 40 per cent over the budget allocation. To minimise the budget slippage, the authorities were forced to introduce expenditure caps in March which are estimated to have reduced spending by some DM 4.4 billion. As is often the case with such *ad hoc* controls, cuts fell disproportionately on investment expenditures.

Budget pressures at the Länder and local government levels have been exacerbated by the rapid accumulation of debt in recent years. Being major employers, they are also susceptible to wage developments. Lower interest rates and a modest public sector wage round were thus instrumental in easing pressures on state and local government budget deficits in 1996. Nevertheless, strict expenditure controls were widely imposed, particularly in public investment.[14] Fiscal pressure was particularly pronounced in the new Länder, which are still highly dependent on transfers from the federal government (Table 8). On the revenue side, local government benefited from significantly higher tax receipts from the local business tax, which accrues to the communities.[15]

The large deficit in the social security system was attributable to both the health and pension funds, and would have been worse if the new long-term care insurance system had not once again earned a surplus.[16] Following the 1995 public pension fund deficit, the pension contribution rate was increased in January 1996 from 18.6 per cent to 19.2 per cent of the wage base. This was intended to produce a slight surplus in the pension funds, so as to re-establish their mandatory one month liquid reserves. However, revenue shortfalls from higher-than-projected unemployment, together with a continuously high inflow into early retirement, resulted in a deficit of DM 10 billion. Eligibility criteria for early retirement have been tightened (see Chapter IV below), but the financial impact will take some time to appear. Revenue shortfalls stemming from high unemployment also affected the health funds, whose collective deficit remained

Table 8. **Public financial transfers to eastern Germany**

DM billion

	1991	1992	1993	1994	1995	1996	1997[1]
1. Gross transfers [2]	**139**	**152**	**168**	**168**	**185**	**187**	**180**
Federal government transfers to the eastern Länder and communities [3]	75	88	114	114	135	138	128
Western Länder and communities [4]	5	5	10	14	10	11	11
Pension scheme [5]	..	5	9	12	17	19	17
Transfers of the Federal Labour Office [6]	24	39	39	27	23	26	21
German Unity Fund borrowing [7]	31	24	15	5	..	..	..
Transfers from the EU [8]	4	5	5	6	7	7	7
2. Receipts	**33**	**37**	**39**	**43**	**45**	**47**	**47**
of which:							
Additional federal tax receipts from the east [8]	31	35	37	41	43	45	45
Additional federal administrative receipts from the east	2	2	2	2	2	2	2
Net transfers (1-2)	**106**	**115**	**129**	**125**	**140**	**140**	**133**
Per cent of:							
All-German GDP	3.7	3.7	4.1	3.8	4.0	4.0	3.6
Western German GDP	4.0	4.1	4.5	4.2	4.6	4.5	4.1
Eastern German GDP	51.5	43.8	41.1	35.3	36.8	35.2	32.4

1. Projections.
2. Without the double count of the federal payments to the Federal Labour Office.
3. 1995 including DM 35 billion federal tax losses caused by the revision of the fiscal equalisation measures.
4. 1993 and 1994 including payments to the German Unity Fund; 1994 including tax losses caused by the revision of the fiscal equalisation measures.
5. Without payments of the federal government.
6. Total deficit east, including federal payments.
7. Without payments of the federal government and Länder.
8. Estimates.
Source: Ministry of Finance.

at around the same level as in 1995. Overall, the contribution rate to the social security system increased from 39.3 per cent of the eligible wage base to 41 per cent in 1996.

The 1997 budget: reconciling conflicting fiscal objectives

The draft 1997 federal budget, presented in August 1996, sought to balance fiscal consolidation with the government's structural reform objectives. A deficit of DM 56.5 billion was projected (1½ per cent of GDP) – DM 22 billion less than the 1996 outcome – while the Solidarity tax surcharge was to be reduced by 1 percentage point and the business capital tax finally abolished. The commitment made in early 1996 to stabilise social security charges was to be pursued by forcing health funds to lower contribution rates at the beginning of 1997 and by keeping contribution rates to the pension funds below 20 per cent.[17]

By autumn 1996, it became apparent that without additional budgetary measures the deficit target for 1997 was unlikely to be realised, the government identifying a shortfall of DM 7 billion. Moreover, the initial draft budget was rejected by the upper house of the parliament, along with social and tax legislation based on the government's programme for growth and employment (see *OECD Economic Survey of Germany* 1996). This pointed to an even larger potential deficit. The authorities therefore decided to introduce additional revenue-raising measures and to reinforce the overall spending restraint. The reduction in the Solidarity tax surcharge, which had been criticised by the new Länder as implying cuts in their future revenues, was postponed until January 1998 and the scheduled increase in the basic income tax allowance was also deferred a year. On the other hand, the unpopular proposal to postpone the increase in child allowances until 1998 had to be reversed and the government stopped collecting the wealth tax (DM 8.7 billion), in response to a ruling of the Constitutional Court. To finance these changes, the inheritance and gift taxes were raised, as was the tax on real estate transactions. In response to strong opposition from the western Länder, the government also had to postpone its plans to eliminate the business capital tax, which is now being introduced in the new Länder.[18] The revised budget was finally approved in November 1996, with a deficit of DM 53.4 billion (around 1.5 per cent of GDP), an improvement of some DM 3 billion over the original version, and DM 25 billion less than the outcome for 1996.

Federal government spending in 1997 is planned to decline by 3.4 per cent relative to actual expenditures in 1996, with the greatest savings in wages and salaries and transfers to the labour office – the counterpart to which will be lower spending on active labour market measures in the new Länder and savings with respect to unemployment benefits and access to early retirement. Personnel in the federal administration are to be reduced by 2 per cent in 1997, which in combination with small tariff wage increases is set to lower the nominal wage bill by $1/2$ per cent. A crucial assumption of the budget was that unemployment would average 3.9 million in 1997, but the government raised its projection of average unemployment by 200 000 to 4.1 million in January 1997, while lifting its projection for the general government deficit from 2.5 per cent to 2.9 per cent of GDP. The official tax estimates which were released in May indicated an overall tax shortfall of some DM 9 billion relative to the government's January projection, about half of which occurred in the federal budget. In response, the federal authorities introduced additional expenditure controls in June and propose to accelerate privatisation so as to meet the constitutional requirement that new debt issues be less than or equal to public sector investment. The new controls are expected by the authorities to save some DM 2 to 3 billion, but this estimate may prove optimistic. Government departments are already under pressure to save around DM 7 billion this year, so that additional savings on discretionary expenditures could prove difficult, while a further cut in investment expenditures has been ruled out on employment grounds. Indeed, concern with the poor state of the construction industry has led the government to initiate an off-budget subsidised loan programme of DM 20 billion to support, *inter alia*, local government investment expenditure. In addition, steps were taken to accelerate infrastructure spending through new forms of private financing amounting to some DM 5 billion.

Despite projected revenue shortfalls, prospects for the Länder seem to be more favourable. According to the November 1996 projections of the Financial Planning Council – a co-ordinating body – the Länder plan to reduce their deficit from DM 47 billion in 1996 to DM 32 billion. Some states have already implemented spending freezes and restraint by the Länder and local governments is supported by the modest wage settlements in the public sector noted above. Although a further reduction in employment appears necessary, it is likely that the Länder will be able to realise their 2 per cent spending growth target for this year. On the other hand, it has not been possible to achieve balance in the social insurance system while keeping to the objective of stabilising contribution rates. Social security charges were increased by more than a percentage point at the beginning of the year. In the health sector the government legislated a reduction of contribution rates by 0.4 percentage points from January 1997 (*Beitragsentlastungsgesetz*), which was supposed to represent a passing-on of savings legislated in 1996. But most health funds expect spending to rise and have counteracted the legislated reduction by increasing contribution rates. With respect to the pension funds, in order to restore the statutory liquidity reserve,[19] the pension contribution rate was increased from 19.2 per cent to 20.3 per cent in January 1997.

Achieving the government's fiscal targets depends rather critically on the high level of savings which are projected in the area of labour market expenditure. The OECD projects a considerably higher unemployment level than assumed in the budget projections: some 300 000 persons more than assumed by the government at the time the budget was passed in 1996, and 100 000 greater than officially projected in January 1997.[20] This would imply additional transfers to the federal labour office and increased outlays for unemployment assistance of some DM 9 billion (0.2 per cent of GDP). Higher unemployment and lower levels of employment are also projected by the OECD to lead to slippage in the pension funds, even though there have been a number of changes to entitlements. On the basis of the OECD's assumptions (see Box 1) the general government deficit is projected to amount to 3¼ per cent of GDP in 1997 (representing a fiscal contraction of around 0.5 percentage points of GDP) (Table 9). At this

---

Box 1. **Assumptions underlying fiscal projections**

The final 1997 federal budget has been incorporated in the projections for the general government deficit, together with measures covering the social insurance funds, with adjustments made to reflect the different macroeconomic framework projected by the OECD. This applies in particular to the level of employment and of unemployment. Projected VAT revenues reflect the weakness of domestic demand. The projections additionally include reduced benefits for asylum seekers and for the unemployed, as well as lower projected interest payments on public debt. Increases in health contribution rates up to April are also incorporated in the projection.

The projections for 1998 are based on the assumption of unchanged policies unless the change has been already mandated. Tax cuts are therefore not included, but an increase in the basic income tax allowance is incorporated. Estimates have been included of legislation curbing social expenditures that became effective in 1996 and 1997. Following the relatively modest wage settlements for 1996 and 1997 public sector wages are projected to grow more rapidly in 1998. Overall, the OECD projects current spending to grow at a rate of 2.3 per cent, marginally less than in the year before.

In projecting gross debt over the period no estimates have been made for privatisation receipts and it has been assumed that the public sector will not increase financial assets by issuing debt.

Table 9. **Appropriation account for general government**

Including social security

	1994	1995	1996[1]	1997[2]	1998[2]
			DM billion		
Receipts					
A. Direct taxes	364.4	387.9	364.4	368.0	378.5
B. Social security contributions	638.3	667.1	698.4	729.9	751.1
C. Other current transfers received	44.2	45.9	48.4	50.8	53.3
D. Indirect taxes	443.6	447.2	451.9	462.6	478.6
E. Property and entrepreneurial income	53.1	41.6	38.2	39.1	40.1
F. Current receipts, total	1 543.6	1 588.7	1 601.2	1 650.4	1 701.6
(Per cent of GDP)	(46.5)	(46.0)	(45.2)	(45.1)	(44.7)
Disbursements					
G. Government consumption	650.2	675.4	695.4	706.6	720.4
of which: Wages and salaries	346.1	355.9	360.4	359.2	364.6
H. Property income payable (interest on public debt)	113.1	129.6	130.6	133.6	138.4
I. Subsidies	67.8	75.4	76.5	76.5	77.3
J. Social security outlays	587.7	620.4	629.6	644.7	654.7
K. Other current transfers paid	107.5	111.8	119.0	124.4	129.3
L. Current disbursements, total	1 526.4	1 612.5	1 651.2	1 685.8	1 720.2
(Per cent of GDP)	(46.0)	(46.6)	(46.6)	(46.0)	(45.2)
M. Saving (F – L)	17.2	–22.8	–50.0	–35.4	–18.6
N. Gross investment	89.7	86.7	81.3	80.9	81.7
O. Net capital transfers received	–32.7	–39.0	–28.9	–28.9	–28.9
P. Consumption of fixed capital	24.6	25.6	26.3	26.9	27.6
Q. Net lending (M – N + O + P)	–80.6	–122.9	–134.0	–118.3	–101.6
Memorandum item:					
Net lending as a percentage of nominal GDP	–2.4	–3.6	–3.8	–3.2	–2.7

1. Provisional estimates.
2. OECD projection.
Source: Statistisches Bundesamt; OECD.

level the 3 per cent criterion could be effectively regarded as being met, the difference being well within the range of normal statistical revision. However, there is a risk that revenues could be weaker than projected due to the unpredictable effects of changes in tax legislation, while labour market expenditures might prove greater than expected. In case of fiscal slippage, the most available and effective instrument would be to raise excise taxes. However, such *ad hoc* tax increases could have a negative effect on confidence and would have to be weighed against the potential costs of budget slippage. Any measures which might have to be taken should be consistent with the general aims of tax and structural reform.

The ratio of public debt to GDP, on the Maastricht basis, rose to around 61 per cent in 1996[21] (Table 10). Unification processes are still having an impact: at the beginning of 1997 the Inherited Debt Fund took over DM 8.4 billion of debt from social institutions at the local authority level, and the fund will also issue debt certificates amounting to some DM 13 billion in the coming months. Overall, it is estimated that more than half of the increase in public debt since

Table 10. **Public debt by government level[1]**

DM billion

	1991	1992	1993	1994	1995	1996[2]
Federal government	586	607	685	712	754	833
Länder west	345	365	391	410	439	469
Länder east	4	19	37	51	65	79
Communities west	120	127	134	136	139	147
Communities east	8	12	18	23	26	28
Unity Fund	50	74	88	89	87	84
Credit Fund	27	92	101	103	..	
ERP Fund	16	24	28	28	34	34
Railways Fund[3]	..	..	..	71	78	78
Inherited debt Fund[4]	..	..	..	..	329	324
Total – territorial authorities[5]	**1 166**	**1 332**	**1 499**	**1 645**	**1 976[6]**	**2 100[6]**
(Per cent of GDP)	(40.9)	(43.3)	(47.5)	(49.5)	(57.2)	(59.3)
Treuhandanstalt	57	110	169	205	..	..
Post Office[7]	81	97	105	124	..	..
Railways[3]	43	53	66	..	..	..
Total – public sector	**1 347**	**1 592**	**1 839**	**1 974**	**1 976**	**2 100**
(Per cent of GDP)	(47.2)	(51.7)	(58.3)	(59.5)	(57.2)	(59.3)
Maastricht definition	**1 184**	**1 357**	**1 522**	**1 675**	**2 009**	**2 149**
(Per cent of GDP)	(41.5)	(44.1)	(48.2)	(50.4)	(58.1)	(60.7)
Financial liabilities	**1 268**	**1 408**	**1 640**	**1 715**	**2 152**	**2 297**
(Per cent of GDP)	(44.4)	(45.8)	(51.9)	(51.7)	(62.2)	(64.9)

1. The Ministry of Finance calculation does not correspond to that published by the Bundesbank and which is reported in the *Economic Outlook*. There are differences in valuation methods and in netting intra-government holdings.
2. Estimates.
3. 1994: reform of railways.
4. 1995: debts of Treuhandanstalt, Credit fund, eastern German public housing sector.
5. Including indebtedness of municipal special-purpose associations and municipal hospitals.
6. Includes debts of two smaller funds not listed in the table.
7. 1995: reform of the Post Office.
Source: Ministry of Finance; Deutsche Bundesbank; OECD.

1989 is attributable to reunification.[22] Public debt is projected by the OECD to continue to rise in both 1997 and 1998 as a share of GDP (Figure 12), reaching around 62 per cent (Maastricht basis).[23]

Fiscal policy in 1998 – fulfilling the medium term programme

The government's medium term fiscal goals are to reduce the level of public expenditures from about 50 per cent of GDP to the pre-unification level of 46 per cent by 2000, while lowering both the tax burden and the budget deficit. Specifically, the intention is to reduce the budget deficit to $1\frac{1}{2}$ per cent of GDP,[24] while lowering the overall social security contribution rate to under 40 per cent. Looking ahead, the government has put forward proposals for a major income tax reform aiming at reducing statutory tax rates for personal and corporate income, so as to improve growth and employment. The major principles of this reform proposal are reviewed in Chapter IV. The package has still to be negotiated, but the overall dimensions are relatively clear. Revenues foregone by cutting personal and corporate income tax rates, and reducing the Solidarity tax surcharge, are projected to amount to some DM 87 billion (more than 2 per cent of GDP) in 1999, which would be partially offset by broadening the tax base and cutting tax expenditures amounting to around DM 43 billion (more than 1 per cent of GDP), DM 53 billion on an accruals basis. In addition, it is proposed to raise indirect taxes. The government envisages a net reduction in the tax burden for the private sector of DM 20 to 30 billion or 0.5 to 0.8 per cent of GDP. It is not intended to alter the medium term consolidation plan, although the government has announced that it would be acceptable for the deficit to stabilise for a while in the course of the tax reform. However, if the medium term consolidation programme is to be met, greater pressures are implied on expenditure reduction, particularly in the area of social spending and subsidies.

Although progress is expected to be made in 1997 in lowering both the deficit and the volume of expenditures (Table 9), the government has had to delay progress in other areas in order to meet the Maastricht deficit criterion. But with fiscal pressure projected by the OECD to ease somewhat in 1998 the way is open for greater priority to be given to structural fiscal objectives. The authorities are committed to cutting the Solidarity surcharge by 2 percentage points in 1998 and they have renewed a pledge to abolish the business capital tax and to cut the business earnings tax. Moreover, it is also proposed to introduce the first phase of

Figure 12. **THE DYNAMICS OF PUBLIC DEBT**[1]
Per cent of GDP

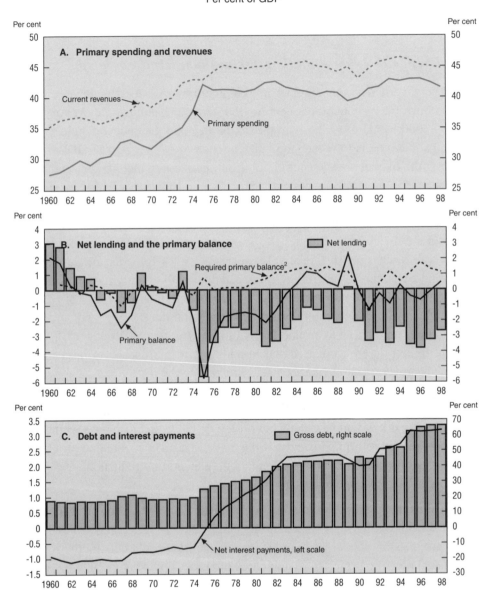

1. 1997 and 1998 OECD projections.
2. Primary surplus needed to stabilize the net debt ratio.
Source: OECD.

the tax reform in 1998 by cutting tax rates on corporate profits and unincorporated business income. In 1998 these measures would be financed by lowering depreciation and other tax allowances, such as loss carry forward provisions, for enterprises. Changes to the business earnings and capital taxes will have to be accompanied by a change in federal/state financial relations for it to be acceptable to local government. Cutting the Solidarity surcharge while at the same time reducing the deficit will be difficult and will require continuing close control of expenditures. The authorities are currently preparing new legislation with the purpose of sharpening the eligibility conditions for obtaining an early retirement pension on account of invalidity. However, significant savings in 1998 could only be expected if "grandfathering" conditions associated with the reform are less generous than in the 1996 reform of early retirement on account of unemployment. In this, as in other areas of expenditure control, a long-term perspective is necessary. Reduced borrowing is necessary in order to meet the constitutional requirement that new borrowing must not exceed the level of public investment. In accordance with this requirement, the federal government is proposing to increase privatisation revenues significantly. The bulk of the planned increase will arise from the sale of a tranche of Telekom shares to a state-owned bank, the intention being to resell these shares at a later date. In addition, proceeds from a revaluation of the dollar currency reserves of the Bundesbank.[25] will be used to reduce the liabilities of the Inherited Debt Fund.

Pension reform

As documented in detail in the previous *Survey*, with no change in policy, demographic developments will lead to increased fiscal pressure from the public pension system, and indeed the government projects that contribution rates would have to rise from 20.3 per cent of eligible gross wages at present to 25.9 per cent in 2030 (Figure 13). An expert commission was established in 1996 to make recommendations for a reform of the public pension system, and their proposals were adopted in draft legislation by the government in mid-1997. This legislation will need to be negotiated in the parliament. By and large, the commission proposed maintaining the present, pay-as-you-go, system without any increase in the mandatory retirement age. To deal with future fiscal pressures, the commission's main proposal is to lower the pension from about 70 per cent of average net wages (after 45 years of contributions) at present to 64 per cent by

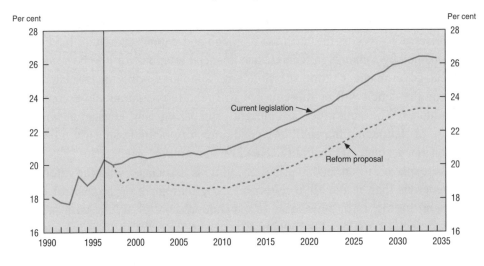

Source: Ministry of Labour and Social Affairs.

2030. To this end, the formula determining the pension level would be amended by a demographic component to capture partly the evolution of life expectancy. As before, Germany would remain the only major country linking pensions to net wages, so that pensioners would share in future productivity increases. In a similar vein, the commission also proposed to extend the eligibility for pensions on account of child-raising, but at the same time recommended that the conditions for obtaining an invalidity pension should be tightened. On the revenue side, the commission suggested extending the contribution base to occasional work and proposed to finance separately additional pension claims arising from child-raising years out of general tax receipts via a "family fund". Funding of pension liabilities was rejected both in whole or in part due to the high level of transition costs and because the commission feared that the funds would gain too large an influence over companies.[26]

Based on the projected evolution of the age structure, the OECD has constructed illustrative scenarios to highlight the dimension of the fiscal burden of population ageing in the pension system (see *OECD Survey of Germany*, 1996).

With the average pension replacement rate lowered to the level suggested by the Commission, public pension outlays would increase from 11 per cent of GDP currently to a peak of 17 per cent in the year 2035. This is 1½ percentage points lower than under the scenario of no change in policy, but still 6 percentage points higher than current spending on pensions. Under the commission's own projections, all proposed measures combined would lead to a decline in contribution rates from 20.3 per cent of gross wages at present to 18.6 per cent in 2011. This would be followed, however, by a steep increase in the contribution rate up to 23.3 per cent in 2035, exceeding the 1997 level by 3 percentage points (Figure 13). In sum, the proposal of the commission would lead to a significant short-run easing of the fiscal burden but implies a considerable increase in the non-wage cost of labour from the second decade onwards.[27] Further steps will be necessary to reduce the longer-run fiscal burden inherent in the system. From this perspective it will be important to maintain – and indeed to strengthen – policy measures designed to raise the effective age of retirement toward the statutory level.

In the absence of more radical reform,[28] it will be important to widen the opportunities for personal choice within the current system. Lowering the average replacement rate to 64 per cent is likely to increase interest by individuals in obtaining additional pension cover, either privately or through schemes operated by their place of work. Yet, as noted in last year's *Economic Survey*, there are significant tax and legal barriers retarding this development. In particular, the development of funded, company-based, schemes has been retarded by tax legislation. The options for developing further private provision of pensions, which would be funded, needs to be looked at more closely.

The pension issue has financial consequences not only in the longer term but also during the period covered by the medium term consolidation plan. This is particularly true with respect to pensions for civil servants (*Beamte*) whose pensions are paid directly from the government budgets, especially those of the Länder and local government.[29] Expenditures for such pensions are projected by the government to double in real terms between 1995 and 2010, resulting in an increase in pensions from 1.6 per cent of GDP to a projected 2.2 per cent, representing a major financial burden. *Ceteris paribus*, the medium term target to reduce expenditures from 50 per cent of GDP to 46 per cent would correspond to a decline of some 5 percentage points of GDP in non-pension expenditures. The government appointed a committee to examine the question and proposals have been presented to levy a contribution of 0.2 per cent on civil servants. However, this proposal has not yet been accepted, since it could change the status of civil servants. In the meantime, three states have proceeded on their own to establish some funding arrangements for these pension liabilities.

Monetary policy

Most indicators of monetary conditions point to a substantial easing during 1996 and into 1997 so that an assessment of current monetary conditions is not subject to the problem of conflicting signals which provided the background to the previous two *Surveys*. Low and stable inflation (Figure 14), excess capacity, and unusually low investment in long term financial assets permitted the Bundesbank to lower the repo rate in August 1996, even though money supply was growing faster than the pre-announced limits. Monetary growth remained rapid going into 1997, while the 10-year benchmark yield has been significantly lower than the historically significant barrier of 6 per cent. In addition, the exchange rate *vis-à-vis* the dollar has fallen considerably. Looking ahead, the framework for monetary policy and for assessing monetary conditions will need to take account of evolving circumstances in the run-up to EMU. This section first reviews recent monetary developments with respect to money and credit aggregates and of the central bank's responses in terms of policy-controlled rates, and this is followed by a discussion of interest rates and exchange-rate developments. It then provides an assessment of monetary conditions and of the challenges facing monetary policy over the next review year, during which time progress towards European Monetary Union could make the formulation and execution of German monetary policy increasingly complex.

Money and credit aggregates

The Bundesbank's preferred monetary aggregate M3 grew by some 8 per cent in 1996, significantly above its target growth range of 4 to 7 per cent.[30] This pattern continued into the first quarter of 1997, although by April the growth rate had declined to around the new upper limit of 6.5 per cent per annum. On a monthly basis, monetary growth was slow in the opening months of 1997, the surge in money supply at the end of 1996 constituting a statistical overhang in

Figure 14. **THE INFLATION ENVIRONMENT**

Percentage change over 12 months

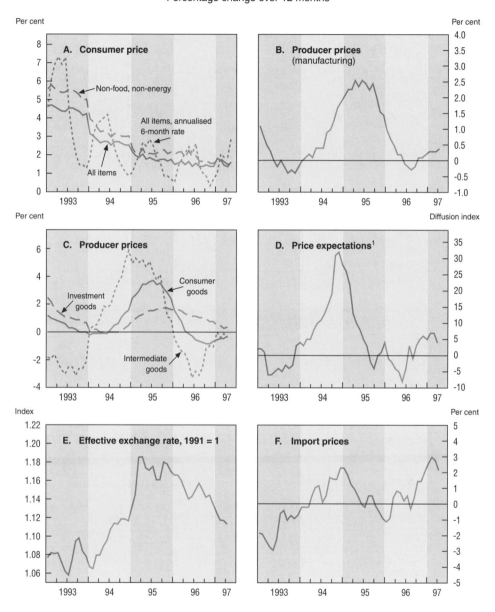

1. Diffusion index. Balance of higher and lower expectations. Seasonally adjusted.
Source: Deutsche Bundesbank, *Monatsberichte;* OECD, *Main Economic Indicators.*

Figure 15. **MONETARY TARGETS AND MONEY GROWTH**

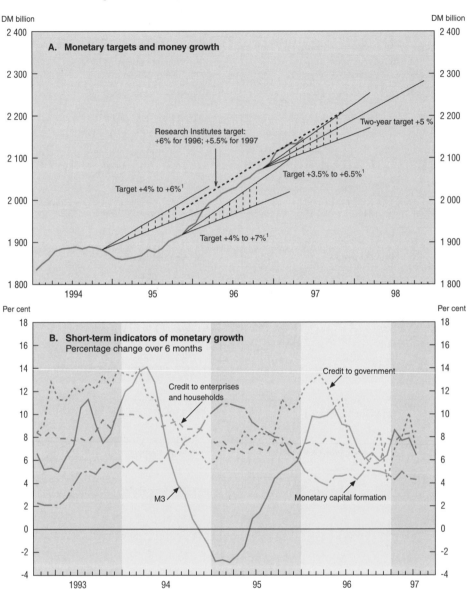

1.   Between the 4th quarter of the preceding year and the 4th quarter of the current year. The target corridor has not
     been shaded until March because M3 is normally subject to major random fluctuations around the turn of the
     year.
Source: Deutsche Bundesbank.

measuring growth relative to the last quarter. Key to the rapid growth of the money supply in 1996 has been the portfolio behaviour of domestic non-banks, which led to a relatively low rate of investment in longer term assets not included in M3 (*i.e.* time deposits with a term longer than four years, savings deposits with a term longer than three months, bearer debt securities) and to a strong increase in special savings deposits carrying higher interest rates (Figure 15). Fears of a sharp drop in bond prices related to expectations of a change in US monetary policy may have reduced monetary capital formation up to the spring of 1996, but since that time, and especially into 1997, German interest rates have declined relative to US rates and monetary capital formation has recovered modestly.

Government borrowing remained strong through 1996 and into 1997, but in absolute terms credit growth in 1996 was dominated by credit to enterprises and individuals. There does not yet appear to have been a change in the trend observed since 1995, whereby credit has been predominantly related to property investment. German banks have not been burdened with difficult property loans as in a number of other countries. Collateral is high and the decline in real estate prices has affected only office building and not housing. In addition, large property loans are usually sold by the banks as mortgage-backed bonds (*Pfand-briefe*) and so do not burden their capital requirements to the same degree as do loans.

Changes in policy rates and operational considerations

Since the last *Survey,* policy-controlled rates have changed only once: in August 1996, when the repurchase rate was lowered by 30 basis points to 3 per cent (Figure 16). The unusually large cut in the most important instrument for influencing money market conditions was taken against the background of very low inflation, a sharp appreciation of the mark against the dollar during July, sluggish activity, and a slowing in the growth of the money supply (which nevertheless remained significantly above its target path). As important as the rate cut itself was the decision to remain with a fixed-rate ("volume") tender rather than move back to the previously-preferred variable-rate tender. In an environment of historically low short-term rates, misjudgements about liquidity demand could result in a rise in the tender rate, which would give a misleading signal to markets about a turning point in the interest rate cycle. In addition, the authorities have wished to avoid the possibility of the repo rate falling too close

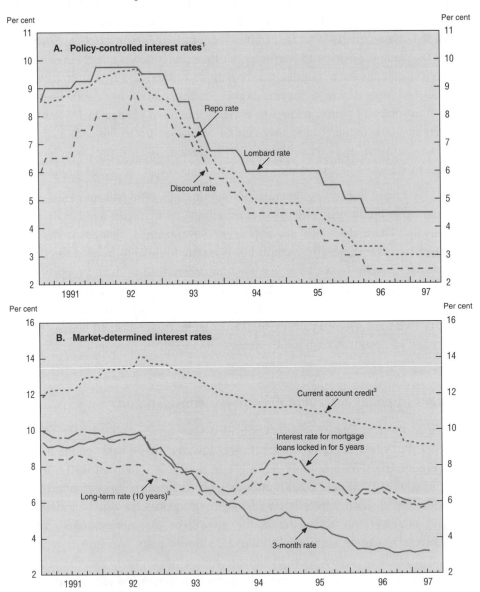

Figure 16. **INTEREST RATE DEVELOPMENTS**

Per cent

A. Policy-controlled interest rates[1]

Repo rate

Lombard rate

Discount rate

1991   92   93   94   95   96   97

Per cent

B. Market-determined interest rates

Current account credit[3]

Interest rate for mortgage
loans locked in for 5 years

Long-term rate (10 years)[2]

3-month rate

1991   92   93   94   95   96   97

1. End of period.
2. Yield on bonds outstanding.
3. Credit of less than DM 1 million.
Source: Deutsche Bundesbank.

to the discount rate, which would stimulate speculation of an imminent cut in this important "floor" rate. Rather, the Bundesbank's strategy over the review period has been to avoid creating the impression that the bottom of the interest rate cycle had been reached and that an increase in rates could therefore be expected.[31]

The development of market interest rates and exchange rates

The stability of policy-controlled rates has coincided with a marked shift in market-determined long-term rates. In particular, a noticeable feature of the development of long-term rates during 1996 and into 1997 was the steady widening of the differential between United States and German yields (Figure 17). With the German rate of consumer-price inflation lower than that in the United States, the real interest rate differential is in favour of Germany (Figure 18). However, shifts in the yield differential have been closely associated with changes in the exchange rate, which depreciated in terms of the dollar when the gap between Deutschemark and dollar yields increased and vice versa (Figure 17). This can be linked to evolving views about monetary policy, although the respective contributions of German monetary stance and a future EMU-based policy on interest and exchange-rate developments are unclear. Despite the downward shift in the level of the yield curve, the slope changed only marginally (Figure 19), suggesting that monetary policy has been successful in steering long-term rates down while maintaining stable expectations as to inflation and to the future course of monetary policy. However, the yield curve has remained relatively steep, indicating that markets still see potential risks for price stability in the future.

Assessment of monetary conditions

Over the review period, monetary conditions have eased significantly and constitute a favourable basis for faster growth. The money supply expanded faster in 1996 than the Bundesbank had intended without inflation expectations picking up (Figure 15). Although part of this growth was related to increased portfolio demand, transactions balances nevertheless grew rapidly: the narrowly defined definition of money, M1, increased by 11 per cent in 1996 and extended M3 by some 6 per cent.[32] Real long-term interest rates are around historical levels, and real short-term rates are at an historically low level (Figure 20). Moreover, short-term rates do not show signs of liquidity shortage and the so-called "monetary conditions indicator" suggests that the overall stance is as easy as at any time

Figure 17. **EXCHANGE RATE AND LONG-TERM INTEREST DIFFERENTIALS**

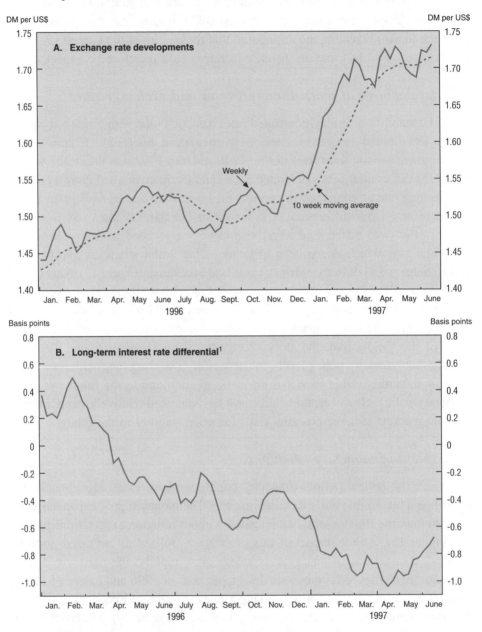

1. Benchmark government bonds (10 years). German bonds minus US bonds.
Source: OECD.

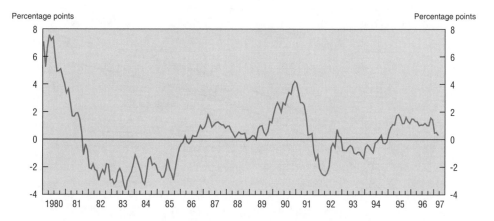

Figure 18. **REAL LONG-TERM INTEREST RATE PREMIA BETWEEN GERMANY AND THE UNITED STATES**[1]

1. Real interest rate for Germany minus real interest rate for the United States. The underlying long-term interest rates are the following:
    Germany: until 1990 7-15 years German public sector bonds, from 1990 yields on listed federal securities with residual maturities of 9 to 10 years; United States: until 1990 US Government bonds, composite over 10 years, from 1990 the benchmark government bonds (10 years).
Source: Deutsche Bundesbank ; OECD, *Main Economic Indicators.*

since the early 1980s (Figure 21).[33] However, it is the exchange rate depreciation which has made the greatest contribution to the easing of overall monetary conditions.[34]

On the assumption that potential output will expand by only a little over 2 per cent in 1997, the Bundesbank has set guidelines for money supply growth for 1997 and 1998 of 5 per cent a year with a band of 3.5 to 6.5 per cent in 1997.[35] The medium-term inflation assumption was set at 1½ to 2 per cent. The monetary target allows for the overshooting of the money supply in 1996 since it was due to portfolio shifts and did not increase inflation risks (Figure 15). By extending the time horizon of monetary targeting to two years, the Bundesbank has reacted to the changed underlying conditions in the run-up to the third stage of EMU. In view of the danger of increasing uncertainties in the financial and foreign exchange market, a clearly-defined monetary target is intended to create confidence in the continuation of a stability-oriented policy stance.

Figure 19. **YIELD CURVES AND THE YIELD GAP**

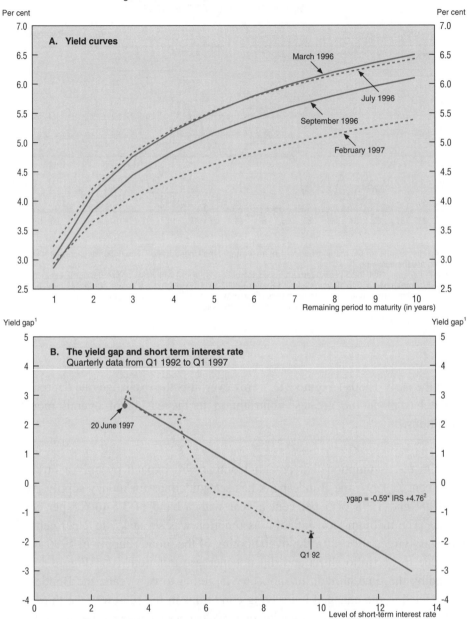

1. Benchmark government bonds (10 years) minus 3-month interest rates.
2. Slope of the regression line estimated using quarterly data from Q1 1980 to Q1 1997.
Source: Deutsche Bundesbank; OECD.

Figure 20. **REAL INTEREST RATES**

Per cent

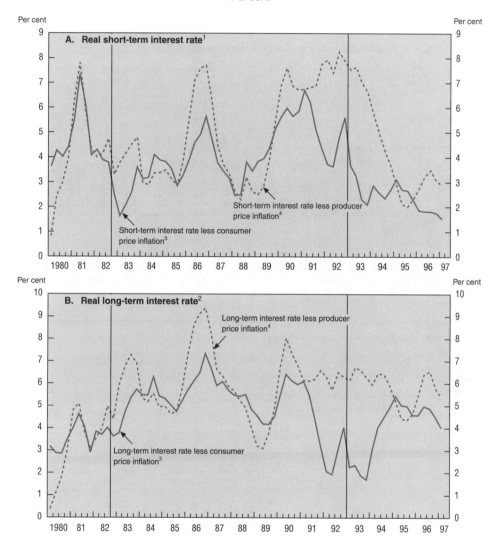

The vertical lines indicate the troughs.
1. 3-month rate.
2. Until 1990 7-15 year German public sector bonds, from 1990 yields on listed federal securities with residual maturity of 9 to 10 years.
3. As measured by the 4-quarter percentage change in the consumer price index excluding food and energy.
4. As measured by the 4-quarter percentage change in the producer price index.
Source: Deutsche Bundesbank ; OECD, *Main Economic Indicators.*

Figure 21. **INDICATORS OF MONETARY CONDITIONS**

Per cent

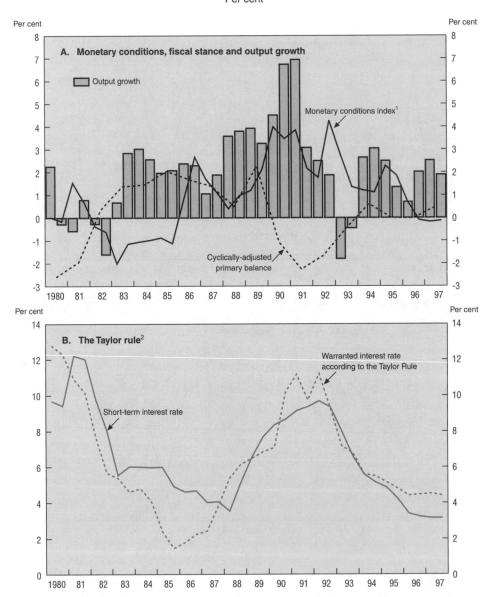

1. See footnote 34 for the calculation of the monetary conditions index.
2. See footnote 33 for the calculation of the short-term rate implied by the Taylor Rule.
Source: OECD.

Based on an extrapolation from 1994, the German research institutes have argued the need for a faster rate of growth of M3 closer to 7 per cent[36] in 1997 (Figure 14). However, as usual, the monetary growth trends will have to be interpreted in a broader perspective, including the development of the exchange rate, financial conditions more generally, and the evolution of output relative to potential. If incoming data suggest weaker growth than projected by the OECD, and forward-looking indicators of inflation are satisfactory, the strategy of matching money growth to potential output growth would call for a decline in interest rates insofar as underlying monetary growth is judged to fall below target.

Over the coming review year the formulation and execution of monetary policy will become increasingly complex in the run-up to European Monetary Union. The most immediate impact could be exchange rate and bond market turbulence arising from market perceptions about which countries will be members of EMU and the likely monetary stance to be taken by the European Central Bank. Exchange-rate and bond-market volatility may increase, making the interpretation of underlying financial conditions difficult. A great deal will depend on decisions about how to convert currencies to the Euro: whether rates will be defined immediately, in which case a monetary union effectively takes place straight away, or whether market rates at the end of the year will be taken as conversion rates.[37] At the same time, interest rates among members of the EMU will converge with DM rates, thereby making money and credit conditions in Germany dependent upon perceptions of the area-wide policy stance which will be followed by the European Central Bank. In the transition period the Bundesbank will probably need to focus increasingly on creating a stable monetary environment in the region as a whole so as not to overburden the new European central bank at its founding when both its credibility and operational techniques are still to be established.

Within such a framework, German monetary policy will exercise a key role. A continuing premium will attach to the type of stability-oriented monetary policy which has been followed in recent years, and the fact that the Bundesbank has specified a guideline for monetary growth in 1998 is important here.[38] However, since output and inflation expectations will increasingly depend on EMU-wide monetary conditions, in the transitional phase to EMU, the range of indicators which will need to be considered in formulating monetary policy will have to be widened. Since German monetary policy will remain the most crucial element in European monetary conditions, flexibility will be even more important in formulating monetary policy in the course of 1997 and through 1998. Most crucially, however, such flexibility needs to be delineated by the overall need to contain inflation expectations and in this respect the Bundesbank's adoption of a monetary target for 1998 should act to prevent instability.

III. Reforming the health sector: efficiency through incentives

Introduction

The quality of health services in Germany is high and access to them universal, accounting in part for widespread popular support of the medical system. Policy measures to reform the health system over the past 20 years[39] have been driven by a concern to preserve these benefits, while avoiding an increase in contribution rates to compulsory health insurance which, given the German practice of financing through contributions equally shared between employers and employees, leads to rising non-wage labour costs. Since the reforms of 1989, policy has focused on cost containment, at first through price caps for medicines and increased co-payments, and since 1993 by the introduction of global budget restraints for hospitals, physicians and for pharmaceuticals. After initial success, contribution rates have nevertheless continued to increase and the statutory health funds incurred deficits in both 1995 and 1996. Underlying this development have been factors common to other OECD countries, such as technological advances and incentives for over-supply, but in the case of Germany the integration of the new Länder has also contributed powerfully to the rise in current and capital expenditures. The institutional structure of health supply is being brought into line with that in the old Länder as health policy aims to achieve a uniform standard of health care throughout Germany. With cost containment policies ineffective and inefficient, most participants in the health policy debate accept that more fundamental reforms, which also aim to increase efficiency of health care suppliers, are now required. Such steps are also necessary to deal with the demographic transition, which will have a major impact on the structure of health demand. Consensus is, however, hard to reach since reforms will undoubtedly affect interest groups in different ways and, with most OECD countries still

67

experimenting with various approaches to health reform, there is no clearly best path to follow.

This chapter analyses the policy issues, focusing in particular on the need to improve efficiency in the provision of health services. The first section reviews health outcomes and overall resource use. It concludes that although health outcomes do not differ from those observed in the OECD area at large, resource use is above average and pressures on expenditures can be expected to increase in the future. The second section identifies areas of inefficient resource use in the health system and seeks to explain these by considering the institutional structure of the health sector and the pattern of incentives facing suppliers of health services. Recent policy measures are also discussed from this perspective. A central theme is the lack of integration in the health system and the weak and sometimes distorted pattern of incentives. The third section considers the general policy issues, against the background of the ongoing reform efforts of the government, and presents recommendations for further policy initiatives.

Size of the health sector and pressures on spending

Health spending has accounted for around 10 per cent of GDP in Germany during the 1990s, and even excluding the high costs arising from unification (*Annex I*), the volume of health expenditures relative to GDP is high by international standards (Figure 22). There has also been a tendency for this ratio to increase at a faster pace than is normal in the OECD area as a whole. Health expenditure per capita is also high even allowing for Germany's relatively high income per capita (Figure 23). Total health expenditures (including investment) drifted upwards relative to GDP throughout the 1980s but surged to over 10 per cent of GDP in 1991 and 1992 with the incorporation of the new Länder into the system (Figure 24); the ratio of health expenditures to GDP is some 13 per cent in the new Länder compared with around 8.5 per cent in the old Länder. There are indications that the ratio has since resumed the previous upward trend. With direct employment of around 1.9 million in 1994 – an estimated further million are employed in closely related occupations[40] – the sector is one of the most important in the economy and represents a dynamic component of the expanding service sector.[41] The impact on the economy and on resource allocation is, however, greater than the GDP contribution alone would suggest: cash benefits to

Figure 22. **THE VOLUME OF HEALTH SPENDING: INTERNATIONAL COMPARISON**[1]

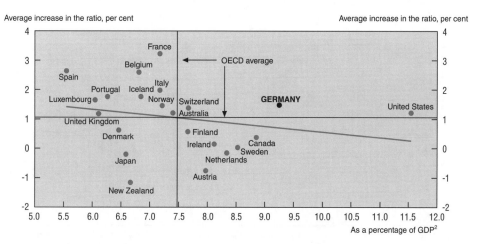

1. During 1970-94. 1970-93 for Belgium, Denmark, Italy, Luxembourg and Sweden 1970-93 ; 1977-93 for Portugal; 1978-93 for New Zealand; 1980-93 for Japan.
2. (Health spending/Health price index)/(GDP/GDP deflator). Average for the period.
3. Unweighted average.
Source: OECD Health Data 97.

Figure 23. **HEALTH EXPENDITURE AND GDP PER CAPITA**[1]

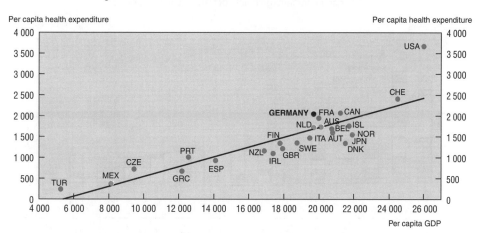

Note: The equation of the regression line is the following:
    Health expenditure per capita = -631.97 + 0.12* GDP per capita
    R squared = 0.74   T: (-2.37) (8.24)
1. Total Germany in 1994. For other countries in 1994 or 1995. Total expenditure on health care and GDP in purchasing power parity exchange rates.
Source: OECD Health Data 97.

69

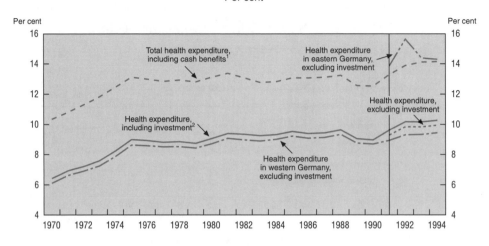

Figure 24. **HEALTH EXPENDITURES IN RELATION TO GDP**

Per cent

1. From 1991 total Germany.
2. The figure for 1996 is an OECD estimate. From 1991 total Germany.
Source: Federal Ministry for Health; *OECD Health Data 97.*

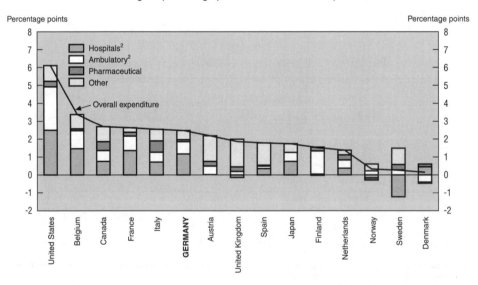

Figure 25. **DECOMPOSITION OF THE GROWTH IN HEALTH SPENDING[1]**

Change in percentage points of trend GDP over period

1. Current spending. During the period 1973 (or the nearest year available) to 1994 (or the nearest year available).
2. For Sweden and United Kingdom public spending.
Source: OECD 97 Health Data.

70

the sick are also an important part of the system and when these are taken into consideration, total outlays are around 14 per cent in comparison with GDP (Figure 24).

Over the period 1970-94 current health expenditures increased by some 2.5 percentage points of trend GDP (Figure 25). Expenditure growth was most pronounced in the hospital sector, but from the international perspective this is not unusual. Of greater concern is the pickup since the late 1980s, when the growth rate of nominal expenditure accelerated and was significantly above the OECD average (Table 11).[42] The causes underlying the recent increase in

Table 11. **The growth of nominal health spending**[1]

	Annual average growth in excess of GDP				As a percentage of GDP	
	1960-70	1970-80	1980-90	1990-96[2]	1960[3]	1996[2]
Germany (western)	**3.1**	**3.8**	**−0.1**	**2.1**	**4.8**	**9.7**
United States	3.6	2.6	3.6	2.4	5.2	14.2
Japan	n.a.	4.2	−0.7	4.0	4.4	7.2
France	3.6	3.0	1.8	2.1	4.2	9.8
Italy	4.0	3.7	1.7	−1.0	3.6	7.7
United Kingdom	1.5	2.6	0.7	2.6	3.9	6.9
Canada	2.8	0.3	2.6	−0.1	5.5	9.1
Australia	1.5	2.9	1.4	1.0	4.9	8.6
Austria	2.3	4.1	−1.1	2.1	4.4	7.9
Belgium	1.9	5.5	1.5	1.2	3.4	8.0
Denmark	5.8	1.3	−0.6	−0.6	3.6	6.2
Finland	4.2	1.5	2.3	−0.7	3.9	7.7
Greece	3.8	0.8	2.0	6.7	2.4	5.9
Iceland	5.0	3.1	3.5	−0.1	3.3	7.9
Ireland	3.8	6.1	−3.2	−0.7	3.8	6.4
Luxembourg	n.a.	5.8	0.6	1.4	3.7	7.0
Netherlands	4.9	3.3	0.5	0.5	3.8	8.6
New Zealand	2.5	1.6	1.8	0.5	5.0	7.3
Norway	4.6	5.0	1.2	−1.7	3.0	7.3
Portugal	n.a.	9.4	1.5	5.1	2.8	8.2
Spain	10.5	5.1	2.3	0.6	1.5	7.2
Sweden	4.8	3.1	−0.7	−3.9	4.7	7.2
Switzerland	5.1	3.7	1.5	3.3	3.3	9.8
EU[4]	4.3	4.0	0.5	1.3	3.5	7.5
OECD[4]	4.1	3.6	1.0	1.2	3.8	8.0

1. Including investment.
2. In a number of cases refers only to 1990 to 1995. For Germany 1990 to 1994.
3. 1970 for Luxembourg, Portugal and Japan.
4. Unweighted average.
Source: OECD Health Data 97.

expenditures in relation to GDP include the cyclical weakness of the economy and the cost of restructuring the health system in the new Länder (*Annex I*). However, even taking account of these special factors, cost increases have been a major problem.

Macro determinants of health spending

Population ageing

Population ageing has not been a major factor pushing up the volume share of health spending over the last few decades, but it is projected to become an important source of spending pressure in the future as the number of elderly people increases sharply. As Figure 26 indicates, health expenditures grow rapidly with age in Germany. For the OECD on average, after the age of 60 health expenditures grow particularly rapidly and a broad rule of thumb is that persons above this age consume about four times as much health care as those below. It has been estimated that, for the OECD as a whole, with unchanged policies and institutions, health care spending would rise by 0.4 to 0.7 per cent

Figure 26. **HEALTH EXPENDITURES INCREASE SHARPLY WITH AGE**
Estimated expenditures per insured by age, 1995

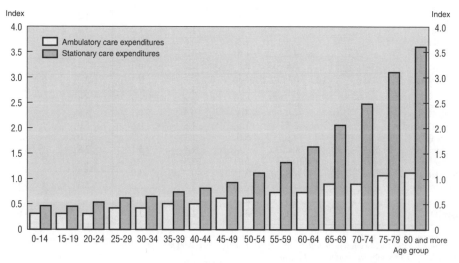

Source: Gesundheitsversorgung und Krankenversicherung 2000, Sondergutachten 1995, Sachverständigenrat für die Konzertierte Aktion im Gesundheitswesen, Nomos, 1995.

Table 12.   **The effects of population ageing on the volume of health expenditure**

Type of expenditure		2000	2005	2010	2020	2030
		Annual average growth rate from 1995				
Ambulatory	Scenario 1[1]	0.7	0.5	0.4	0.2	0.1
	Scenario 3[1]	0.8	0.7	0.6	0.4	0.3
Dentists	Scenario 1	0.1	−0.0	−0.3	−0.3	−0.5
	Scenario 3	0.3	0.2	0.2	−0.1	−0.2
Hospitals	Scenario 1	0.9	0.8	0.7	0.5	0.4
	Scenario 3	1.0	1.0	0.9	0.7	0.6
Pharmaceuticals	Scenario 1	1.0	0.9	0.8	0.6	0.5
	Scenario 3	1.1	1.1	1.0	0.8	0.7
Medicines	Scenario 1	0.8	0.7	0.6	0.3	0.1
	Scenario 3	0.9	0.8	0.7	0.5	0.3
Dental replacement	Scenario 1	0.7	0.6	0.4	0.0	0.2
	Scenario 3	0.9	0.8	0.6	0.3	0.1
Total expenditure	Scenario 1	0.7	0.6	0.6	0.4	0.2
	Scenario 3	0.9	0.8	0.7	0.6	0.3

1.   The two scenarios are based on different assumptions about the development of the group above the age of 60 relative to the age group 20 to 60 years. Scenario 3 results in a higher share of the population aged 60 and over.
Source: Sachverständigenrat für die Konzertierte Aktion im Gesundheitswesen, Sondergutachten, 1995, *Gesundheitsversorgung und Krankenversicherung 2000,* Table 1.

per annum between 2000 and 2020 simply due to ageing.[43] OECD simulations for Germany suggest that spending could rise by some 1.5 percentage points of GDP by 2030. A good deal of the projected additional expenditure arises not from increased longevity but from the projected rise in the numbers of the elderly: increased life expectancy may not have a great effect on health costs *per se* since these appear to remain concentrated in the period shortly before death regardless of actual age (compression of morbidity) and recent research indicates that health costs incurred in treating those of advanced age might not be as great as expected. In addition to increased expenditures, the composition of demand is also projected to change significantly, with pharmaceutical expenditure and stationary care projected to grow particularly strongly (Table 12).

Rising relative prices

The relative price of health care in Germany, as conventionally measured in the national accounts and relative to the GDP deflator, has been steadily rising over time, at about the rate common for the OECD area. However, there has been

Figure 27. INTERNATIONAL TRENDS IN RELATIVE HEALTH CARE PRICES
Index 1970 = 100[1]

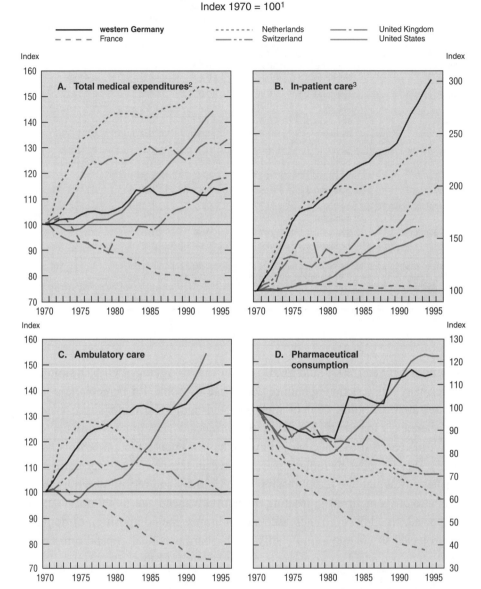

1. Deflator for health-expenditure deflated by the GDP deflator.
2. Including investment.
3. Data for Switzerland have been estimated by the OECD for the period prior to 1978.
Source: OECD Health Data 97.

some acceleration in the 1990s. Most of this rise can in turn be traced to the hospital sector where prices have risen two-and-a half times faster than general inflation since 1970 and have accelerated further in the 1990s (Figure 27). In addition, pharmaceuticals prices have also been rising rapidly after marked declines in the 1980s and the movement of relative prices has closely followed that in the United States, but not those in other European countries. By contrast, prices in the outpatient sector – mainly reflecting the development of wages – have shown little tendency to rise since the beginning of the 1980s. A rising relative price for health services is generally to be expected. Productivity gains in such labour-intensive areas as in-patient treatment are not measured but are often considered to be less than those in manufacturing. However, this principle of inevitable relative cost rises should not be taken too far when considering the constraints on health sector spending. For example, the greater use of medicines could reduce hospital costs and ambulatory care significantly.[44]

Costs and performance

Price statistics in the area of health services need to be treated with a great deal of caution, but comparisons carried out as part of the investigation of purchasing power parities point to a relatively low price level in Germany – with the notable exception of pharmaceuticals purchased directly from pharmacies by the public, and medical supplies (Figure 28). Again, these prices refer to the costs of inputs, not cures, and estimates of value-for-money are more accurately based on comparisons of performance and total inputs used.

In general, the quality of health services is high in Germany and access to such services is universal. The relationship between the inputs of health care and the health status of the population is complex, being influenced by factors such as life style. Moreover, the concept of health status is itself multi-dimensional. On the whole, health status appears average in comparison with the OECD area (Figure 29). Infant mortality at 5.6 per 1 000 live births in 1994 is among the lowest in the OECD. Expectation of life at birth in 1993, though still below the OECD average, has risen to 79.3 years for women and 73.8 years for men. However, a better measure of health status – and a useful indicator of outcomes of the health system – is "potential life years lost" (PLYL), which represents the shortening of life expectancy due to avoidable disease. Figure 30 indicates that the number of years lost is slightly above the OECD average, even though health

Figure 28. **COMPARISON OF PRICE LEVELS IN THE HEALTH SECTOR**[1]

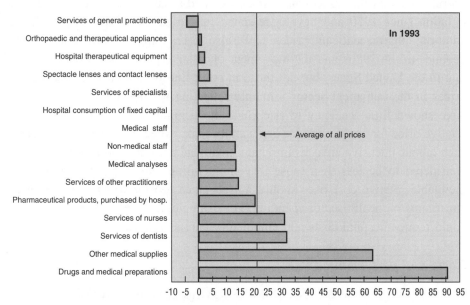

In 1993

Services of general practitioners
Orthopaedic and therapeutical appliances
Hospital therapeutical equipment
Spectacle lenses and contact lenses
Services of specialists
Hospital consumption of fixed capital
Medical staff
Non-medical staff
Medical analyses
Services of other practitioners
Pharmaceutical products, purchased by hosp.
Services of nurses
Services of dentists
Other medical supplies
Drugs and medical preparations

Average of all prices

-10 -5 0 5 10 15 20 25 30 35 40 45 50 55 60 65 70 75 80 85 90 95

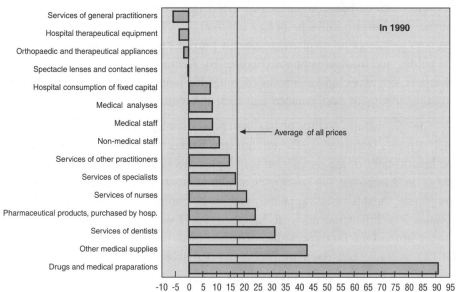

In 1990

Services of general practitioners
Hospital therapeutical equipment
Orthopaedic and therapeutical appliances
Spectacle lenses and contact lenses
Hospital consumption of fixed capital
Medical analyses
Medical staff
Non-medical staff
Services of other practitioners
Services of specialists
Services of nurses
Pharmaceutical products, purchased by hosp.
Services of dentists
Other medical supplies
Drugs and medical praparations

Average of all prices

-10 -5 0 5 10 15 20 25 30 35 40 45 50 55 60 65 70 75 80 85 90 95

1.   Difference between Germany and the EU countries, using the relevant PPPs.
Source: OECD, *Purchasing Power Parities and Real Expenditures.*

76

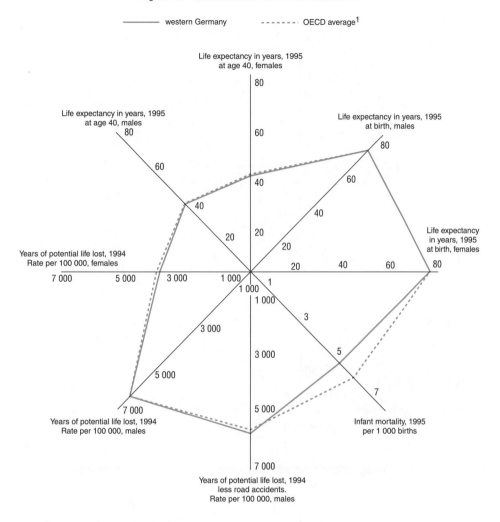

Figure 29. **INDICATORS OF HEALTH STATUS**

——— western Germany   - - - - - - OECD average[1]

1. OECD average less Czech Republic, Hungary, Mexico, Poland and Turkey.
Source: OECD, Health Data 97.

spending as a percentage of GDP is now significantly above average. In addition, Germany has not been particularly successful in improving relative performance over several decades: potential life years lost has declined in line with the OECD average even though the expenditure increase was above average (Figure 31).

77

Figure 30. **HEALTH EXPENDITURES AND HEALTH OUTCOMES**[1]

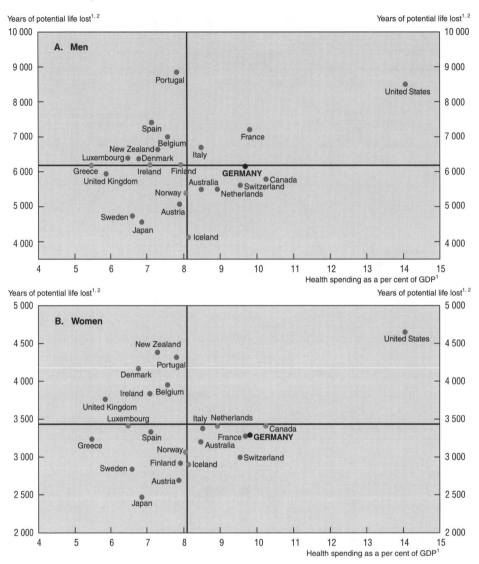

1. Western Germany in 1994, for other countries latest year available. Health spending includes investment.
2. Rate per 100 000 male/female population, aged 0 to 64. These data, based on the "avoidable mortality" concept, provide a crude measure of premature mortality embracing both somatic and mental causes of death which could have been prevented if medical knowledge had been applied, if known public health principles had been in force, and if risky behavioural stances had not been so prevalent.
Source: OECD Health Data 97.

Figure 31. **CHANGES IN HEALTH EXPENDITURES AND IN HEALTH OUTCOMES**

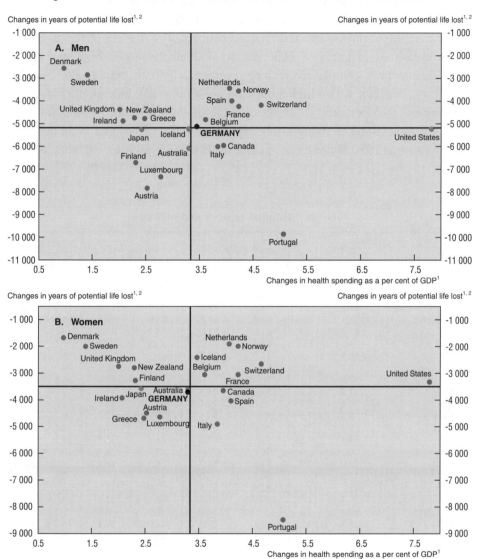

Changes in years of potential life lost[1,2]

Changes in years of potential life lost[1,2]

A. Men

Denmark
Sweden
Netherlands
Norway
United Kingdom ● New Zealand
Spain ●
Switzerland
Ireland ● ● ● Greece
France
Belgium
Japan   Iceland   **GERMANY**   United States
● Canada
Finland   Australia   Italy
Luxembourg
Austria

Portugal

Changes in health spending as a per cent of GDP[1]

Changes in years of potential life lost[1,2]

Changes in years of potential life lost[1,2]

B. Women

● Denmark
Netherlands
● Sweden   Norway
United Kingdom
● New Zealand   ● Iceland
Belgium
Switzerland   United States
● Finland   France
Australia
Ireland ● Japan **GERMANY** ● Canada
Austria   ● Spain
Greece   Luxembourg   Italy ●

Portugal

Changes in health spending as a per cent of GDP[1]

1. Western Germany. Between the end of the 60s and the mid-90s. Health spending includes investment.
2. Rate per 100 000 male/female population, aged 0 to 64. These data, based on the "avoidable mortality" concept, provide a crude measure of premature mortality embracing both somatic and mental causes of death which could have been prevented if medical knowledge had been applied, if known public health principles had been in force, and if risky behavioural stances had not been so prevalent.
Source: OECD Health Data 97.

79

Most indicators of direct resource use indicate that health outcomes which are about average for OECD countries are associated with high inputs, including hospital services, physicians and pharmaceuticals. The density of the stationary sector measured in terms of beds per 10 000 inhabitants is high and this is associated with a comparatively long average length of stay (acute cases of 13.9 days), together with a high admission rate (Table 13). Indeed, the number of admissions is 15 per cent above the average of the European Union. However, there are indications of rising efficiency: the number of hospital beds has been declining since 1980 although the rate of decline has only been half that in other

Table 13. **Hospital capacity and utilisation**

	Beds for 1 000 inhabitants		Average bed occupancy (per cent)		Average length of hospital stay (days)		Admission rate of population (per cent)	
	1970[1]	1994[1]	1970[1]	1994[1]	1970[1]	1994[1]	1970[1]	1994[1]
Germany (western)	**11.2**	**10.0**	**88.5**	**83.9**	**24.9**	**14.9**	**15.4**	**20.6**
United States	7.5	4.1	80.3	66.1	14.9	8.8	15.5	13.0
Japan	12.7	16.2	81.6	83.1	55.3	45.5	5.4	8.9
France	9.2	8.9	83.2	81.2	18.3	11.2	7.4	22.7
Italy	10.5	6.5	77.9	72.7	19.1	10.8	15.7	16.0
United Kingdom	9.4	4.9	82.1	80.6	25.7	10.2	10.9	23.0
Canada	7.0	5.4	80.4	84.2	11.5	12.6	16.5	12.5
Australia	11.7	8.9	81.6	74.5	..	14.0	..	16.5
Austria	10.8	9.3	86.4	79.4	22.2	10.9	15.5	24.7
Belgium	8.3	7.6	85.7	83.5	20.7	12.0	9.3	19.8
Denmark	8.1	5.0	80.6	83.8	18.1	7.5	14.4	20.4
Finland	15.1	9.3	91.0	87.7	24.4	11.8	18.2	25.4
Greece	6.2	5.0	76.0	70.0	15.0	8.8	10.5	13.5
Iceland	12.9	15.9	98.3	84.0	28.3	16.8	16.4	28.0
Ireland	12.6	5.0	80.1	77.0	13.3	7.7	12.4	15.5
Luxembourg	12.7	11.1	82.6	81.4	27.0	15.5	13.4	19.4
Netherlands	11.4	11.3	90.9	88.6	38.2	32.8	10.0	11.1
New Zealand	10.8	7.3	..	57.3	16.1	6.9	9.3	14.1
Norway	15.7	13.5	83.1	83.0	21.0	10.1	13.2	15.0
Portugal	6.5	4.1	74.1	71.0	23.8	9.8	6.9	11.3
Spain	4.7	4.0	69.0	76.7	18.0	11.5	7.1	10.0
Sweden	15.3	6.5	83.6	82.1	27.2	7.8	16.6	18.5
Switzerland	..	20.8	84.6	82.6	26.0	25.2	13.1	15.0
EU countries[2]	10.1	7.2	82.1	80.0	22.4	12.2	12.2	18.1
OECD[2]	10.5	8.2	82.8	78.9	23.1	14.0	12.4	17.2

1. Or nearest year available. For Germany 1994.
2. Unweighted average.
Source: OECD Health Data 97.

Table 14. **Indicators of resource use in the health sector**

	Average growth (number of physicians)		Physicians per 1 000 population	Proportion of specialists	Ambulatory sector	
					Contacts with physicians per capita per year	Prescriptions per capita
	1970-80[1]	1980-95	1994[2]	1994[2]	1994[2]	1994[2]
Germany (western)	**3.4**	**4.6**	**3.4**	**47.4**	**6.1**[3]	**12.8**[3]
United States	3.4	2.8	2.6	50.9	6.0	6.5
Japan	2.8	2.9	1.8	..	16.3	..
France	5.2	3.2	2.9	49.4	6.3	52.0
Italy	4.9	2.8	1.7	..	11.0	21.1
United Kingdom	2.7	1.7	1.6	..	5.8	9.3
Canada	3.6	2.4	2.2	41.8	6.8	..
Australia	5.4	3.6	2.2	34.4	10.6	9.2
Austria	2.0	3.7	2.7	53.3	6.3	17.4
Belgium	4.8	3.7	3.7	40.5	8.0	10.4
Denmark	4.9	2.2	2.9	5.1	4.8	7.6
Finland	6.8	3.6	2.8	56.5	4.1	6.0
Greece	5.1	4.0	3.9	55.7	5.3	21.0
Iceland	5.3	3.6	3.0	..	4.8	16.0
Ireland	2.5	2.2	1.7	17.4	6.6	12.5
Luxembourg	4.9	2.6	2.2	62.7	..	..
Netherlands	5.2	3.3	2.5	33.3	5.7	8.0
New Zealand	5.2	2.9	2.1	26.9	3.8	8.8
Norway	4.1	2.8	2.8	4.2	3.8	6.9
Portugal	9.0	2.8	3.0	66.1	3.2	19.8
Spain	6.6	4.8	4.1	..	6.2	14.8
Sweden	5.7	2.5	3.1	71.4	3.0	6.4
Switzerland	5.4	2.7	3.1	34.8	11.0	19.0
Turkey	7.0	6.5	1.1	42.1	1.2	..
EU[4]	5.4	3.6	2.8	46.6	5.9	15.7
OECD[4]	4.8	3.2	2.6	41.8	6.4	14.3

1. United Kingdom 1979-80; Australia 1971-80; Belgium, Ireland 1971-80.
2. Or nearest year available. For Germany 1994.
3. Total Germany.
4. Unweighted average.
Source: OECD Health Data 1997.

European countries.[45] Greater progress has been made with respect to reducing admissions and the average length of stay. Public health investment (mainly in hospitals) has been almost the highest in the OECD area, although in recent years the special demands of reunification have played a role in this regard. The only indicator which has been comparatively low is the number of nursing staff, though this has been increasing rapidly in recent years in response to a policy initiative. With respect to the outpatient sector, Germany is characterised by a high density of practising physicians (Table 14). The number of drug prescriptions per capita is also higher than in a number of countries and in terms of expenditures per capita, Germany has the third highest level after France and Luxembourg. The relatively high price of pharmaceuticals is clearly one factor influencing this level.

Problems with the institutional setting

Major features of the health system

Germany follows the social insurance model for the provision of health care, which is in principle similar to the systems operating in Austria, France, the Netherlands and Japan. This model, described more fully in *Annex I*, is characterised by:

- *Compulsory coverage* for most employees, apprentices, pensioners and those on social benefits with income beneath a threshold level by non-profit public sector health funds (*Gesetzliche Krankenkassen*, GKV). Dependants are automatically insured so that the system covers about 90 per cent of the population. The funds are financed by contributions from employers and employees and they account for nearly a half of all health expenditures including cash benefits to the sick (Figure 32). Until 1997 consumer choice as to which health fund to join was quite restricted.
- The system is *self-governing,* with incorporated bodies representing health funds, doctors and hospitals negotiating important aspects of health policy. Overall regulatory responsibility for health policy is shared between the federal authorities and the Länder, with the latter having a great deal of authority.
- The *solidarity principle* is a key aspect of this statutory health system with contributions linked to gross wages (up to a limit) without reference to health risk and with household dependants co-insured without additional contributions. The insurance aspect of the statutory system has thus been very limited.

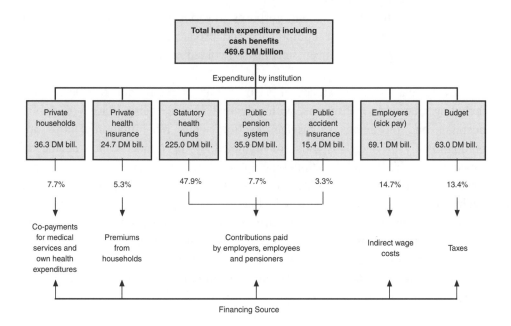

Figure 32. **INSTITUTIONAL STRUCTURE OF EXPENDITURES AND SOURCES OF INCOME OF THE HEALTH SYSTEM, 1994**

All Germany

Source: Federal Ministry for Health.

– *Voluntary health insurance for those with income above a statutory level and for the self-employed.* They may stay in the statutory system or opt out to private health insurance in which case they no longer pay contributions to the system. Once having left the statutory system it is practically impossible to return.

– *Co-existence of private risk-based health insurance with the solidarity-based statutory system.* For those who opt out of the statutory system private health insurance is available with premiums based on risk profiles. Insurance rates for young people are much lower than in the compulsory system and insurance companies compete actively for young clients in particular. Problems have arisen with the insurance of older people. A total of 7 million people were fully covered by private health insurance in 1995 and a further 6 million had supplemental policies in addition to their compulsory coverage.

– There is for all intents and purposes *freedom of choice* of physician and hospital in both the compulsory and private systems and rationing of health services has been steadfastly avoided on the grounds of equity.

Health care services are provided by a mix of public and private entities including charitable institutions, with principal reliance being placed on public hospitals and physicians in private practice, while rehabilitation centres are predominantly private. Hospitals are regulated by the Länder which decide on capacity, speciality and location but, apart from the provision of investment funds, they are not responsible for their financing. This is provided almost exclusively by the health funds which are also responsible for financing the ambulatory sector. Physicians are also organised mainly on a Länder basis through a statutory organisation which controls their number and location. In combination with the solidarity principle and universal access to services-in-kind, the role of price signals has been minimal, resulting in an essentially bureaucratic system for managing resources.

Since reunification, the structure of the west German health system has been extended to the new Länder, which has required extensive restructuring. Health funds have been established whose finance is independent from that in the old Länder. The ambulatory sector in the GDR was based around large outpatient clinics (polyclinics). In the absence of a long-term commitment by the Länder, the clinics have been running down rapidly, with specialists leaving to set up private practice. A network of practising physicians and dentists has been established surprisingly quickly. There has been significant financial help from government programmes in doing this and the debt level of many practices is said to be high. The hospital sector was burdened by a large number of long-term patients and by under-investment. Patients requiring long-term nursing care have now been transferred from the acute care sector and there is a special programme of hospital investment amounting to some DM 21 billion, shared equally between the federal government, the Länder and the health funds, spread over the period 1995 to 2004. Health costs are higher than in the west and with contribution income weaker, contribution rates are relatively high. The two health systems

Box 2. The three stages of the current phase of health reform

The first phase of the current health reform took place in 1989 and, amongst other things, emphasised the need to control expenditures on pharmaceuticals. In 1992 the major parliamentary parties and the Länder agreed to the so-called second phase reform which was passed by the parliament and entered into force in 1993 (*Gesundheitsstrukturgesetz*, GSG). The background to the initiative was the need to avoid a projected major increase in contribution rates in 1993 and 1994, but after the disappointing experience with previous reform measures, the need for a deeper structural change was also addressed. The objectives of the reform were therefore to: prevent health expenditures growing faster than contributions to the statutory health funds over the period 1993-1995; and to take steps to establish a self-managing and efficient health system, which would ensure stability of insurance contribution rates through the introduction of more market incentives. In pursuit of these objectives, global budgets were introduced for hospitals, doctors (and dentists) and for medicines, which were to be phased out in a third stage of reforms taking effect in 1997. Measures were included to control the over-supply of doctors, to improve the incentives for hospitals to increase efficiency and to improve co-operation between doctors and hospitals. Measures were also taken to prepare the statutory health funds for competition, which was to become the principal organising framework of the system; a fund to balance different risk profiles between health funds was set up in preparation for introducing the freedom to choose funds by individuals in 1997.

Not all the elements of the law were put into operation due in part to disagreements with Länder which retain a great deal of legislative authority, in particular over hospitals. A positive list for medicines was not introduced. Hospital budgets have also been exceeded due to exceptions introduced at the Länder level while, after a marked initial decline, the pharmaceuticals budget has started to rise again. Contribution rates have risen further.

The third stage of the health reform has as its primary objective to: stabilise and lower contribution rates; establish competition between the health funds; strengthen self-management at all levels of the health system and increase cost-consciousness on the part of patients. The stage involves a number of legislative actions. One law (*Beitragsentlastungsgesetz*) reduced cash benefits paid by the health funds, curtailed treatment of spas and cut dental replacement and also legislated a reduction in contribution rates in January 1997. Performance related reimbursement was introduced into hospitals in 1996, but a major piece of legislation to change the structure of the health system was rejected by the upper house of parliament. In 1997 two laws (*Neuordnungsgesetz*) to replace the 1996 initiative were passed by the lower house of Parliament in March and entered into force in July; copayments were increased and the exempted population widened, increases in contribution rates of the individual health funds will be linked to increases in co-payments; clients will be able to switch funds immediately following any rate increases; and budget limits on total expenditures for physicians and for pharmaceuticals have been lifted with details of a new system to be determined by negotiations between the associations representing the doctors and the health funds. More generally, the possibilities for the two associations to negotiate have been widened.

– and in particular the health funds – are set to merge when the level of income in the new states exceeds 90 per cent of the western average.

The institutional setting has been undergoing extensive change since the beginning of the 1990s as part of the government's reform programme, and further measures have been implemented in July 1997 (see Box 2). The objectives of the reforms have been to achieve stability of – and more recently to reduce – contribution rates to the statutory funds, through the introduction of better incentive structures. The rationale behind them has been that high and rising costs and inefficient use of resources are the direct results of the pattern of incentives faced by the suppliers of health services, related to the institutional setting as well as to the lack of incentives for people to economise on health care. This section therefore assesses the pattern of incentives as it has evolved in response to the reforms in progress, and considers how they might ultimately influence behaviour.

Declining contribution base for financing the statutory health funds system

A feature of the German system is that about 60 per cent of total health expenditures are financed from wage-based contributions from both employers and employees. The bulk of these (around 80 per cent) accrue to the statutory health funds. The average contribution rate to these funds has been steadily increasing, reaching 13.5 per cent of wages and salaries liable for contributions (Figure 33). Even so, from 1992 to 1995, a period when health policy was attempting to contain costs, contribution income rose by 7.3 per cent whereas health expenditures increased by 10.3 per cent – deficits in 1992 and again in 1995 and 1996 being covered by running down reserves. The institutional structure of the health funds is such that any deficit must lead to increases in contribution rates, since they are self-financing and hence do not receive direct support from the budget. The increasing contribution rate to the statutory health funds has reflected to an important extent the development of the contribution base and in particular, gross wages. Total wages have been rising more slowly than GDP for some time (Figure 34), mainly due to the structural shift towards sectors with a lower wage share. In addition, since the mid 1980s the upper limit for wages on which contributions to the statutory health funds must be paid has risen more slowly than average wages since health policy has also sought to

Figure 33. **CONTRIBUTION RATES FOR COMPULSORY HEALTH INSURANCE**

Per cent

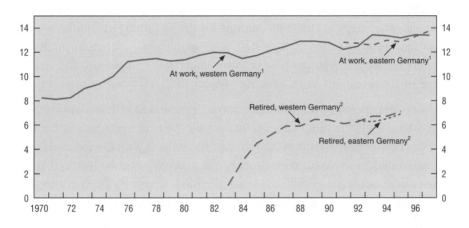

1. Average contribution rate across all health funds on wages and salaries liable for contributions, on 1 January.
2. On total income.
Source: Federal Ministry for Health.

Figure 34. **GROWTH OF THE CONTRIBUTION BASE**

Annual growth rate

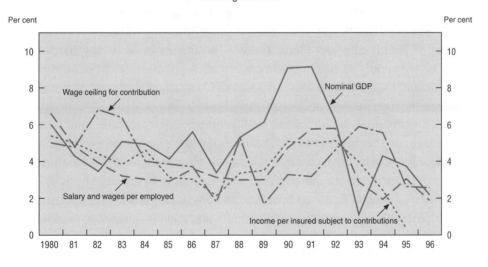

Source: Federal Ministry for Health.

"make room" for voluntary private health insurance. As a result, the growth of wages subject to compulsory contributions has grown even more slowly than wages and salaries per capita. Other influences include the rise in unemployment (the labour office pays health contributions for the unemployed, but the contribution revenue is lower than if they had been employed), increased numbers of pensioners whose contribution base is lower than for the employed, and a relative increase of those employed in jobs not subject to social security contributions.

Unless expenditures are stabilised through increased efficiency, or the contribution base expands more rapidly than in the past, the prospect is for health insurance contribution rates to rise more rapidly in the future. On the basis of past experience such increased contribution rates might not be fully offset by decreases in direct wage costs, so that employment would be likely to decline. It is this scenario which has focused policy deliberations on ways to improve efficiency.

Limited contractual relations between health funds and suppliers of health services

A key feature of the health system which recent reforms have aimed to correct has been the passive nature of financing by the health funds. The contractual relationships between the health funds and the suppliers of health services (physicians and hospitals) have been limited, allowing little control over the actions of health care providers. There is no institution with any incentive to integrate the supply of health care between all suppliers so as to minimise costs of treatment: the system remains segmented. Contractual relations are maintained between the associations of doctors, health funds and hospitals. Direct relations between individual health funds and hospitals are generally not permitted – although at a regional level the health funds deal as a group with individual hospitals in some matters (see below) – even though the fund may be the main source of finance, and the same applies with respect to funds and physicians. The imposition of budget limits on hospitals and physicians since 1993 has meant an end to passive financing and has forced efficiency gains, but it does not address the lack of integration and sometimes makes it worse as each group seeks to defend its own budget limit. The exchange of information is also limited: medical information which could assist health funds to identify best or worst practice hospitals and doctors could not be given to health funds on the grounds of confidentiality. The 1993 reform has improved the flow of information to the health funds but has not significantly extended the direct relationship between health funds and health providers. The most recent reforms which entered into force in July 1997 widen significantly the matters to be decided by negotiations between the associations but do not widen the scope for direct relations between individual funds and suppliers.

The system of health finance is itself fragmented, leading to possible inefficiency due to lack of co-ordination. Thus, rehabilitation institutions are financed for most people by the pension insurance system while long-term nursing care is financed separately by a wage-based contribution. The inherent danger in such a system is that efficiency-enhancing measures may be rejected by one of the institutions which views the change as simply a way of shifting costs in its direction.

Low integration between hospital and ambulatory care

Inefficiencies in the health sector as a whole are related in part to the low level of integration among providers of health services. There are a number of aspects to this. Under German law, there has been a strict segregation between ambulatory and hospital-based physicians resulting in a lack of systematic exchange of information between the two sectors and a frequent duplication of diagnostic procedures. In a number of Länder there are now agreements between the associations representing doctors, hospitals and health funds which aim to improve information flows, but their effectiveness will ultimately depend on the incentive structure confronting health suppliers to control costs. In addition, the gate-keeper function of general practitioners is weak. A physician who refers a patient to a specialist runs the real risk of losing the patient and therefore income because of the fee-for-service system. They have therefore had an incentive to refer a patient to a hospital rather than to an ambulatory specialist who could often perform the procedure in an outpatient setting at lower cost. One recent extensive study[46] came to the conclusion that 15 per cent of medical cases handled in hospitals could have been handled by the ambulatory sector where total costs were about half of those in the hospital. Potential savings on a total hospital budget of the GKV of around DM 80 billion were estimated by the study at around DM 7.5 billion for 1996. Moreover, hospitals have created informal networks of referring physicians, since there is effectively no control as to which hospital a patient chooses to visit.[47]

Another aspect of the problem is the underdeveloped nature of outpatient services in hospitals. This was recognised as a problem with the 1993 reforms, which increased the possibilities for greater outpatient treatment but it has not expanded to any great extent.[48] One reason for this appears to be the relatively low reimbursement which hospitals can obtain. While hospitals have pushed for greater freedom in the area of ambulatory care – and in the area of surgical procedures in particular – the association of doctors has strongly resisted the move, which is viewed as unfair competition. In the event, ambulatory surgery has been increasing, but it appears to be an additional health service since surgery performed in hospitals has not declined. Overall, there is a lack of incentives for both physicians in the ambulatory sector and the hospitals to package care for patients.

Hospital sector

Although at one time or another all cost components have shown a tendency to rise rapidly in relation to contribution income (Figure 35), hospitals (in-patient care) have been a major cost element of the system and their costs rose by 20.4 per cent over the period 1992-95.[49] Direct indicators point to considerable inefficiency in the hospital sector. Inefficiency has a number of dimensions besides the fact that hospitals might handle cases which could be more cost efficiently handled in the ambulatory sector. Procedures might be undertaken which are ineffective; patients might be kept in hospital longer than medically necessary; and overhead costs might be unnecessarily high:

- Many diagnostic procedures prescribed by doctors in both hospitals and in the ambulatory sector are regarded by the medical profession as not necessary. As an example of the wider problem, around a third of X-ray tests were judged by the German Association of Radiologists to be unnecessary while for bone tests the relevant association regarded only a fraction of the tests as useful.[50]
- International comparisons of similar medical procedures indicate that the duration of stay in hospital is extraordinarily long. For example, with a birth performed by caesarean section the average length of stay is around twelve days while in twelve other similar countries the average was

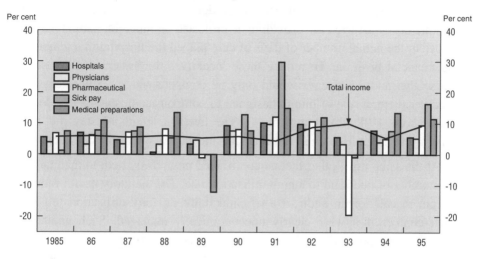

Figure 35. **HEALTH INSURANCE OUTLAYS BY TYPE OF EXPENDITURE**
Western Länder
Annual growth rate

Source: Federal Ministry for Health.

around seven days. More detailed studies of other procedures reveals a similar pattern.

- Investigations indicate that for hospital patients over 60 years of age, over one-third remain in hospital longer than medically necessary, while for those under 60 years the proportion is 40 per cent. For all patients the average length of stay could thus have been 2.6 days less which translates into some 85 000 excess beds and 26 million excess days of care.[51]
- Benchmarking across hospitals for the same procedure is difficult, but those which have been done in Germany indicate that total costs might vary as much as 50 per cent. The difference in cost extends across all aspects of the procedure including surgery, medicines, overheads and basic accommodation. Moreover, costs vary significantly between the Länder.

Incentive structures in the hospital remuneration scheme

The system of hospital remuneration has favoured high admission rates and relatively long stays in hospitals. Prior to 1986, hospitals operated on the basis of full cost recovery; for planning purposes, hospitals merely added their projected non-investment expenditures for the coming year and divided the sum by the number of prospective days of care to be delivered. With the per diem set to cover all costs incurred in providing a projected number of patient days, an increase in the actual number of days of care placed the hospital in a temporarily good financial position. To reduce these incentives the system was changed in 1986 so that additional days would only be compensated at 25 per cent of the agreed per diem, a rule of thumb designed to compensate hospitals only for their variable costs ("flexible budgeting"). The average length of stay did indeed decline up to 1992. However, the financial incentives were still not very strong.

At the same time, other factors contributed powerfully both to maintaining a large number of beds and to a high utilisation rate. The statutory health funds had the right to call for an audit of a hospital if its capacity utilisation fell below 85 per cent or if it were clearly uneconomically managed. Such audits were limited, but the possibility of such a control has been an incentive for hospital administrators to keep capacity utilisation above that level. This was underpinned by the incentive structure facing the powerful directors of hospital departments (*Chefarzt*). The chief physicians have usually negotiated a contract with the hospital that allowed them to offer services in the hospital to privately-insured patients. Such income could be a multiple of the public salary. Because the number of beds in a department has often been related to the number of public beds, which in turn depended on the utilisation rate, there has been a strong incentive for these chief physicians, as key influences on discharge decisions, to maintain high activity levels and a relatively long length of stay.

The 1993 reform did away with the principle of automatic cost recovery, and since that date hospitals have been permitted to make a cash profit or a loss.[52] From 1993 to the beginning of 1996 the system was based on a per diem payment (which covered both hospital and hospital-based physician services) subject to a global hospital budget; no hospital was to spend more than it had in 1992, apart from adjustments to reflect the annual growth of gross wages – the basis of income for the statutory health funds. However, in the case of a loss due to low utilisation the per diem of the current year was adjusted to compensate for some or all of the loss of the previous year.

Although the average length of stay and the number of beds declined further after 1993, the reform did not achieve its immediate objective. Hospital budgets have been exceeded over the entire period although expenditures declined surprisingly in 1996. There were several reasons for budget overruns. First, there were many exceptions, including provisions for increasing employment levels of nursing staff (*Pflegepersonalordnung*), increased costs via mandated reduced hours of work and special provisions for public service pay settlements. The former two have contributed powerfully to continually rising costs since 1993. Second, some Länder passed laws making adherence to budgets of subsidiary importance to the provision of health care – with predictable results. The 1993 law also increased the proportion of income from private patients which head doctors had to pay hospitals. Nevertheless, pressures to lower capacity were muted. With fixed costs high, efforts to reduce the length of stay would simply result in less income, which would require the funds to increase the per diem payment the following year to account for some of the financial shortfall. Fixed costs are high in part because hospital staff often have civil servant status and as such it is very difficult to reduce employment levels.

The 1993 reform defined a new system of performance-related financing which was voluntary up to the end of 1995 – only a few hospitals adopted the system – but which became compulsory for all hospitals in 1996. The system changes the pattern of incentives significantly and should eventually place hospitals with above average costs under considerable pressure to improve efficiency. It is oriented toward the reimbursement of therapy provided, so that it avoids in principle the danger of lower service quality sometimes associated with diagnostic-related payments systems. Four methods of hospital reimbursement have been defined:

- a flat rate fee per case (*Fallpauschale*) which covers all services related to a therapy for a set number of days;
- a special therapy related reimbursement fee (*Sonderentgelte*) which covers only some treatments, usually surgical procedures, the length of hospital stay being covered by a per diem;
- a ward-specific per diem rate (*Abteilungspflegesatz*) which covers only medically related services not reimbursed by either of the first two methods;
- a basic per diem rate (*Basispflegesatz*) which is hospital specific and which covers hospital-wide services not rendered by medical staff.

Therapy-based payments currently cover about 15 to 20 per cent of the total procedures performed (mostly surgical), amounting to around 20 per cent of the hospital budget. More procedures are expected to be covered by therapy-based payments in the future which will in the short run increase budget flexibility: the per diem budget is tightly controlled, with budget overruns being subject to partial reimbursement by the hospital so that the hospital gains more flexibility as the proportion of remuneration covered by therapy-based payments increases.[53] The original intention was that the per diem budget would be subject to a global budget restriction at the level of each Land and that eventually the per diem rate would be based on the average cost of all hospitals so that it would resemble a market price. These last two intentions were opposed by both the Länder and the hospitals and have not been realised in the legislation passed in 1996. Before the new system could fully take effect the government changed it in important ways, in response to the high level of budget appropriations requested by hospitals for 1996.[54] A budget cap was placed on individual hospital budgets for 1996, allowing only for increases related to the expected growth of public sector pay rates. A complex system of reimbursements for overruns in all four systems of payments was temporarily introduced to control excess expenditures.

The impact on hospital behaviour of the move toward performance-related reimbursements has been immediate. Hospitals have now started to introduce cost accounting systems and have become sensitive to the length of stay in hospital for those cases covered by therapy-based fees. The introduction of long-term care insurance for the elderly will also allow hospitals to cut the length of stay for those who do not require specific medical treatment. In addition, they have become much more sensitive to costs in various departments because of the ward-specific per diem. However, other less desirable incentives are also present to some extent: there appears to be a tendency to "optimise" payments by carefully selecting the therapy category while, given the uncertainty about the transition process, the rational strategy for a hospital at present remains to use its budget limit to the full.

Regulation of capacity and controls on investment

A major problem for the hospital system over the years has been the financing of investment. Hospital capacity is regulated by the Länder; they are responsible for investment expenditures but also determine the number of beds through their role in licensing hospitals. Since the Länder were not at the same time responsible for financing operating costs, or for covering deficits, there was a strong incentive to expand hospital capacity, thereby creating local employment and satisfying political pressure from cities and communities. This may account for the high density of beds and also for another noticeable feature: the large number of small and medium-sized hospitals. The Länder were, however, responsible for maintenance and replacement investment (depreciation), but a court decision in 1993 ruled that there was no constitutional basis for this. Since then the statutory health funds have also had to finance these costs, which are ultimately due to decisions beyond their control, leading to a legal challenge in 1996. While health funds will remain responsible for such costs in the future, from 1997 to 1999 they will be able to levy a DM 20 surcharge on each member of the statutory health funds to cover this investment-related gap.

The hospital system is thus characterised by dual financing; despite political agreement on the desirability of moving to a unified system, it continues to be a feature after the most recent reforms. Under dispute have been the powers of health funds *vis-à-vis* individual hospitals and the need to restrict the Länder to specifying only a general framework for hospitals within their borders. As a result, from the perspective of efficient hospital management there is little possibility of using investment in order to rationalise and to reduce operating costs. In private hospitals such rationalisation has sometimes taken place.[55] Moreover, the allocation of investment between hospitals is subject to many non-efficiency related factors. Nevertheless, there has been some progress. Budget pressures have forced the Länder to start to rationalise hospitals under their control by consolidating specialist departments. The lack of unified budgeting has also had an impact in another area: outpatient care. As noted above, an objective of the 1993 reform was to improve integration by allowing outpatient surgery in the hospitals. This possibility has not been used, in part because of the lack of general investment funds on the part of the hospitals.

The provision of long-term care

Rising pressures on social assistance provided to the elderly by communities led to the introduction of insurance for long-term care in 1995, with contribution rates of 1 per cent of eligible wages, and in July 1996 this was extended to stationary care and the contribution rate lifted to 1.7 per cent. The intention of the second phase is to encourage the development of special institutions to provide long-term nursing care and to relieve the burden on acute-care hospitals which are relatively expensive. It was intended that Länder and local governments would provide investment funds for this development on the basis of savings they would make from a reduction in social assistance payments. This has not happened, states and local government maintaining that there are no additional resources available for this purpose. The long-term care funds had an unexpected surplus of DM 6 billion in 1995 and this has extended into 1996. The surplus is due to a greater number of families than expected opting for cash benefits to support nursing at home rather than selecting benefits in kind. Perhaps as a result, hospitals have been able to reduce the number of long term care patients in wards (especially in the new Länder), helping to lower the average length of stay. As operating costs in hospitals might be reduced by increased investment in long-term care, the example illustrates the problems arising from the split financing of the German health system.

The ambulatory sector

At the end of 1995 the ambulatory sector comprised approximately 119 000 practising physicians and about 60 000 dentists. Only 26 500 of the former were in group practice, although it is often the case that doctors will form a group to collectively provide diagnostic testing. Doctors and dentists are organised into 19 regional organisations (KV, *Kassenärztliche Vereinigung*) for the purpose of negotiation and payment but they also regulate the number of practising doctors: the supply of physicians in the ambulatory sector is tightly controlled, via licenses to receive reimbursements from the GKV system. In 1993 the right to set up practice was severely restricted, and doctors above 55 years of age are prohibited from being granted a license. This has increased still further the barriers between the hospital and ambulatory sectors. There is no licensing restriction for physicians in the hospital sector. For some time now there have been controls on the number of medical students. Despite these controls, there is felt to be an oversupply of practitioners.

The structure of financial incentives

The method of finance for the ambulatory sector is basically a fee for service, which tends to lead to supply-induced demand, and this might have contributed to the high density of doctors: by 1993 there was widespread agreement among policy makers that there was an excess supply of physicians. Some 2 000 services are specified in the fee system, with points assigned to each service through negotiations between the doctors association (KV) and the association representing the GKV. In line with the emphasis on cost containment, from 1993 until 1997 each regional KV (including dentists) has been subject to a budget limit which was permitted to increase by the growth rate of wages (*i.e.* the growth of income of the health funds) each year. Doctors and dentists submit the total number of points which have accrued each quarter to their local KV which, after dividing the budget by the total number of points, reimburses them accordingly: there is no mechanism for the budget to be unused. Some of the regional associations also specify budgets for individual specialities. Doctors as a whole are thus effectively on a capitation system, but each individual doctor still has an incentive to increase output in order to gain the largest possible share of the KV budget and to increase their income. This danger implicit in the payments system became reality in 1996 when the total number of points submitted rose by an impressive 30 per cent and there has been a tendency for the number of services per case to increase. Much of the increase for the year was in the area of consultation; in order to encourage greater contact between doctors and patients, and to discourage technical testing, the relative number of points for each procedure was changed at the end of 1995. With the marginal cost of increasing consultations low, the incentives to increase the number of points to be reimbursed (''output'') has been high. This has been reinforced by uncertainty about the ultimate value of points so that the rational strategy for an individual doctor has been to strive for above average ''output'' increases.

At the same time, the fee-for-service system subject to a global budget restriction resulted in considerable uncertainty about the value of points, making medical practices difficult to manage. Starting in 1998, the point value will be fixed in advance by negotiations between the KV and the health funds. Each physician will have an individual reimbursement limit – determined and administered by the doctors associations rather than by the health funds – above which the value of points will decline. However, the system would only apply to a proportion of the current services (to be negotiated between the doctors' association and the health funds), the remainder being reimbursed separately. At the time of writing (June 1997) important details were outstanding so that it was not possible to judge whether the new system appeared to be financially sound or whether, as initially feared by the health funds, the system was being liberalised prematurely.

Prescribing medicines

The amount of medicines prescribed by doctors is relatively high by international standards and there are indications of significant wastage. A ceiling on expenditures was defined by law in 1993, after which time the health funds had some leeway to raise the level.[56] If this ceiling is exceeded, the amount above the limit could be recovered from doctors in the ambulatory sector – and from the pharmaceuticals industry in the first year of the scheme. The initial impact in 1993 was that the number of prescriptions fell by 11 per cent and expenditures declined by 18 per cent, in part due to lower drug prices (see below). Noticeable shifts also occurred within drug groups, with doctors tending to prescribe less expensive drugs. The radically-changed prescription behaviour of doctors created a number of problems as the impression was created that many past treatments had been unnecessary.[57] In addition, it appeared that some doctors preferred to refer a patient to a specialist, so that if there were to be individual pharmaceutical controls they would be attributed to the specialist. Despite these measures, expenditures on medicines continued to rise in the following years (Figure 36), increasing by 6.7 per cent in 1996, although in the last months of the year a collapse in prescriptions similar to 1993 occurred as doctors feared the possibility of the need to make reimbursements. Doctors in the new Länder seem especially prone to prescribing expensive drugs, and in large volumes, so that they have been the first to exceed their budgets and thus faced the threat of having to reimburse the health funds.

With the health funds either refusing to increase the pharmaceuticals budget or insisting on a very slow increase, the stage was set for large scale reimbursements by physicians in 1997. However, the legal requirement to reimburse cost overruns was not enforced by the authorities, resulting in a damaging loss of credibility. One reason for not enforcing the penalty was that it was impossible to identify the value of prescriptions issued by individual doctors. Thus the group liability would have required *ad hoc* payments by individual doctors which might have been particularly damaging for physicians in the new Länder, who have been especially prone to prescribe expensive medicines. For the second half of

Figure 36. **GROWTH OF EXPENDITURE ON PHARMACEUTICALS**

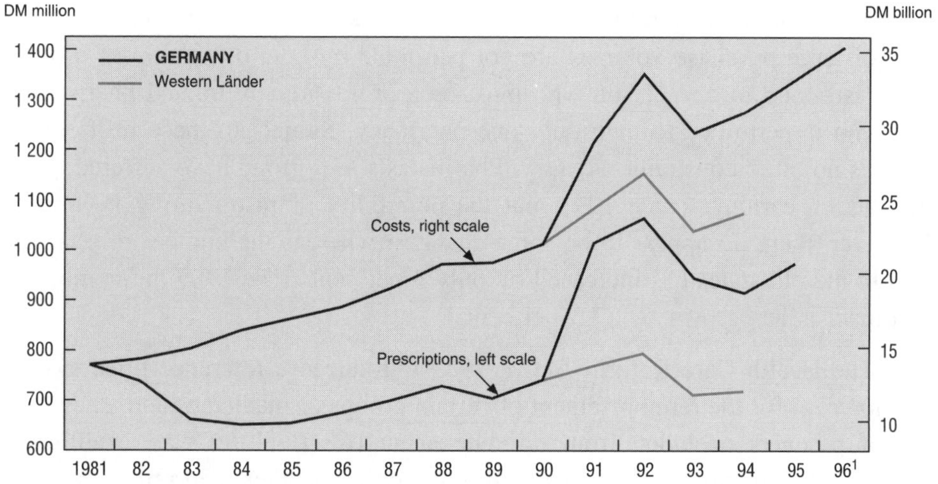

DM million   DM billion

1. Preliminary estimate for 1996.
Source: Federal Ministry for Health.

1997, the system has been changed by a new law with volume guidelines, rather than budgets, to be issued to individual doctors. If they exceed the limits by a given percentage they can be subject to checks and in extreme circumstances to the need to reimburse the health funds. The advantage of a volume guideline over a value one is that expensive drugs, which might be efficient, would not be forced out of the market. The disadvantage is that it will be exceptionally hard to control. While the government has decided on the general features of the new system, the all important implementation details have been left for the associations to negotiate. It will be important that the new system contains sufficient checks and balances to encourage careful prescribing practices by physicians.

The pharmaceutical sector

The high level of pharmaceutical expenditures in Germany is partly due to the relatively high price of pharmaceuticals, which in turn might be associated with the retail structure of the market. Medicines may be dispensed only by pharmacies, which are subject to heavy regulation, ranging from the prices of prescription drugs, which have to be the same throughout Germany, to the criteria for establishing and operating a pharmacy. Pharmacy chain stores to take advantage of large purchase volumes are not permitted by law; ownership of a pharmacy is bound to one person who must be a professionally trained pharmacist, and who is permitted to own only one pharmacy. Subject to these restrictions, there is no other constraint on entry. Pharmacists as a group have suffered sharp declines in earnings since 1993, but the possibility of restructuring is limited. However, there do appear to be some changes: whereas the number of pharmacies in the old states has increased by only 3 per cent since 1985 the number of pharmacists has grown by 37.5 per cent.

The Health Care Reform Act of 1989 introduced a reference price system (*Festbetrag*) for the reimbursement of certain groups of medicines and a negative list of products excluded from reimbursement (*Negativliste*) was established. Both regulations are still in effect and have been extended. The reference price system (*Festbetrag*) sets a fixed maximum reimbursement for drugs whose main components are in the same or similar category.[58] The statutory funds do not reimburse costs above the limit. This has the effect of price controls from the perspective of most manufacturers since consumers are often unwilling to pay the difference themselves. The system applies to about two-thirds of the pharmaceuticals which the GKV are required to pay for. The negative list designates medicines completely excluded from reimbursement and is partly defined by indication (*e.g.* colds and sore throats) and there is an additional list covering drugs regarded as uneconomical. The success of the 1989 reforms in containing costs was only temporary. There were disproportionate increases in the prices of drugs not subject to the reference price system and there was a tendency for larger packages than necessary to be prescribed by doctors. However, the price of pharmaceuticals did fall in relation to the European averages.

The 1993 reforms sought to influence not only price but also the quantity and the composition of prescribed drugs. In addition to a global pharmaceutical budget for the ambulatory sector (described above), the measures included:

- Price moratorium: effective January 1993 until the end of 1995, a government decree lowered the price of prescription medicines not covered by the previous maximum reimbursement reform by 5 per cent and the prices of non-prescription medicines for which pharmacies have a monopoly by 2 per cent.

- New co-payment regulations: co-payments were increased in 1993 depending on the price category of the drugs. From 1994 the amount of co-payment depends on the size of the package which could paradoxically lead to an increase in the quantity purchased for any given ailment.
- Positive list: a list determining those medicines which could be reimbursed was foreseen and such a list was presented in April 1995. It was, however, never introduced, one of the reasons being that it would inhibit innovation.

In 1996 the share of parallel imports amounted to 1.5 per cent of drug sales in pharmacies and for around 1.7 per cent of the pharmaceutical costs of the health funds. Prices for imports tend to be 10 per cent lower than the original price. Although pharmacies have not been obliged since 1996 to favour the imported drug, imports are still increasing. The use of generic drugs has increased by 10 percentage points since 1990 and now accounts for some 30 per cent of turnover and for some 58 per cent of the market for multi-source drugs.

Co-payments

Prior to the reform measures in 1989, co-payments by patients were rather small and, although the effects are still subject to a great deal of controversy, might have contributed to the large number of visits to doctors and to the high usage of medicines. Since then co-payments have assumed an increasing importance, but are subject to ceilings of 2 per cent of gross income up to a limit (for incomes greater than this level the ceiling is 4 per cent). Since 1994, co-payments have been levied for medicines (including fixed reimbursement prices for some drugs), and for a range of dental treatments and other health services. For hospitals there is no co-payment for a simple visit, while for treatment the cost sharing is limited to DM 12 for a maximum of fourteen days per year. There is no co-payment for visits to a physician. It is difficult to place an overall sum on the size of cost sharing, but the authorities estimate it at around DM 9 billion or 4 per cent of health fund expenditures in 1995.

The introduction of co-payments appears to have had a significant impact on expenditures on medicines by the health funds, although it is difficult to separate the effects from those associated with the introduction of budgets for medicines. And whether they have reduced overall health costs is also an open question. Both patients and doctors have shown a greater interest in cheaper generics and consumers might also have substituted self medications. In 1995, self-medication products purchased in the pharmacies increased by 8 per cent and now account for 16 per cent of the DM 46.4 billion market for pharmaceuticals in Germany.

Policy issues

The available direct indicators, together with the pattern of incentives implicit in the institutional structure, all point toward continuing inefficiencies in the German health system going into 1997. Financing of health care has assumed a passive role, leading to significant supply-induced demand. Moreover, although the health system has been in the process of reform, the measures taken up to the present – although an important step in the right direction – have not essentially changed the situation. Inefficiencies are particularly pronounced in the hospital sector, and the imposition of budgets – as was expected – can only be a temporary solution. But inefficiency is also apparent in the ambulatory sector and in the interaction between the two; in short there is not an institutional arrangement to package or integrate health services in an economically efficient manner. Budget ceilings might have been effective in the short run but they are associated with severe deficiencies if prolonged too long: they serve to fix the allocation of resources between branches of the health system and as between individual suppliers whereas health reform will certainly require shifts of resources between health suppliers.

This section reviews the policy issues arising from the inefficiencies discussed above, drawing where possible on international experience. It begins by discussing the options for improving the cost efficiency of suppliers, concluding that experience points to the need to develop a system of purchasers of health services. These would have an incentive to integrate (*i.e.* package) the provision of health care for patients from different suppliers and sectors which currently operate in a financially independent manner. Such a system could, in principle, be run either by a universal health fund or by competing health funds, but it is crucial in either case that the operating environment of the fund(s) be specified in a coherent manner. In this respect the section assesses whether the current operating environment of the statutory health funds is consistent with the expressed intention of the government to improve efficiency of the health system via competition between health funds. Finally, the strategic choice concerning the type of financing system, as between a ''solidarity'' or insurance-based scheme, is reviewed, the section arguing that equity objectives and operational considerations preclude moving toward a risk-based health insurance system.

Influencing consumer behaviour

An important issue in all health systems, but particularly those relying on solidarity finance, is to minimise excessive use of what appear to be free health services by consumers (''moral hazard''). Granting rebates based on actual usage is one approach, but this in effect results in risk-oriented financing. Another approach would be to improve the information available to consumers. This is particularly important in Germany, since health care is provided in kind. The most recent move by the government to inform patients more fully about costs of treatment is therefore welcome, but how this principle will be implemented after negotiations by the associations of health suppliers and the health funds will need to be closely monitored.

Another possibility is to increase further cost sharing on the part of patients (co-payments) and this is an important and controversial feature of the government's health reform approach. It has taken the form of direct payments, which could increase from DM 9 billion to DM 14 billion, to encourage the more economical use of medical services, and of increases in contribution rates so as to encourage the insured to move between health funds.[59] There are still differences of opinion about the effectiveness of co-payments in limiting demand in an efficient manner. For the most part, the proportion of the cost of health care borne by the consumer is low and this means that even with a small price elasticity of demand, the impact of a significant rise in price through cost sharing could be significant.[60] A recent indicator of the effectiveness of co-payment increases may be seen in the decline in demand for treatment at spas which has fallen by a half since 1996 following an increase in the per diem co-payment.

A generally acknowledged problem with co-payments is that they may conflict with the fundamental objective of equity. For example, there is convincing evidence in Germany and elsewhere that health status and hence health care need are negatively correlated with income. This means that the incidence of co-payments falls disproportionately on the sick and poor and, in turn, this usually leads to additional measures to exempt these categories. Indeed under the recent measures to increase co-payments some eight million adults with low incomes and twelve million children are said to be excluded (*Härtefälle*) and for those with chronic diseases, co-payments have been limited to 1 per cent of their income. However, such provisions also tend to raise administrative costs and sometimes to promote fraud. On balance, some increase in co-payments appears warranted but they should be regarded as only one element of health reform to help control frivolous demand.

Improving the cost efficiency of suppliers

The analysis presented in this chapter suggests that a major, if not the most important, problem in the German health system is inefficiency in the hospital system and in ambulatory care. The imposition of global budgets – which applies also to pharmaceuticals – while perhaps warranted as a transitional measure to prevent the sharply increasing volumes which have been observed in other countries during reform, does not address the efficiency issue and could indeed make it worse (as was indeed the case with remuneration of physicians in 1996, and the marked swings in prescription behaviour at the end of the year). The longer budget caps remain, the more agents will adjust to the distorted pattern of incentives which they imply, whereas an efficiency-oriented health reform implies implementing a system which promotes the transfer of resources between sectors and individual suppliers. Such transfers are frustrated by the current budget cap system, which is mainly oriented toward stabilising contribution rates. From this perspective, the effective termination of existing budget restrictions on physicians and on their pharmaceutical prescriptions effective from mid-1997 and into 1998 is a step in the right direction. However, it remains to be seen whether the system, which has still to be negotiated, will either promote cost effective supply of medical services or control expenditures. The introduction of therapy-based reimbursements for hospitals is a step in the direction of making hospitals more cost conscious, but in itself it is not powerful enough to stimulate efficiency and to facilitate the reallocation of resources.

The general outline of options for a practical, efficiency-oriented health supply system are becoming clearer as a result of experience in other countries,[61] as well as in Germany where there have been some experiments in managed care at local level.[62] The health system needs to become more integrated as between the stationary and ambulatory sectors and also with respect to rehabilitation and long term nursing care, in the sense that incentives need to be present for medical practitioners to choose the most cost effective treatment regardless of health supplier. A strengthened gate-keeper function for physicians appears to be crucial in this regard but methods of remuneration would also need to be altered: capitation payments for the individual doctor could be necessary – rather than collectively as in the system up to July of this year – combined with some fee-for-service components to avoid adverse selection problems (*i.e.* avoiding patients with an adverse health record since remuneration would only be a one-off payment and could be less than actual costs). For hospitals, the new system combines a mixture of prospective or therapy-related payments as well as some fee-for-service elements and should avoid adverse selection of patients. However, the system also needs to include an integrated treatment of investment to improve the mix of capital and current expenditures, although the precise institutional arrangements will depend upon whether active purchasers of health care evolve.

Incentives to raise efficiency in the use of pharmaceuticals raise other issues. Some cost sharing on the side of health care providers appears indispensable through techniques such as performance-related payments for hospitals and cost sharing by physicians or some form of diagnostic system with best practice prescribed. In view of relatively high pharmaceutical prices in Germany, initiatives are also required at the retailing level. Consideration needs to be given to allowing the development of chains of pharmacies – while retaining the important role of qualified pharmacists – which could stimulate a reduction of prices. However, the single price regulation which sets price margins for the country as a whole would need to be relaxed and incentives to use parallel imports restored.

Toward active purchasers of health care

An efficiency-oriented health care system most importantly requires organisations that can act as purchasers of health services (on behalf of patients) from suppliers. At this stage of the health reform in Germany there has been little movement towards establishing purchasers of health services although this is implicit in the government's objectives. Several policy issues need to be addressed: deepening contractual relations, reforming hospital structures, and limiting the freedom of patients.

- Under the current system of cartel relations between health funds, hospitals and doctors, direct contracting of individual health funds with individual suppliers is scarcely possible, so that a purchasing system would not be able to develop. The new health care reform bill which entered into force in mid-1997 does allow for experimentation in the system, but this must be agreed between the existing associations of health providers. In view of the fact that any efficiency based system will have major impacts on health suppliers and their associations, such experimentation may proceed too slowly, and close too many options, to form a reliable basis for developing health policy.

- Public ownership of many hospitals makes it difficult to change staffing levels and internal structure, while rationalisation of hospitals (*i.e.* closing some, merging others or consolidating departments) is also difficult because the internal structure of hospitals is often more in the nature of an association of medical departments than an overall organisation. Significant reforms would seem to depend on changing the management structure of hospitals, with enhanced powers for the central administration. If a new system of health purchasers were to evolve contracting directly with hospitals, it is not clear that they should at the same time assume responsibility for financing investment in hospitals. This could remain with the Länder although the way in which finance would be allocated, and the manner in which they could be used by hospital administrations, would certainly have to change. Such a system would also avoid the possibility of health funds coming to directly own hospitals.
- The insured are in practice free to use the hospital and doctor of their choice at present, and this appears to be valued highly by policy makers. It could prove difficult to preserve this freedom in a system based on health purchasers, so that trade-offs will be necessary, but could be compensated by the new freedom to shift between health funds.

Establishing competition between the statutory health funds

A system of health purchasers – rather than passive financers of health services – may be organised around one health fund (including many individual funds which are constrained to act as if they were one universal fund) or a number of competing funds. Developing a competitive system of health funds is not in itself sufficient to establish health purchasers and is indeed associated with many practical difficulties.[63] In particular, it involves a number of policy issues related to the efficiency of a competitive market in health insurance. The government has formally chosen to pursue the path of competing health funds, although a number of arrangements in the 1997 law concerning relations with suppliers in particular are more indicative of a single universal fund. Further policy initiatives to improve the consistency of the system are required.

The health reform of 1993 foresaw that, starting in 1997, individuals would be free to choose any of the 600 or so statutory health funds (see *Annex I* for a description of their structure).[64] At the time, contribution rates varied between 11.0 per cent and 14.9 per cent mainly on account of the different demographic structure of membership since all funds provided essentially identical services. In order not to distort competition and to avoid the possibility of adverse selection (*i.e.* funds competing to acquire low risk individuals), a risk equalisation fund was introduced in 1994 together with a legal obligation to accept all applicants who wished to be insured by a fund and a prohibition on discrimination. The risk equalisation fund covers standardised risks, including wage levels, family size (important given that one contribution covers all dependent family members), age, gender and invalidity. Even though health expenditures vary by Länder, the arrangement covers the new and the old states as a group separately, so that there is also an element of fiscal equalisation within each region (see *Annex I* for a description of arrangements in the new Länder). The initial effects of the risk fund have been pronounced. Contribution rates have tended to converge: in 1993, 64 per cent of insured paid up to 1 percentage point above or below the average, but in 1996 this had increased to 86 per cent. The consequences for individual funds have also been marked: some of the previously occupational-organised funds and enterprise funds (*Ersatzkassen* and *Betriebskassen*) have been major contributors to the area-based funds (AOK) and one large health fund pays around a half of its contribution revenues to the risk equalisation fund. Not all risks it should be noted are covered by the risk fund: difficult cases which are associated with high costs are concentrated in the area-based health funds and are not compensated.

The risk fund has become a subject of controversy, some claiming that it will prevent competition and in effect lead to a single universal health insurance fund. There are, for example, demands to reduce the demographic component gradually in future years by raising the age limit for compensation from 40 years to over 60 years, and cities such as Berlin are seeking to be treated as a special risk. The fundamental objective of universal access, the possible immobility of large parts of the population between health funds and the requirement to accept every applicant as a member, all necessitate the continuation of risk equalisation. Nevertheless, if the intention is to base the health system on competition, the treatment of risk will need to be refined (although not in the direction of city-based risk which is a question for fiscal equalisation arrangements). The current risk-equalisation system does not cover all risks and the risk profiles are still being refined since adequate survey data has been lacking. It therefore seems likely that the current system could still provide an incentive for funds to practise risk selection. This is formally illegal but experience in the rest of the world suggests that when incentives are strong enough it will happen in one form or another.[65] Greater transparency with respect to premiums in different health insurance funds would help diminish the risk. Competition in such a health insurance system could, in theory, be unstable, leading to either bankruptcy of funds or preventative mergers. Even though the German system is different from private insurance systems in that contribution rates are set (generally speaking) for the whole fund and not on the basis of the individual risk profile (*i.e.* there is risk pooling in the individual fund), such an outcome is likely. Indeed, since the announcement of the reforms, there have been a number of mergers mainly of territorially organised funds. Such market-based restructuring is not in itself a problem and indeed the 1993 law did make it easier for funds to merge. However, in order to avoid any policy changes during the process of consolidation, it is important that the likely consequences be understood at the outset.

The more important policy questions concern the framework for competition between the health funds and here the situation is particularly fluid. Although the intention has been to establish competition – presumably also with respect to contribution rates – the approach has been one of tight regulation. Legislation was passed forcing all statutory funds to lower contribution rates in January 1997 although funds have by and large avoided doing this. In addition, since March 1997 certain increases in contribution rates by an individual health fund are linked to an increase in the co-payments of its members. Competition between funds in 1996 via marketing expenditures – one of the few channels open for competition to increase market share[66] – were met with threats from the government to introduce new controls.[67] Under the rubric of preventative care, a number of marketing schemes had been developed, especially by the regional funds which have been losing members. While opening-up genuine preventative care,[68] the marketing schemes have been struck from the list of available medical services, although they only account for around 0.7 per cent of health fund expenditures. By and large, the approach has been only to accept competition in principle if contribution rates are lowered while at the same time seeking to avoid any alteration to the principle of solidarity financing toward more risk related premiums.

The fundamental rationale for competition in the health sector is to lower health costs, but here the health funds are hampered in two ways: funds cannot effectively compete on the basis of health service provision and contracting relations with health care suppliers remain restricted. Policy consistency needs to be established. With respect to health services several policy alternatives were available. One which has often been put forward is to specify a package of basic health care allowing the funds to offer supplementary care in exchange for higher premiums and competition would focus on this area. An alternative approach is to specify some services in which there would be room for manoeuvre by the funds (*Gestaltungsfreiheit*) in specifying content. Such services would also form a voluntary part of the health care package allowing room for funds to compete. The major drawback with the former concept is that it is enormously difficult to specify a minimum package which is both cost effective and medically appropriate. With respect to elective services, the fear was also expressed that under the limited conditions of competition which were being specified, such health services would simply cease to exist. In the event, little has been changed. Given the constraints implied by remaining in a system characterised by universal access and solidarity-based financing, the decision is reasonable. However, in this case the desire to base the health system around competition between health funds requires greater freedom of manoeuvre in relations with health suppliers. The ability to contract with health suppliers has been extended somewhat, but only for the funds acting as a group within the current structure of cartel relations: contractual relations at the level of individual funds and suppliers remain very limited.

Risk-based versus solidarity-based insurance and private health insurance

At present, the health system is based on pooled risk for large segments of the population with contributions based on income (an alternative is of course to finance the system from general taxation). Since the level of benefits is unrelated to the level of the contribution payment in the solidarity approach, contributions resemble to some extent a tax. However, as noted above, the present system also combines elements of individual risk-based insurance, and the logic of competition could imply a further move in this direction. However, moving to a risk-based insurance market system for everybody would raise a number of issues concerning income distribution, universal access and the efficiency of the system. The current health system has a significant impact on income distribution and concerns about this limit policy choices when considering reform options. Income distribution is currently affected in the following ways:

– Wage-based contributions (the solidarity principle) up to a wage ceiling redistribute income toward those most at risk of illness and to those with low incomes, but may also favour those with incomes above the ceiling. It also discriminates in favour of those with non-wage income, although the ultimate effects are unclear due to the higher private insurance premiums which families with a greater proportion of non-wage income, who have opted out of the statutory system, might have to pay.

– Premiums are lower for the old-aged, being based on a limited contribution base but expenditures are relatively high, resulting in a shift of income distribution toward the retired. One estimate is that insured employees subsidise the health coverage of pensioners by more than three percentage points of their contribution base.[69]

– Co-insurance of dependants shifts income towards families as do a range of maternity related benefits.[70] Health contributions are not paid during maternity leave but full membership rights are maintained. The total cost of both factors is estimated by one source at around DM 58 billion.[71]

Such redistributive elements are not compatible with risk-based insurance and would have to be achieved through the fiscal system, thereby increasing the complexity of health reform. Of greater importance for policy, however, is that private health insurance markets are always associated with the danger that insurers will select only the best risks ("adverse risk selection"), which makes it very difficult to ensure universal coverage. Indeed, similar problems are already being encountered with optional private health insurance in Germany (Box 3). The emphasis given to universal access and to broad inter-generational risk

pooling thus suggests the need to maintain the present statutory, solidarity-based,
system. Even so, significant efficiency improvements could be made.

The present co-existence of a solidarity-based system covering 90 per cent
of the population and a risk-based one covering the remainder, with the two

systems competing at the margin raises several policy issues. This arrangement, although offering flexibility and choice for those with higher incomes, also serves to reduce the income base of the statutory system while at the same time worsening its overall risk portfolio (Box 3). It is thus important that competition between the two systems be efficient. Current conditions do not create a level playing field. The statutory system is burdened by expenditures related to family policy (*e.g.* dependant spouses are co-insured) and statutory health funds are not liable for taxation. With individual health funds now competing for members both amongst themselves and, for some clients, with the private funds, competitive conditions need to be reviewed.

Widening and simplifying the contribution base

Given that an insurance-based system is ruled out, the current wage-based contribution system appears to be inefficient from two perspectives: it gives rise directly to pressure on labour costs and is sensitive to business cycle developments – and perhaps even to longer run developments in income distribution. Moreover, the wage-based contributions are being utilised to finance important redistribution programmes to pensioners and to families. As such, a number of ideas for reform have been put forward to widen the contribution base as well as to shift the financing of some elements to general taxation. Many of the policy issues are closely related to the fundamental decisions discussed in the preceding paragraphs.

The rapid rise in contribution rates has been driven only in part by rising health expenditures, the relatively slow increase of wages and salaries subject to contributions also being an important contributory factor. While this latter influence might be expected to be temporary, over the longer run factors are also at work such as the ageing of the population which could serve to shift factor income in favour of property at the expense of wages. A simple expedient would be to raise the threshold level for contributions to the statutory system which would, however, reduce numbers privately insured so that the gains in net income may not be great. In addition, there are more fundamental questions related to opting out from the statutory system which would need to be addressed. Another policy proposal which has been put forward is to widen the contribution base to include other sources of income. Several aspects need to be considered. Widening the contribution base to include non-wage sources of income would allow contribution rates to be lowered, however, it is difficult to see how basing contributions on total income could be made compatible with a system of competing health funds: it would be more compatible with a universal fund financed from general taxation. A case could be made, however, for widening the contribution base for people in retirement and indeed this is already being done to some extent. In addition, a proposal is often made to include wages which are not at present subject to contributions such as casual work (*geringfügige Beschäftigung*). As argued in the 1996 *Survey,* any improvement in contribution income would have to be offset against a possible decline in such employment, which might be particularly sensitive to increases in social charges. As most employees in such work are often already covered by an employed spouse, an increase in contributions would amount to a costly way of reducing the income transfer to families which is an important part of the present system. In sum, with the exception of widening the contribution base for retirees, little might actually be gained by moving away from the wage base for financing the statutory health system. However, in view of the potential efficiency losses associated with wage-based contributions, there is a case for financing more distributional-oriented programmes such as those supporting families by general taxation.

Contributions are divided equally between employers and employees and this has limited reform options: some proposals to encourage competition between funds and to promote consumer sovereignty have needed to be balanced by complex proposals to freeze the employer's contribution. One reform path which suggests itself, therefore, has been to unify contributions for the employee, grossing wages in the process. This would make the true cost of health insurance more transparent for the employee although it need not reduce wage cost pressures fully if the social partners negotiated on the basis of real net wages. Although there is little economic reason for contributions to be divided, since most evidence would suggest that employees as a group eventually carry most of the burden either in the form of lower net-wages or reduced employment, the system has other advantages which could be utilised. Splitting contributions provides a rationale for the employers to be represented on the boards of the health funds (*i.e.* to participate in the social consensus) and in this role to underpin caution in raising contribution rates. Given that the thrust of reforms is to increase the autonomy and financial responsibility of statutory health funds this motivation loses some, though not all, of its significance. However, if the

Box 4. Recommendations for further reform of the German health care system

Based on the analysis presented in the chapter, further policy initiatives are needed to *i)* improve incentives for households to use health care services economically and to place more emphasis on prevention, *ii)* provide incentives for health suppliers to reduce costs in a sustainable manner; and *iii)* strengthen the integration of the health system both between the ambulatory and stationary sectors as well as between the health insurance system and the rehabilitation and long term care sectors. To meet these objectives will require changes in the way health funds operate and in the institutional structure of the health system more generally so as to encourage competition between suppliers. Within the context of the self-managing structure of the health system, the government has an important role in establishing the legal and regulatory framework to promote changes in the behaviour of doctors, hospitals and health funds. From this perspective the government's most recent measures, which came into effect during 1997 represent an additional step towards a more coherent structure. The chapter identifies the need to move ahead in the following areas:

Influencing consumer behaviour

- *Improve information available to consumers and use co-payments to control frivolous demand.* The most recent measures which introduce an obligation to provide information is welcome but implementation needs to be closely monitored.

Improving cost efficiency of suppliers

Therapy and diagnostic procedures need to be assessed systematically with a view to promoting technologies and practices which are cost-effective. The large gap between the most cost effective methods and those currently in use needs to be closed. Realising these potential savings requires improving incentives facing health suppliers along the following lines:

Hospital reform

- *Place hospitals under pressure to provide more cost-effective services.* The new method of therapy-based hospital remuneration needs to be further developed. Fixed budget limits need to be eventually replaced, so as to facilitate a shift of resources between hospitals which will become more important in the future.
- *Public owners should take steps to alter the managerial structure of hospitals along more efficient lines and the Länder need to reform investment financing to promote more rational decision making by hospitals.*
- *Control access to hospital treatment by strengthening the gate-keeper function of doctors.* The effectiveness of the recent measure to strengthen this function on a

(continued on next page)

(continued)

voluntary basis needs to be closely monitored. The incentives for doctors to refer patients to hospitals rather than specialists also needs correcting.

Medical practice

- *Encourage a change in the system of remuneration for doctors.* With the effective termination of the budget cap there is a danger that the amended fee-for-service system – which has still to be negotiated between the doctors and the health funds – will result in over-supply of services. The system could be supplemented by some form of capitation payment which amounts to a form of supply-side cost-sharing. Remuneration rules should allow the development of group practices.
- *Monitor pharmaceutical expenditure and prescribing practices.* Details of the new guideline system are still to be negotiated between the self-governing bodies and if the system is associated with wide limits and weak sanctions the government might need to reinforce the legal framework.
- *Liberalise the ownership of pharmacies to permit the development of chains and more actively promote the use of parallel imports.* Pharmaceutical prices are high and these two measures would improve the bargaining position of retailers *vis-à-vis* manufacturers.

Developing active purchasers of health care

- *Improve the integration of the health system at all levels including rehabilitation and long-term care in order to lower the cost of health care while maintaining quality.* This might be best achieved by moving from passive financing of health care suppliers towards a system of health purchasers which have an incentive to package the provision of health care from disparate, currently separated, branches.
- *To this end, broaden the ability of individual health funds to set contracts with individual hospitals and practitioners.* This would introduce a degree of competition between hospitals and would be a necessary complement to reforming the provision of investment funds and in moving to more flexible budgeting.

Defining the competitive environment of the statutory health funds

The need to develop active purchasers of health care is compatible with either a universal health fund or competing funds but the policy requirements are quite different and system coherence is vital. If health funds are to be competing, in line with the government's stated intentions, then clearer direction is needed in the following areas:

- *Create greater possibilities for individual competing health funds to evolve into active purchasers of health care.* The present institutional arrangements need to be made less restrictive, including the requirement that experimental forms of health care need to be approved by all the current health supply organisations.

(continued on next page)

(continued)

- *Maintain a suitable risk equalisation fund to avoid the danger of adverse selection and enforce universal access.*
- *Allow employers to search for health funds with lower contribution rates.* Employers could have both the knowledge and incentive to seek out the best opportunities, but this would need to be made compatible with the solidarity-based system which does not currently permit contributions to differ between members of a health fund.
- *Specify a negative list which should be available against individual related premiums and should be self-financing.* Specifying a basic list of health services which should be provided by each health fund is difficult to do in a medically efficient manner and there is a risk that optional services could be driven from the market threatening the objective of equal access.

Specifying a reliable and fair system of financing

It would be difficult to achieve the equity objective of universal access and high quality of health care with a purely risk-based health insurance approach, so that maintaining a solidarity-based system will require the following:

- *Steps need to be taken to place potential competition between statutory and private health funds on an equal basis.* With the present system allowing some individuals to opt out of the statutory system in favour of private insurance competition will develop at the margin between the two health insurance systems. This could prove inefficient unless competitive conditions are equalised.
- *While wages should remain the primary contribution base, with the income of retirees and the self-employed, free cover for dependants, which is a part of family policy, should be paid to some extent out of general tax revenue.*

---

system is to be characterised by genuine competition between health funds, efficiency could be strengthened by permitting enterprises to seek cheaper statutory health insurance for their employees: with the split system any benefits would, at least initially, partly accrue to them. Enterprises may be better informed and more able to find lower cost opportunities. The main objection to such a proposal is that it violates the consumer's rights and may lead to reduced labour mobility and to lower quality health care. These are valid criticisms but the argument of lower quality loses some of its force if health care remains standardised across all health funds as is proposed. A more fundamental objection might be that health funds could be inclined to grant special terms to large firms, thereby moving the system away from its solidarity-based financing toward a risk-based system.

In sum, the process of health reform which began in earnest in 1993 is beginning to move the health system toward more market based mechanisms for remunerating providers of health services, while at the same time increasing the responsibility for consumers to decide about their own health needs. The present system must, however, be regarded as transitory since many of the new mechanisms are either not yet fully in operation (*e.g.* therapy-related payments for hospitals) or are still blocked by inappropriate institutional settings. The legislation which became effective in 1997, while moving the reform process forward in a number of areas, does not deal with the fundamental issues which now need to be tackled. In particular, the competitive operating environment of the health funds needs to be clarified and a basis established for them, either as a group or individually, to evolve into purchasers of health services. Moreover, the integration of the health system needs to be facilitated by reducing the barriers not only between the stationary and ambulatory sectors but also rehabilitation and long-term care. A synopsis of policy recommendations, building on recent reforms, is given in Box 4.

IV. Implementing structural reform: a review of progress

Introduction

Within the framework set out by the *OECD Jobs Study*, the 1996 *OECD Economic Survey of Germany* provided a set of detailed policy recommendations[72] to reduce Germany's high level of structural unemployment and to increase employment creation. The underlying causes of the current high level of unemployment were diagnosed as complex, covering rigidities in the labour, capital and goods markets as well as features of the tax and benefits system. In the past, wage bargaining institutions have not taken the unemployment situation sufficiently into account. Wage differentiation has remained deficient, while restrictive employment regulations relating to hiring and dismissals have reinforced the negative impact of high wage costs on labour demand. The social insurance system has contributed to high non-wage labour costs which, to the extent they have not been absorbed in lower wages, have reduced labour demand, while benefit schemes have not produced the correct incentives for re-employment of the unemployed. The tax and regulatory systems have inhibited entrepreneurship. These factors taken together may help to explain the difficulty in reallocating manpower resources in response to industrial restructuring, as well as the lack of capacity-expanding investment, especially in the new Länder, where the high subsidy- and transfer-induced growth of wages has led to a relatively high price of labour and an excessively capital-intensive development.

Recognising the complexity of Germany's unemployment problem the *Survey* argued that an improvement of labour market outcomes depended on actions being taken along the following lines:

– *Increased wage and labour cost flexibility*: greater wage differentiation with respect to skills, regions, sectors and firms should be encouraged, in part by the greater use of opening clauses in wage contracts, which would delegate greater decision making to the enterprise level. Market pressures would be increased by changing the social security system to stimulate re-entry into work and by reducing financial incentives to early retirement. The tendency toward more differentiated wage developments in line with economic fundamentals in eastern Germany needs to be supported.

– *Reduction of the distortions arising from unemployment insurance and related benefits*: the long duration of benefit payments needs to be reduced, and the criteria for not accepting offers restricted and the penalties strengthened; job-search controls and benefit sanctions need to be tightened. Social security contribution rates need to be lowered, especially for low earners. The personal tax system needs to be drastically simplified and marginal tax rates lowered; the generosity of sickness benefits should be reduced and incentives to avoid abuse strengthened.

– *Increased working time flexibility and easier employment security provisions:* regulations underpinning inflexible working practices need to be reformed. The possibility for renewing fixed-term contracts needs to be liberalised and part-time work facilitated; dismissal protection needs to be relaxed so as to encourage new hiring by reducing the uncertainty and costs of dismissal.

– *Enhanced active labour market provisions:* participation in active labour market programmes should be excluded from the requalifying period for unemployment benefits, and measures need to be more closely targeted on at-risk groups; the practice of providing employment subsidies on condition that wages are set below negotiated rates should be strengthened.

– *Improved labour force skills:* the attractiveness of the dual system needs to be preserved or restored in some areas and its relationship to higher education needs to be clarified; higher education needs to be aimed at shorter and more occupational-oriented studies.

– *Enhanced creation and diffusion of technological know-how:* the development of venture capital markets needs to be fostered and regulatory barriers to new activities reduced; new subsidies need to be avoided.

– *Supporting an entrepreneurial climate:* the establishment of new enterprises needs to be facilitated; efforts need to be made to increase the
business acumen of the new owners of enterprises in the new Länder.
– *Increased product market competition:* planning approvals need to be
simplified; shop-closing hours should be liberalised further; competition
in the network sectors (electricity, gas, telecommunication) needs to be
encouraged, and exclusive concessions more tightly controlled; services
provided by communities need to be more closely market-tested;
privatisation opportunities need to be pursued and industrial subsidies
reduced.

Progress in tackling these issues over the last year has been significant, and
has taken place within the framework of the 50-point action programme for jobs
and investment which was adopted by the government in January 1996 (see
OECD Economic Survey of Germany, 1996). Measures which were already
mandated were dealt with in that *Survey*, but action on many measures was
outstanding at that time. Since then, a number of key elements have either entered
into force or are in an advanced stage of preparation and are reviewed below. A
number of other proposals were rejected by the Länder in the upper house of
parliament (*Bundesrat*), either on the grounds of political unacceptability or
because they would have adversely affected the states financially. Progress is still
needed in these areas. In addition, the government is moving ahead in the key
areas of tax and pension reform. The expert commissions have presented their
reports and the government has now taken policy decisions which still need to be
approved by the parliament. The general features of the tax reform proposals are
discussed below, pension reform being covered in Chapter II.

Progress in structural reform

Increasing wage and labour cost flexibility

The tendency towards more decentralised wage bargaining has continued
over the last year. The number of firms with company-specific tariff agreements
increased from 4 500 at the end of 1995 to 4 700 at the end of 1996. Some branch
tariff agreements have allowed for temporarily reduced wages for newly-hired
employees, particularly, for those previously unemployed. Overall, agreements

were associated with commitments to secure existing employment. In the construction sector, wage flexibility has been hampered by a tariff agreement on minimum wages, designed to protect German construction workers against low-wage competition, which was declared binding for non-contracting parties (*Allgemeinverbindlichkeitserklärung*).[73] Encouraging more decentralised agreements continues to be of primary importance for generating a wage structure which conforms better with employment expansion. Although wage increases in the new Länder were more moderate than in 1995, the catch-up with wages in the west continued, with detrimental consequences for job creation.

To support the development of a more appropriate wage structure, market signals need to be strengthened, particularly with regard to older workers. Eligibility for early retirement has been restricted, for the unemployed and, more recently, for both women and the long-term insured.[74] With respect to the unemployed, generous transitional rules are likely to restrict the effectiveness of the measure quite seriously for some time to come. A phased increase in the early retirement age for women from 60 to the standard retirement age of 65 years will

Figure 37. **INFLOW INTO EARLY RETIREMENT**[1]

New early retirement pensions as a percentage of total new pensions

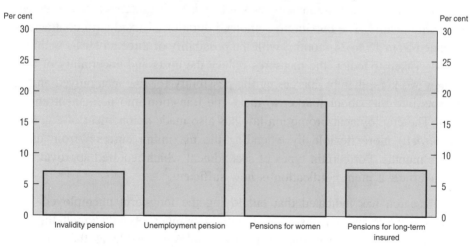

1. In 1995.
Source: Deutscher Bundestag, *Rentenversicherungsbericht 1996*; OECD.

take place between 2000 and 2004 and for the long-term insured from 63 to 65 years, in the years 2000 and 2001.[75] In 1995, two-fifths of all women retiring received an early-retirement pension, and 7 per cent of all retirees utilised the early retirement scheme for the long-term insured (Figure 37). The eligibility criteria for early retirement on account of invalidity have been exploited by companies to reduce their workforce at the expense of the government in recent years and as a result this scheme has gained importance.[76] The government has tabled legislation to deal with this loophole.

Increasing working time flexibility and easing employment security provisions

Legislation easing employment protection provisions and widening the scope of fixed-term contracts came into force in October 1996. The employment ceiling for enterprises above which employment protection is applicable was raised from five to ten employees per firm. The number of enterprises which are not subject to the general job protection law was thereby increased by some 15 per cent. These companies employ some 30 per cent of all employees. There is, however, a three-year exemption from the new regulation for all employees who were employed at the time the law became effective. With respect to large-scale redundancies, the general requirement to consider social criteria in selecting employees to be made redundant was relaxed, with greater emphasis given to economic factors. The maximum combined duration of fixed-term contracts was extended from 18 to 24 months, with the possibility of three renewals within this period. Taken together, the measures reduce the costs and uncertainty of taking on new workers, thereby increasing the possibility for the unemployed and new entrants into the labour market to make the transition into permanent employment. The employment promotion law has also made secondment of employees (*Leiharbeit*) more flexible by extending the maximum duration from nine to twelve months. For certain types of secondment which required approval of the labour office, a mere notification is now sufficient.

Research has indicated that employing the long-term unemployed – and some other groups – is associated with a number of risks, including high absenteeism.[77] To reduce such risks for employers, while at the same time breaking a vicious circle for the unemployed, a special type of work contract (job insertion contract, *Eingliederungsvertrag*) for this group has been in effect since

April 1997. Such contracts cover a period of between two weeks and six months, during which time the previously unemployed person has the chance to establish themselves in the company, with the goal of making the transition to regular employment. For the periods that the employee does not work, such as sickness spells and holidays, the labour office reimburses employers for wages and social security contributions. In addition, the labour office may pay wage subsidies that are targeted at long-term unemployed. The employment contract can be terminated any time. It is an advantage of the insertion contract and the associated support by the federal labour office that they are linked to employment in the primary labour market, which should reduce the risk of crowding-out regular employment by subsidised work inherent in some employment-creation measures. It will be important to monitor the operation of this innovative approach and to evaluate it against other active labour market policies, in particular direct employment creation measures. This might suggest a shift in the relative importance of different active labour market instruments. It remains true, however, that wage subsidies can be no substitute for properly functioning labour markets, which give the unemployed the opportunity at an early stage to price themselves back into employment.

The tendency to increased work-time flexibility in tariff agreements continued in 1996. This development mostly takes the form of "working time accounts," allowing companies to deviate temporarily from the agreed average weekly working time by compensating the worker with free time within a specified period .[78] Some tariff agreements – predominantly those in the new Länder – now include a "hardship" clause which permits working time to be reduced at the company level, with corresponding cuts in wages, if warranted by the financial situation of the company. The latter usually means that the company is close to bankruptcy. However, exercising the clause is conditioned on employment guarantees and requires the approval of the union and the employers association; in some cases, approval has taken up to six months and involves the danger that the company's financial situation will become well known and therefore often fatal. These features restrict the applicability of such clauses.

At the time of the previous *Survey*, a new policy had been introduced to encourage part-time work by older workers: provided a company compensates for reduced working hours by hiring unemployed or newly-graduated apprentices,[79] a premium is paid by the labour office to guarantee an earnings level of 70 per cent of the employee's former full-time net income. Such part-time work contracts may be concluded on an individual basis, but some tariff agreements have reduced this new flexibility and also specify higher payments to older workers. There is no information available at present about the take-up rate for this programme, which amounts to a job-sharing approach rather than one oriented to increasing labour utilisation.

Measures have been introduced to increase flexibility in the public sector. A new law has reformed the employment conditions for civil servants (*Beamte*) increasing transferability between posts and restricting the tenure in management positions. It also provides for more performance-oriented remuneration and restricts health benefits. In a break with tradition, part-time arrangements have been made for teachers in the new Länder. Due to a drastic drop in the birth rate in eastern Germany, there is significant overstaffing of elementary schools. The new Länder have therefore made arrangements which phase in part-time employment for teachers over several years, with a proportional cut in salaries. Part-time employment is on a voluntary basis and associated with a job guarantee. In later years, the working time will gradually increase.

Reducing the distortions arising from unemployment insurance and related benefits

Since April 1997 changes to the employment promotion law have curbed unemployment-related income support, and narrowed the grounds for refusing job offers (*Zumutbarkeit*) by recipients of unemployment benefits or assistance. In particular:

- Redundancy payments (*Abfindungen*) are now generally credited against unemployment insurance benefits up to a limit, whereas in the past this was only the case in restricted circumstances, which were generally easy to avoid. Redundancy payments were formerly used by enterprises to supplement unemployment and early retirement benefits, hence increasing the acceptability of lay-offs and avoiding legal disputes relating to the fulfilment of the provisions of the dismissal law. The change should increase the incentives for job search and reduce the indirect subsidisation of lay-offs, particularly by large companies. On the other hand, it has been suggested that dismissals could now become considerably more costly, leading to a decline in labour demand. The new regulations

– including changes in the dismissal law – therefore need to be closely monitored to see whether the equity and efficiency objectives of the regulation are being fulfilled.

– The incentives for workers to price themselves back into employment have been increased to the extent that the minimum age for receiving unemployment benefits for more than a year has been raised by three years.

– Job offers can no longer be refused on the grounds that they do not correspond to the vocational qualification of the unemployed. The new system also introduces an internal auditing system of the labour office to support tighter controls of the eligibility criteria.[80]

– From the beginning of 1998 onwards, training periods will not re-establish eligibility for another entitlement period.

The measures to extend crediting of redundancy payments and to increase the minimum age for receiving unemployment benefits are subject to generous transition arrangements, which imply that persons who have an uninterrupted employment record of at least three years will be affected by the new regulation only if they become unemployed after March 1999.

The statutory level of sick pay to be paid by employers for the first six weeks of an absence has been reduced from 100 per cent of gross wages to 80 per cent since October 1996. Following the change in the legislation, which was pending at the time of the last *Survey*, the social partners agreed in many industries to a continuation of the full replacement of gross wages in the case of sickness. In some sectors the negotiations were accompanied by strikes. However, in many cases it was agreed to exclude overtime wage premia from the gross wage base, and bonuses have also been reduced. Firms also appear to have become more active in checking sickness spells of their employees.

Enhancing active labour market provisions

Support by the Federal Labour Office for training the unemployed has been extended. Since April 1997, the unemployed have continued to receive unemployment benefits while they are participating in training programmes offered by private employers or educational institutions, provided the training increases the chances of integration into the labour market. According to the old law, participation in such programmes could lead to a loss of the entitlement. In addition, outlays in connection with the training are reimbursed to the unemployed.

Work creation measures (*ABM*) need to act as a temporary supplement to normal employment opportunities and to this end, wage subsidies for ABM projects have normally only been granted if the associated wages do not exceed 90 per cent of negotiated wage rates. However, in recent years the judgement has been that ABM jobs were coming to represent a secondary labour market, particularly in eastern Germany. In order to restore the original objective, the difference between tariff wages and subsidised wages has been widened to 20 per cent[81] since April 1997, and the maximum wage capped in absolute terms. At the same time, a floor was established for the minimum subsidised wage so as to secure a differential with respect to social assistance benefits, and provide an incentive to seek work opportunities. This represents, at most, a second best solution: the first best would have been to control the level of social assistance payments more closely, which is actually required in the relevant legislation. Overall, these measures should, nevertheless, increase the incentive for the unemployed to make the transition to normal work if offers arise.

A major problem with work creation programmes in the new Länder is to ensure that the projects are useful, and to this end, the co-payments by the body organising the project have been raised. In the new Länder, the share of grants paying 100 per cent of the wages in employment-creation measures has been restricted to no more than 30 per cent. (Normal wage subsidies pay 90 per cent of the total wage bill.) Government plans to lower effective wage subsidies for job creation measures to 75 per cent of the wage base by the year 2003, which is the normal level of support in western Germany, have been dropped. It remains important, however, to phase out the preferential treatment for eastern Germany as soon as possible, since this would increase the pressure on the social partners to negotiate wage agreements more conducive to increased employment.

Improving labour force skills

Apprenticeship curricula are continuously under revision, with the purpose of modernising and making more attractive the dual vocational education system. Revised curricula are scheduled to become effective in August 1997, and some entirely new occupations have been defined, mainly in the services and multimedia branches. However, fundamental problems remain in the provision of training places. Surveys indicate that the provision of training places by enterprises is set to decline in the future, while the number of possible apprentices will continue to increase. Yet, at the same time, 85 per cent of the sampled enterprises considered vocationally-trained employees for their company as being important or very important, although an expansion of more sophisticated services appears to be increasing the relative importance of tertiary training.[82]

Enhancing the creation and diffusion of technological know-how

In the government's 50 point programme to promote investment and employment, a great deal of emphasis was given to measures improving the operation of capital markets, and particularly to facilitating the supply of risk finance. The intention has now progressed to the stage of draft laws (*Drittes Finanzmarktförderungsgesetz* amongst others) which have now been circulated to interested parties for comment. The proposed reform is focusing on the functioning of the stock exchange, investment funds, and equity participation in non-quoted firms. An important feature is the proposed easing of the criteria for admission of companies to the stock exchange, with the purpose of fostering the flotation of new and smaller enterprises. Regarding investment funds, the proposed law allows for new types of institutions, notably nested funds and closed-ended funds, and widens the spectrum of admissible investment instruments (foreign real-estate claims, swaps, OTC-options, repurchase contracts). Potentially of great importance, the period of liability during which an investment advisor can be sued for bad advice is to be lowered from 30 years to three years. To foster the provision of equity capital to small firms which are not quoted on the stock exchange, restrictions concerning investment, refinancing, and the legal form of specialised intermediaries (*Unternehmensbeteiligungsgesellschaften*) are to be lifted. In addition, it is also proposed to change the framework of corporate governance, reducing the number of directors on the supervisory board of directors (*Aufsichtsrat*) and limiting the proxy voting rights of banks for shares held on behalf of clients where the bank holds more than 5 per cent of a company's capital.[83] Take-overs will also be easier, while in an effort to stimulate better shareholder value it is proposed to allow firms to buy back up to 10 per cent of their own shares.

Supporting an entrepreneurial climate

Previous *Economic Surveys* have identified the tax system as not only distorting resource allocation through tax expenditures, high marginal taxes and narrow tax bases, but as also possibly serving to restrict entrepreneurial activity. This assessment is shared by the authorities, who specified tax reform as a major priority in the programme for growth and employment. The government has now tabled a tax reform law (Box 5). As the programme still needs to be negotiated with the upper house of the parliament, it would be premature to review the reform in detail here.

In the previous two *Surveys,* the wealth and inheritance taxes were criticised as having features likely to adversely affect the entrepreneurial climate. A great deal of progress has been made in this area. The wealth tax has not been collected since the start of 1997, in response to a ruling of the constitutional court.[84] In the past, wealth was taxed at both the corporate level (0.6 per cent of the company wealth) and the shareholder level (0.5 per cent of private wealth), implying double taxation of proprietors bringing their company to the stock market. Furthermore, the basis for the wealth tax differed across legal forms. In addition, the inheritance tax as related to company wealth has been reduced provided the heirs, who need not be family members, maintain ownership of the enterprise for at least five years. Reduced taxation is achieved by a lower valuation of company assets. This is potentially an important measure, since numerous small and medium-sized companies are expected to be subject to inheritance in the near future. On the other hand, as noted in Chapter II, the upper house of the parliament once again rejected the government's plan to abolish the local tax on enterprise capital (*Gewerbekapitalsteuer*), which will now probably have to be introduced in eastern Germany.

Increased product market competition

The previous *Survey* identified the need to improve the regulatory framework in retailing, planning approvals and telecommunications. Progress has been made in many of these areas. First, shop opening hours were relaxed in November 1996 with permitted opening times being extended by one and a half hours on a working day and by two hours to 4 p.m. on a Saturday. According to a recent survey, extended shop opening hours have been utilised by 86 per cent of retailers which were sampled in February 1997.[85] Almost all firms with

Box 5. **Principal features of the proposed tax reform**

Following the report of an expert commission, the government presented laws to reform both the corporate and income tax systems to the parliament in June 1997. At the time of writing, the proposals were being negotiated between the parliamentary parties. The objectives of the reform are to simplify the tax system and support employment and growth by improving international competitiveness. To this end, the government proposes a significant reduction of statutory tax rates for personal and corporate income, together with a reduction of tax concessions and a broadening of the tax base. At the same time, in combination with other reforms, the overall share of indirect taxes may rise. The present plan calls for a net tax relief of DM 20 to 30 billion (see Chapter II).

Although the present system of family-based taxation and linearly rising marginal tax rates would be maintained, the lowest income tax rate would be cut from 25.9 per cent to 15 per cent and the top rate from 53 per cent to 39 per cent (Figure). The top marginal tax rate on income from unincorporated business activity would be reduced from 47 per cent to 35 per cent. For corporations it is proposed to lower the tax rate on retained profits from 45 per cent to 35 per cent, and for distributed profits from 30 per cent to 25 per cent.

The reform proposes to widen the tax base by including other sources of income and by reducing tax concessions. Exemptions such as tax allowances for farmers or for small and medium sized companies would be abolished or reduced. Half of retirement benefits would be subject to income tax, since employees' contributions (50 per cent of total contributions) are considered to be made out of already-taxed income, while employers' contributions are paid out of previously untaxed revenues. Premia from work at night, Sundays and holidays, which are largely untaxed in the current system, would be included in the tax base (to be phased in over several years) so as to treat all forms of income in a similar manner. With respect to corporation tax, generous depreciation allowances would be reduced and rules for the valuation of assets and for accruing reserves against prospective losses tightened. The reform law also restricts the possibilities of carrying losses forwards and backwards and abolishes the possibility of forming untaxed reserves for the purpose of financing specific future company liabilities. However, small and medium-sized companies would be treated more generously.

Reducing the entry tax rate for households would increase the difference between income from work and income from benefits (*Economic Survey of Germany, 1996,* Chapter III) and could result in a significant increase in income for many families. Taxing new sources of income should not change this conclusion. For corporations, tax rates will be closer to world levels and foreign investors would be placed on an equal footing: lower taxation of distributed profits, as well as a planned cut in the withholding tax on dividend payments from 25 per cent to 15 per cent, would mainly benefit foreign investors since domestic residents can deduct these taxes from their individual tax burdens. In addition, the neutrality of the tax system would increase because companies

(continued on next page)

(continued)

PROPOSED MARGINAL AND AVERAGE INCOME TAX RATES
Per cent

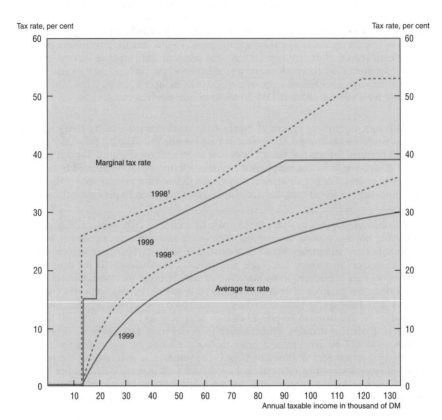

1. 1998 has been used for comparison so as to incorporate mandated changes in the basic tax allowance.
    The Solidarity tax surcharge is not included.
Source: Statistisches Bundesamt.

would be treated more equally: capital-intensive firms and those with a great deal of weekend and night work have been subsidised in the past by others and this effect would be significantly reduced. But some of the measures, such as narrowing the possibilities of carrying losses forward and backward, which are intended to apply from 1997, will not always improve the economic efficiency of the tax system and should not be introduced simply for financing reasons. It is not possible at this stage to assess the potential impact on investment since all aspects of the reform need to be considered.

50 employees or more have made use of the new possibilities, but extended hours are less widespread among small firms. Around 15 per cent of the sampled firms employed more personnel than before, of which almost 60 per cent were full-time or part-time with the obligation to make social security contributions. Second, planning approval procedures have been revised, with the purpose of accelerating investment. Monitoring whether the new regulations speed up the processing of permits and reduce costs will be important. Third, although Telekom was partly privatised by issuing new equity capital on the stock exchange in a record flotation, at the time of writing (June 1997) the regulatory authority was still not in place. Under European directives, full liberalisation will occur at the start of 1998.

From April 1997, air transport has been liberalised along the lines of the directive by the European Commission. The federal government sold its remaining 35.7 per cent stake in Lufthansa to a state owned Bank (*Kreditanstalt für Wiederaufbau*), with the shares to be sold to the public in the second half of 1997. The reason for the delay is the need to establish a mechanism which would ensure a majority of German nationals in the shares of Lufthansa after privatisation. This is considered to be a necessary condition for a further privatisation, since without a domestic majority, some bilateral air traffic agreements with other states would become invalid.

The government has tabled a revision of the energy law to introduce more competition in the electricity and gas industries. Mutually reinforcing exclusivity clauses in concession contracts between communities and suppliers, together with demarcation contracts between suppliers themselves, currently prevent competition. The proposed energy legislation aims at abolishing both types of exemptions from the German cartel law. The draft of the energy law has been rejected by the Länder chamber of the parliament and will probably go to a mediation process between the two houses of the parliament. An important motive for the rejection was concern by the communities that the proposed legislation would halve their DM 6 billion concession income, and that locally-owned utilities could be threatened by competing companies. In anticipation of increased competition resulting from a new regulatory framework, utilities have already commenced large-scale investment programmes to increase their efficiency, so as to be able to offer lower prices. More generally, little progress appears to have been made in persuading local governments to economise in the provision of public services, a priority identified in last year's *Survey*. In addition, the government's intention to subject all public sector bodies to the same tax regime as private companies to ensure competition has not been realised.

Subsidies (comprehensively defined) amounted to 8.6 per cent of GDP in 1995,[86] having declined from 9.5 per cent in 1994, and their reduction remains a high priority.[87] As part of its medium-term fiscal plan, the government proposed a gradual reduction in subsidies to the coal industry, but in the face of industrial action and protests by affected Länder, the proposal was diluted: the federal subsidy is scheduled to decline from DM 8 billion in 1997 to DM 3.8 billion by the year 2005. Over this period, employment will be halved from the current level of 85 000. The government has also initiated a subsidised loan programme through state-owned banks which favours the construction sector (see Chapter II above). One area which needs to be investigated more fully concerns the government guarantee for the debt of the public Länder banks.[88]

The major subsidy programmes for eastern Germany, comprising investment credits, investment grants and special depreciation allowances, which amounted to some DM 16.5 billion in 1995, have been reviewed by the federal government.[89] When introduced in 1991, these programmes were limited in duration until 1996, reflecting the expectation that by then the restructuring of eastern Germany would have proceeded sufficiently to support self-sustained growth. In 1996 the government judged that this condition had not been met, and most of the programmes were prolonged until the end of 1998 pending a final review. The government considers it necessary to continue a high level of support to eastern Germany until 2004, with the purpose of further upgrading the infrastructure and broadening the industrial base. Legislation restructuring the support programme by concentrating aid on industry and simplifying the system in favour of investment allowances was passed by the Parliament in June.

In the past, subsidies for eastern German enterprises were rationalised as compensating investors for excess costs arising from the former division of Germany, notably a lack of a modern infrastructure – roads, railways and public transport, energy supply, telecommunication, public administration –, deficient capital markets, and legal impediments like unclarified property rights. Compensation for such deficiencies was intended to raise the rate of private investment in the new Länder, thereby "buying time" for a simultaneous improvement of the infrastructure by the government. In this respect, it is important to note that a poll among eastern German industrial enterprises in autumn 1996, which sought to identify problem areas, revealed that about half of them still felt their development to be hampered by inadequate infrastructure. However, the enterprises judged other factors to be even more important in lowering their competitiveness: the two problems ranked highest in their response about major barriers were excessive costs for personnel and rapidly rising social security contributions (Figure 5). Such disadvantages have led to pressures for additional subsidies but these have been rejected by the government on the grounds that they do not constitute a legitimate policy response. However, the difference in practice between legitimate and distortionary subsidies is often unclear with a great deal depending on the programme modalities adopted. Unless carefully designed, subsidies to compensate for externalities through support for investment can raise labour costs by encouraging excessive wage agreements and, indeed, this appears to have happened to some extent.

Overview and scope for further action

Over the last year, there have been a wide range of developments, including substantial legislative initiatives, which can be expected to improve the functioning of the labour market. With exceptions, such as the binding minimum wage in construction, the general thrust has been to increase labour-cost and working-time flexibility and reduce non-wage labour costs, while also making progress towards a regulatory environment based on greater competition, enterprise creation and technology diffusion. An overview of the original *Jobs Study* proposals, subsequent developments and assessment of what remains to be done is given in Box 6. When interpreting the actions taken so far in terms of actual results, it is, however, important to keep in mind a number of qualifying factors: *i)* the immediate effectiveness of the measures is often reduced by generous "grandfathering" clauses, which delay their impact substantially; *ii)* ultimately, the social partners rather than the government are responsible for implementing a higher degree of wage flexibility and where the government takes initiatives, implementation requires their co-operation; and *iii)* the overall effect of measures taken so far is still dependent on implementing the whole job-creation strategy, including elements relating to tax and pension reform, utility deregulation, and the pressing issue of subsidy reduction. Implementation of government proposals

Box 6. **Implementing the OECD Jobs Strategy – an overview of progress**

Since the last review a wide range of policy measures in the spirit of the *OECD Jobs Strategy* have been implemented. However, some important measures have been rejected by the Länder house of the Parliament.

Job strategy proposal	Action taken	OECD assessment/ recommendations
I. Increase wage and labour cost flexibility		
• Encourage wage differentiation, greater plant-level bargaining and opening clauses.	Minimum wage in construction was declared binding.	Wage bargains should incorporate greater flexibility.
• Facilitate the employment of older workers and reduce incentives for early retirement.	Early retirement age to be increased; part-time work of older workers is subsidised.	Reform eligibility for invalidity pensions; consider further means to curb early retirement (stricter eligibility criteria, actuarial discounts for pension benefits) and avoid long transitional arrangements.
II. Increase working-time flexibility and ease employment security provisions.		
• Reform regulations underpinning inflexible working practices.		Review effects of regulations.
• Liberalise terms for renewing fixed-term contracts.	Renewal period and admissible frequency of renewals increased; scope for secondments extended (period extended, approval requirement reduced).	Monitor employment effects and continue with reforms if necessary.
• Facilitate part-time work.	More flexible work arrangements in the public sector; subsidies to part-time work for the elderly.	Avoid further subsidisation of part-time work for the elderly.
• Reform dismissal protection.	Exemption from general dismissal law widened; social criteria for dismissals relaxed.	Monitor the effects on hiring and the costs of dismissals.
III. Reduce the distortions arising from unemployment insurance and related benefits		
• Reduce the generosity of benefits.	Minimum ages for receiving unemployment benefits increased by three years; redundancy payments credited against unemployment benefits.	Abolish the extended period of receiving unemployment benefits for the elderly; increase the gap between social assistance payments and the earnings of low-income families.

(continued on next page)

(continued)

Box 6. Implementing the OECD Jobs Strategy – an overview of progress

Since the last review a wide range of policy measures in the spirit of the *OECD Jobs Strategy* have been implemented. However, some important measures have been rejected by the Länder house of the Parliament.

Job strategy proposal	Action taken	OECD assessment/ recommendations
• Restrict the criteria for not accepting job offers, strengthen penalties, tighten controls.	Qualification no longer reason for rejecting job offers; definition of acceptable wage narrowed; controls tightened, internal auditing introduced of criteria.	Monitor the revised criteria for refusing job offers or taking up employment and narrow if necessary.
• Lower social security contribution rates.	Spending curbed in the pension and health funds and in the federal labour office, but social security contribution rates increased; presentation of a pension reform plan by an expert commission.	Curb social spending; consider other measures to place the pension system on a sustainable base (retirement age, basic pension, funding).
• Simplify the personal tax system and lower marginal taxes.	Taxation reform proposal.	Implement the proposed tax reform.
• Reduce the generosity of sickness benefits and strengthen incentives to avoid abuse.	Statutory sick pay lowered from 100 per cent to 80 per cent.	Maintain policy.
IV. Enhanced active labour market provisions		
• Exclude measures from the requalifying period for unemployment benefits.	Training periods will not re-establish eligibility for another entitlement period.	Continue reform.
• Target measures at at-risk groups.	Support schemes for training of unemployed extended; more flexible work contracts for formerly unemployed.	Monitor effectiveness; monitor the efficiency of work-in contracts, in particular in relation to employment provision measures.
• Base employment subsidies on wages below market rates.	Admissible wage base lowered. Special conditions for the new Länder will be phased out.	
V. Improve labour force skills		
• Preserve and restore the attractiveness of the dual vocational training system, clarify its relationship to higher education.	Curricula for apprenticeships revised and new occupations introduced.	Continue to revise vocational training schemes.
• Shorten higher education and focus it on more occupational-oriented studies.	No action.	Shorten higher education and make it more occupationally oriented.

(continued on next page)

(continued)

Box 6. **Implementing the OECD Jobs Strategy – an overview of progress**

Since the last review a wide range of policy measures in the spirit of the *OECD Jobs Strategy* have been implemented. However, some important measures have been rejected by the Länder house of the Parliament.

Job strategy proposal	Action taken	OECD assessment/ recommendations
VI. Enhance creation and diffusion of technological know-how		
• Foster venture capital markets and reduce regulatory barriers.	Laws tabled to liberalise financial markets, ease access of companies to equity capital and change corporate governance.	Implement proposed legislation.
VII. Support an entrepreneurial climate		
• Facilitate the establishment of new enterprises.	Accelerated depreciation allowance for newly-founded enterprises; wage subsidies for small new-founded firms.	Continue to examine regulatory impediments.
• Increase the knowledge of the new owners of enterprises in the new Länder.	No major changes.	Support projects to diffuse knowledge.
• Reduce the overall tax burden.	Abolition of wealth tax; reduction of the inheritance tax; trading capital tax being introduced in the new Länder; tax reform proposal.	Implement proposed tax reductions and abolish tax expenditures.
VIII. Increasing product market competition		
• Simplify planning approvals needs to be simplified.	Approval procedures simplified.	Monitor the effectiveness of the new regulations and continue reform if necessary.
• Liberalise shop-closing hours.	Statutory shop opening hours extended.	Liberalise further statutory shop opening hours.
• Encourage competition in the network sectors.	Law tabled allowing competition in energy sector.	Implement the energy law proposal and monitor whether regulations to enforce the opening up of networks are sufficient.
• Market test services by communities need to be more closely market-tested.	No major changes.	Abolish preferential VAT treatment of public utilities.
• Pursue privatisation.	Telecom partly privatised.	Step up privatisation.
• Reduce subsidies.	Subsidies benefiting construction increased and reduction of coal subsidies slowed.	Avoid new industrial subsidies; set up schedule for reducing existing subsidies.

(continued on next page)

in these areas are dependent upon the Länder chamber of the parliament, and in some cases have been delayed or blocked entirely.

Delays in implementation and transitional arrangements will mean that several of the measures listed above will take some time to have a major effect. In particular, although the legislated increase in the early retirement age is a necessary step towards encouraging older workers to stay in the labour force and to lower financial pressures on the pension system, the adaptation period is very long and retirement on account of invalidity could increasingly serve as a loophole for companies to reduce their workforce unless the criteria for obtaining this benefit are reviewed. Also, the immediate impact of the measures to relieve the burden of job protection is reduced by exempting from the new regulation for three years all employees who were employed at the time the law became effective. The immediate effectiveness of measures to credit redundancy payments against insurance benefits and to increase the minimum age for receiving unemployment benefits for an extended period, has also been seriously impaired by generous transition arrangements.

A further complication is that the effectiveness of labour-market deregulation depends on the co-operation of the social partners. The legislated reduction in minimum sick-pay provisions from 100 to 80 per cent of pay, for example, has generally not been adopted in wage agreements, but there may have been a dampening impact on negotiated wages and overtime wage premia are now usually excluded from the gross wage base. Existing possibilities for plant-level bargaining still need to be more frequently exploited by collective contracts. The trend towards decentralised agreements has been associated more with preserving than creating jobs. Exercising "hardship clauses" in tariff agreements is usually conditioned on employment guarantees and requires the approval of the union and the employers' association which is difficult to achieve in time and restricts the applicability of such clauses. A higher degree of flexibility would require that more general opening clauses could be exercised by agreement at the company level without the need to refer back to the tariff partners, while, more generally, the trend towards framework agreements which leave greater scope and flexibility for local bargaining still needs to be encouraged. Furthermore, a recent study indicates that smaller companies are using flexible working-time arrangements to a lesser degree than large companies.[90] This finding is attributed in part to complex legal provisions in the labour code (Arbeitszeitgesetz). This suggests that the working time law still needs to be scrutinised for simplifications, with the purpose of improving its applicability, particularly for smaller companies which must seek to avoid costly legal advice.

Perhaps most importantly, despite actions to curb benefits, the social welfare system in Germany still has to be put onto a sustainable base. The overall contribution rate has continued to increase, driven by, among other factors, developments in the labour market (Chapter II), making the government's objective of lowering the overall contribution rate to under 40 per cent by the year 2000 difficult to attain. The general issues facing pension reform are discussed in Chapter II, while health reform measures were covered in detail in Chapter III.

As far as product-market competition is concerned, the deregulation of shop hours appears to have already had a beneficial effect on employment, but remaining regulations still appear restrictive and could be liberalised further, giving market forces more scope to determine the actual opening hours. Important progress has been made in the liberalisation of air transport and the energy sector. But it is important that the energy law eventually adopted should not allow locally-owned utilities to continue their monopolisation the energy supply. Communities have the power to force local utilities to become more competitive, and need to utilise them. More generally, at the local level, further efforts need to be made to open up the provision of public services.

One of the most pressing outstanding issues is to reduce the level of subsidisation. Some measures, such as the continuation of coal subsidies at a higher level than originally planned by the government and shipbuilding subsidies are counter-productive in this respect. Although the government has made it clear that economic activity will continue to be subsidised in eastern Germany after 1998, the current restructuring of subsidisation policies presents an opportunity to reduce and streamline the level of support. In implementing policies during the coming year, several objectives thus need to be given priority:

– The volume of subsidies should be made regressive and a date for their termination should be set. Some regression in the provision of aid is contained in the government's new law.
– Subsidies should be linked to potential competitiveness. The government's decision to utilise the expertise of financial intermediaries for the provision of loans is welcome in this respect.

- The number of programmes needs to be curtailed and co-ordination improved. At present, the different levels of government and public sector banks offer a multiplicity of subsidy programmes for the new Länder. Although 90 per cent of the overall volume is covered by five main programmes,[91] this diversity has been criticised by analysts as well as eastern German companies[92] as being non-transparent, over-bureaucratic and wasteful. For a more efficient allocation of resources, it therefore appears important to reduce the number of programmes to a few only. The government's decision to abolish the special depreciation allowance is welcome in this respect. But a higher degree of co-ordination between the federal government and the Länder governments is required.
- Overall, subsidisation always runs the risk of preserving or creating enterprises which would not be able to pass market testing in the longer term if state aid were withdrawn. The developments in the mining and shipbuilding industries in western Germany stand as an example that aiding uncompetitive structures cannot durably and effectively solve social problems.

The stated goal of the government and both sides of industry is to halve unemployment by the turn of the century. In view of past labour-market performance this is an ambitious goal and one which will require continuing efforts to improve the operation of labour, capital and product markets. A great deal has been achieved in the past year but it is important that current legislative proposals be implemented, including tax reform and improvements to financial markets. Continuous monitoring of the regulatory environment to identify barriers to growth and employment will remain important. It would be unrealistic to expect a dramatic improvement in the labour market at this stage, since a number of reforms will only take effect gradually and it will take some time for behaviour to change. A basis is, however, being put into place for improved performance in the future.

Notes

1. The quarterly pattern was highly erratic. Output fell by 8.5 per cent in the first quarter but grew by 10 per cent in the second. The second half growth rate is heavily influenced by the second-quarter weather-related surge, the underlying rate in the course of the second half being much more modest.

2. For empirical support see J. Clostermann, "Der Einfluss des Wechselkurses auf die deutsche Handelsbilanz" *Deutsche Bundesbank Diskussionspapier*, 7/96.

3. For this comparison, unit labour costs in the west and the east have been derived by dividing gross compensation per employee by nominal value added per employee. Normally, value added in constant rather than current prices would be used to derive unit labour costs. In this case, average unit labour costs in eastern Germany would have increased by some 15 per cent since 1991 and be more than 65 per cent higher than in the west. However, given the dramatic changes in relative prices after reunification such a measure overstates the true increase in unit labour cost in eastern Germany over the period. Comparing nominal values should be a better approximation.

4. Estimates provided by the Deutsche Bundesbank as well as those published by the Council of Economic Advisors indicate that the average gross yield on fixed assets of producing enterprises in overall Germany increased between its trough in 1992 and 1996 by around 1.2 percentage points. The two sets of estimates differ, however, in the methodology applied. While these estimates allow the conclusion that the profitability of investment has increased they refer to the average profitability of the capital stock rather than the profitability of new investment at the margin.

5. From the national accounts perspective, the increase in profit share is in part due to higher profits in the service sector. Closer examination shows that most of this increase is in "other services", which includes imputed rents for owner-occupied housing. Lack of data prevents the identification of the development of business profits separate from this imputed item. See Boss *et al.*, "Deutsche Konjunktur weiter aufwärtsgerichtet", *Die Weltwirtschaft*, 1997.

6. See Deutscher Industrie und Handelstag, *Wirtschaftslage und Erwartungen – Februar 1997*, Bonn 1997.

7. There is great concern in Germany that foreign investment is at the expense of domestic investment. While it is not possible to rule this out, it needs to be stressed that FDI is relatively small: less than 6 per cent of total domestic investment although in some branches of manufacturing it is quite high. However, it should also be kept in mind that the concept of foreign direct investment differs markedly from the national accounts definition of domestic

investment. Purchases of existing enterprises abroad are counted as FDI but a similar domestic transaction would not be regarded as investment from the national accounts perspective.

8. See Institut für Wirtschaftsforschung, *Strukturbericht 1995*, Munich 1995.

9. Deutscher Industrie und Handelstag, *Produktionsverlagerung als Element der Auslandsinvestitionen*, Bonn 1996.

10. In April 1997, 451 000 persons were participating in such programmes, 64 000 less than in April 1996.

11. The tariff agreement in the metal and electrical industry permits a reduction of the general working time by up to five hours matched by a proportionate decline in monthly wages if employment is guaranteed. In the textile industry, the tariff partners agreed on an opening clause which allows the suspension of wage increases by agreement at the company level if economic conditions deteriorate and provided that redundancies are avoided (see Chapter IV).

12. Revenues foregone from these measures are estimated to amount to DM 30 billion or 0.85 per cent of GDP in 1996.

13. The federal government received revenues of DM 2.1 billion from selling its remaining 35.7 per cent stake in Lufthansa to a state owned bank (Kreditanstalt für Wiederaufbau). The shares are scheduled to be sold in 1997 after mechanisms have been put in place to ensure that a majority of shares remains in the ownership of German nationals. The public offering of Deutsche Telekom in November 1996, representing the largest privatisation offering ever, raised DM 20.1 billion but left the budget unaffected since the proceeds accrued to the company thereby offsetting the large debt burden which was transferred from the public debt to the company. The stake of the government in Deutsche Telekom was reduced to 74 per cent.

14. At the local government level, other factors have been important. Social assistance payments declined as a result of the new long-term care insurance, which took over some of the financial responsibilities from them.

15. The increase in the business tax is attributable to both increasing profits of the enterprises and the fact that the three successor companies of the post office had to pay business tax for the first time.

16. The unexpected surplus in the long-term nursing care insurance system was in part due to an unexpectedly large number of families opting for cash benefits rather than benefits in kind, which would have involved care in expensive facilities. In July 1996 the system was extended to cover in-patient care, financed by a simultaneous increase in the contribution rate from 1.0 per cent to 1.7 per cent.

17. The pension funds must hold the equivalent of one month's payment in liquid reserves otherwise contributions need to be increased. Regulations were changed in 1996 so that a variety of real estate investments could be treated as liquid reserves which therefore lowered the required increase in pension contribution rates.

18. The Federal government at first proposed that the tax not be enforced in the new Länder, but despite the potentially adverse effects on companies and on employment many communities proceeded anyway with implementation.

19. Restoring the statutory liquidity reserve of the pension funds requires a surplus of some DM 12 billion.

20. The official tax estimate released in May was derived on the basis of the higher rate of unemployment projected by the federal authorities in January.

21. The OECD utilises the banking definition of financial liabilities used by the Bundesbank which also issues another series closer to that of the Ministry of Finance based on financial statistics. The former series is regarded as more compatible with national accounts methodology and financial liabilities on this basis were 65 per cent of GDP in 1996.

22. *Deutsche Bundesbank Monthly Report*, March 1997, p. 19.

23. Financial liabilities as a proportion of GDP is projected by the OECD to reach 66 per cent in 1998.

24. *German Convergence Programme*, Federal Ministry of Finance, December 1996 and *Deutsches Konvergenzprogramm: Neuere Entwicklungen seit Dezember 1996*, Federal Ministry of Finance, February 1997.

25. Initial proposals called for a revaluation of the gold stocks to be used in a similar fashion. Revaluation will now take place only in 1999 in conjunction with the third stage of monetary union, and the disposition of the reserve will have to be decided within the legal framework of the European Central Bank.

26. *Vorschläge der Kommission: Fortentwicklung der Rentenversicherung,* Bundesministerium für Arbeit und Sozialordnung, Bonn, 1997.

27. Demographic developments leading to population ageing can also be expected to reduce labour supply thereby easing the unemployment problem. This does not imply that labour might be taxed higher in the future. For the spending pressure arising from population ageing to be financed, conditions favouring a high level of employment and economic growth are required.

28. An alternative option to the Commission's proposals would be to introduce a basic, income tax-financed, pension which would be supplemented by a mandatory funded component. A tax-financed basic pension has the advantage that it broadens the financing base to include capital income and is better suited to handle different forms of labour force participation, including part-time work.

29. The increase in pension liabilities is not an ageing problem *per se* but the consequence of the huge build-up of civil servants between 1960 and 1980.

30. The increase in the M3 money stock during 1996 overstates the growth of liquidity of the domestic non-bank sector. This is suggested by the fact that the money stock M3 extended (which includes in addition to M3 euro-deposits, the certificates of domestic and foreign money market funds and the short-term bank debt securities held by domestic non-banks) expanded more slowly than M3 because of shifts from euro-deposits and money market fund certificates to components of M3. Such shifts have an impact on the growth of M3 but not on the overall liquidity situation of the economy. Nevertheless, M3 extended increased by some 6 per cent in the course of 1996, which still indicates liquidity being readily available in the economy.

31. Moreover, the Bundesbank announced its terms for securities repurchase agreements one and two weeks in advance following meetings of the bank's Central Council. In addition, the issue of a new tranche of 30 year bonds for the Federal government in 1997 was accompanied by a number of statements that this should not necessarily be construed as a turning point of the interest rate cycle.

32. A strong increase in special savings deposits and the simultaneous weakness of monetary capital formation point to the great importance of domestic non-banks' portfolios behaviour in the buoyancy of monetary growth in 1996. A considerable part of monetary expansion is likely to be attributable to the store of value function rather than to the transaction function of money. On the other hand, this should not be read as suggesting a shortage of transaction balances; M1 – the narrowly-defined money stock definition – increased by more than 11 per cent in 1996.

33. This is also suggested by the so-called Taylor rule calculated as:
$r = r^* + ep + 0.5 (p - tp) - 0.5(GDP^*/GDP)$
where r is the short rate implied by the Taylor rule; r* is the neutral short rate; ep is expected inflation; p is actual inflation; tp is the central bank inflation objective; GDP* is potential output; and GDP is actual output. The neutral rate is set at 3.5 per cent in real terms, the inflation target at 2 per cent and expected inflation proxied by actual year-ahead inflation and by projected inflation for the last observations.

34. The monetary conditions index combines developments in short-term money-market interest rates and the exchange rate, using variable weights designed to reflect the openness of the economy. By construction, the MCI can measure changes in monetary conditions in relation to an average, but for want of neutral objective yardsticks, it reflects only the relative degree of tightness of monetary conditions.

35. "Strategy of monetary targeting in 1997-1998", *Deutsche Bundesbank Monthly Report*, January 1997.

36. "Die Lage der Weltwirtschaft und der deutschen Wirtschaft im Herbst 1996", *DIW Wochenbericht*, 43-44/96.

37. One problem concerns the commitment to convert the Euro and the Ecu at a rate of one for one and that conversion should not modify the external value of the Ecu. The problem arises from the different membership of the EMU and the Ecu which means that exchange rates from 1 January 1999 might have to be used. For a review of issues see D. Begg, *et al.*, *Getting the End Game Right*, CEPR, London, 1997, and D. Gross and K. Lannoo, "The Passage to the Euro", *Working Party Report*, No. 16, Centre for European Policy Studies, 1997.

38. The target corridor will be specified at the end of 1997.

39. Since 1977 there have been 46 pieces of legislation concerning the sector and 6 800 regulatory actions, and in 1996 alone, ten significant pieces of legislation have been considered by the parliament.

40. Sachverständigenrat für die Konzertierte Aktion im Gesundheitswesen, Sondergutachten 1996, *Gesundheitswesen in Deutschland: Kostenfaktor und Zukunftsbranche*, 1996, p. 218. OECD statistics are based on a different methodology, and employment was estimated as 2.3 million in 1995.

41. In the period 1976/1994 as well as 1992/1994 branches of the health sector accounted for four of the top branches in terms of employment creation in western Germany. The branches include private and public hospitals. *The Health Care System in Germany: Cost factor and branch of the future*, Advisory Council for the Concerted Action in Health Care, Special Report 1996, Summary, Bonn, 1996, Table 7.

42. For purposes of comparison, 1994 has been chosen as a cut-off date so as to avoid distortions which could arise from the transfer of responsibility for some long-term nursing care from the social assistance to the health system.

43. "New Directions in Health Care Policy", *Health Policy Studies*, No 7, OECD, Paris, 1995, p. 13.

44. One study suggests that a $1 increase in pharmaceuticals expenditure is associated with a $3.63 reduction in hospital care expenditure and that government imposed rationing of pharmaceuticals has led in some cases to increased use of hospital care. See F. Lichtenberg, "The Effect of Pharmaceutical Utilization and Innovation on Hospitalization and Mortality", *Paine Webber Working Paper Series on Money, Economics and Finance*, Columbia, 1996 and the references therein.

45. M. Schneider *et al.*, *Gesundheitssysteme im internationalen Vergleich*, BASYS, Augsburg, 1995, p. 218. Between 1980 and 1992 the rate of decline was 0.6 per cent in western Germany and 1.5 per cent in the European Union.

46. *Nationaler Bericht zur Prüfung der Notwendigkeit der Krankenhausbehandlung* as quoted in *Süddeutsche Zeitung*, Nr 17, 22 January.

47. By law it should be the closest hospital but this is not effectively enforced.

48. For a review of experience see R. Strehl, "Hindernisse und deren Überwindung bei der Erbringung ambulanter Leistungen durch Hochleistungskrankenhäuser", in M. Arnold and D. Paffrath, *Krankenhaus Report 95*, Fischer, 1995.

49. Hospital expenditures stabilised in 1996 but it cannot be concluded that the underlying pressures on costs have been brought under control.

50. See Sachverständigenrat, *op cit.*, 1996, Chapter 5 for more examples and also Sachverständigenrat für die Konzertierte Aktion im Gesundheitswesen, Sondergutachten 1995, *Gesundheitsversorgung und Krankenversicherung 2000*.

51. Schneider *et al., op cit*, p. 224.

52. After allowing for depreciation changes, hospitals have been in a position to register losses since 1986.

53. Until 1998 a hospital is to deduct from its overall budget the revenue from the two therapy-based payments. The remainder net budget is subject to controls. Starting in 1998 the hospital must make this deduction using actual cost data.

54. There were a number of reasons for this high request including the need of the hospitals to catch up on neglected maintenance costs. however, others also appeared to believe that they could make up for budget decreases incurred since 1992. See U. Neumann, "Das neue Entgeltsystem in der Praxis", in M. Arnold and D. Paffrath, *Krankenhaus-Report 96*, Fischer, 1996.

55. For an example see Sachverständigenrat, 1996 *op. cit.* p. 198.

56. Four indicators were specified which would permit a change of the budget: population growth and age structure, prices of medicines, changes in the mandated coverage of the health funds and changes in efficiency.

57. Frank Munnich, M. Wiegand, "Reform des deutschen Gesundheitswesens", *Wirtschafts politische Blätter*, 6/1993.

58. The medicines subject to the control fall into three classes: drugs with the same active ingredients; drugs with comparable active ingredients; drugs with a similar therapeutic effect. In 1995 157 drugs fell into class one, 22 active ingredient groups with 162 individual active agents in class two, and 15 combinations in class three.

59. If a health fund raises contribution rates, co-payments for that fund must also be raised.

60. For a review of some empirical studies see R. Ellis and T. McGuire, "Supply-side and demand-side cost sharing in health care", *Journal of Economic Perspectives*, 7, 4, 1993.

61. OECD, "New directions in Health care Policy", *Health Policy Studies* No. 7, Paris, 1995.

62. F. Knieps, "Die Domestizierung von *Managed Care* – Chancen und Perspektiven neuer Formen des Gesundheitsmanagements", in M. Arnold and D. Paffrath, 1996, *op. cit.*

63. For a selective review of issues and literature see D. Cutler, "Public Policy For Health Care", *National Bureau of Economic Research Working Paper Series*, 5591, 1996.

64. After a wave of mergers many of these 600 funds are operated by enterprises and are open only to their own workers so that the number of funds actually available to the general public is substantially less; at the state level there may be around ten funds.

65. See the references in Joseph Newhouse, "Reimbursing Health Plans and Health Providers: Efficiency in Production Versus Selection", *Journal of Economic Literature*, September 1996. pp. 1236-1263.

66. The objective of the statutory non-profit health funds is to increase market share subject to the constraint that costs will not rise requiring a rise in contribution rates. The motivation for the emphasis on market share is that the wage system links salaries of the officers of a health fund to the number of clients administered. In the short run this can lead to some strange decisions such as competition to acquire people on social assistance (bad risks) by cutting contribution rates.

67. "Seehofer droht mit Zwangsmanahmen", *Handelsblatt*, 4 July 1996. Among the developments which come in for criticism has been the rapidly rising expenditures on health promotion measures.

68. Preventative care such as periodical checkups and controls in the case of dentistry is treated as a normal health expense so that the cost accounting line referred to here covers only a limited range of special measures.

69. *OECD Economic Survey of Germany*, 1996.

70. For a study on the redistribution within the public health insurance system see Henke, K.D., and Behrens, C.F., *Umverteilungswirkungen der gesetzlichen Krankenversicherung*, Bayreuth, 1989.

71. Institut der Deutschen Wirtschaft, Köln, 1996.

72. See OECD (1996), *Economic Survey of Germany*.

73. The agreement is valid between January and August 1997.

74. Employees are long-term insured if they have made contributions for 45 years.

75. For women, this change accelerates the adjustment of the retirement age, which was scheduled for the period between 2001 and 2012 according to the 1992 pension reform law. The long-term insured can still obtain a pension between the age of 63 and 65 years but only at a level reduced by 0.3 percentage points per month.

76. This mode of reducing a company's workforce is not confined to the private sector. The post office has also utilised early retirement on account of invalidity to reduce its workforce.

77. See for example, G. Scharf *et al.* "Wege in die Wiederbeschäftigung: Empirische Ergebnisse über eine Reintegrationsmanahme für Langzeitarbeitslose", *WSI Mitteilungen,* 12/1995.

78. Tariff agreements covering overtime presently often require that overtime premia be compensated not only in cash, but also by reduced work at a later date.

79. See *Economic Survey of Germany* 1996.

80. Although no data are available about the frequency of not-admissible job refusals the number of sanctions appears to be low. In January 1997, out of a total of 3 593 068 recipients of unemployment benefits and assistance, 2 288 were sanctioned by a waiting period, and 559 by a withdrawal of benefits.

81. As an exception the old rate applies if the wage paid in the work provision scheme follows the reduced rate for long-term unemployed.

82. Survey conducted by the Bundesinstitut für Berufsbildung, *Handelsblatt,* 22-23 February 1997. 60 per cent of enterprises providing training plan to hold their number of apprentices constant over the next three years, while 23 per cent expect a reduction, but only 17 per cent an increase, in the number of apprentices.

83. For an extensive discussion of corporate governance issues see OECD *Economic Survey of Germany,* 1995.

84. See *Economic Survey of Germany,* 1996.

85. Survey conducted by the Hauptverband des Deutschen Einzelhandels; quoted after *Süddeutsche Zeitung,* 31 March 1997.

86. Boss, A. and A. Rosenschon, "Subventionen in der Bundesrepublik Deutschland – Bestandsaufnahme und Bewertung", *Kieler Arbeitspapier,* No. 793, 1997.

87. According to the European Commission, subsidies to the manufacturing sector amounted to 4.8 per cent of value added between 1992 and 1994. See *Fifth Survey on State Aid,* European Commission, Brussels, 1997.

88. The guarantee was recently criticised by the Council of Scientific Experts of the Ministry of Economics.

89. The scale of the subsidy programme to the new Länder is such that in the period 1992-94, annual average state aid per employee amounted to ECU 11 610, an increase from ECU 5 415 in the period 1990-1992. For western Germany the figure is ECU 553. See *5th Survey on State Aid,* European Commission, Brussels, 1997.

90. Dörsam, Pia, *Flexible Arbeitszeitgestaltung in mittelständischen Unternehmen,* Mittelstands Institute, Bonn, 1997.

91. See Sachverständigenrat zur Begutachtung der gesamtwirtschaftlichen Entwicklung, *Jahresgutachten 1995/96*.

92. See Institut für Wirtschaftsforschung Halle, Deutsches Institut für Wirtschaftsforschung, Berlin, and Institut für Weltwirtschaft an der Universität Kiel, *Gesamtwirtschaftliche und unternehmerische Anpassungsfortschritte in Ostdeutschland*, Fünfzehnter Bericht, Halle, 1997.

Annex I

The German health care system

Social insurance

The structure of the German welfare system was outlined in last year's *OECD Economic Survey* and, in addition to a wide range of benefits and social assistance provided from general taxation, comprises five social insurance pillars:

- Pension insurance
- Unemployment insurance
- Accident insurance
- Health insurance
- Long-term nursing care insurance.

Both health and long-term nursing care cover are compulsory for most employees and apprentices and are financed by contributions levied on gross wages up to a limit – for health insurance it is currently 75 per cent of the annual earned income ceiling set for the social security pension insurance system and is around DM 6 150 per month in the old states and DM 5 325 in the new Länder. Compulsory health insurance also covers dependants without additional contributions. Contribution rates currently range from 9 per cent to 15.3 per cent (with an average of 13.4 per cent) depending on region and health fund, half of which is borne by the employer. For long-term nursing care the contribution rate is currently 1.7 per cent.

Legislative and regulatory responsibility

Regulatory responsibility for the health care system rests with both the federal authorities and the Länder. The latter supervise the regional statutory health funds, register physicians and plan the development of hospitals including their size and speciality. Any hospital not so approved cannot qualify for reimbursement by the health funds. The Länder also provide a major share of investment funds to the hospitals. In addition, they are responsible for a wide range of public health issues. The federal authorities supervise the non-regionally based health funds and the public corporations which are responsible for implementing regulation and for running the health system. The ability of the federal government to formulate health policy is limited by the need to reach agreement with the Länder especially in the area of hospitals and in other areas affecting them both financially and administratively.

Organising institutions

The health system comprises two types of institutions: public corporations and voluntary associations. The former comprise all statutory health insurance funds (*Gesetzliche Krankenkassen*, GKV) and regional associations of doctors and dentists (*Kassenärztliche Vereinigungen*, KV and an equivalent organisation for dentists) whose members practice under contract to the health insurance funds. These public corporations are empowered by the government to design and direct some aspects of health care policy and to establish legal obligations. They are self-administered in the sense of negotiating with each other important aspects of the health system such as prices of medical services. Voluntary associations are not granted any executive authority and are not part of the self-administration system but may be involved in negotiating terms and conditions for the provision and finance of health services. They include:

- Four associations of pharmaceutical manufacturers (one for those undertaking research)
- The German Hospital Association
- The Association of Private Health Insurers
- Associations of GKV and voluntary associations of doctors and dentists.

Statutory health insurance funds

The statutory funds all offer largely the same range of services and currently provide health care benefits for about 90 per cent of the population; private health insurance companies cover around 9 per cent of the population so that very few people are without cover. The statutory funds finance around half of all health care expenditures. For historical reasons the statutory funds fall into two groups: primary funds (*Primärkassen*) and substitute funds (*Ersatzkassen*). The primary funds include regional funds (AOK), company funds usually run only by large companies (BKK), and funds covering farmers, seamen, miners and some other occupations. The substitute funds were often established in the 19th century and cover both blue-collar and white-collar workers.

Membership of a fund was closely regulated until recently: employees were required to belong to a fund set up by their employer (BKK) or a fund covering their trade or profession. If such a fund did not exist, an individual would be covered by a regional fund (AOK). The funds must accept any applicant and their dependants who meet the charter of the fund. Until 1997 the only freedom of choice given to individuals required to have compulsory insurance was to switch to a suitable "substitute" fund. Individuals with incomes exceeding the legally-defined limit have always had freedom to choose any available health insurance coverage. As of January 1997, all individuals required to have compulsory insurance will also be permitted to choose their health insurer freely.

As a result of historical development and the allocation of individuals to different funds, contribution rates vary, as does the risk structure of those insured. Since 1994 there has been a risk equalisation fund (*Risikostrukturausgleich*) to compensate for this, but not all risks are covered. Some of the "substitute" funds and those based at firm level are net payers to the regional funds where the risk structure is the most unfavourable.

The services to be rendered by the statutory funds include the promotion of good health, the prevention of illness, the treatment of illness, the provision of intensive nursing care and flat rate benefits to cover long-term nursing care, sick pay and maternity allowances. The only possibility for the funds to compete is in the range and quality of health-promotion programmes and some other health services they offer accounting in total for about 2.5 per cent of their expenditures. A key aspect is that benefits are provided principally in kind: members of statutory funds never see the bills submitted by health providers to the statutory funds.

Private health insurance funds

A total of 7 million people were fully covered by private health care insurance in 1995 and a further 6 million had supplemental policies in addition to their compulsory coverage. In contrast to the contribution rates of the statutory funds, private insurers calculate their premiums on the basis of risk profiles and contributions must be paid for all dependants. As a result, private insurance rates for young people without dependants are much lower than those of the statutory funds. To provide for future risks arising from ageing of the insured, the insurance companies must build reserves. In recent years these have been too low as companies have competitively cut rates to attract young clients.[1] At the same time, there have been significant increases in rates for older clients.

Since July 1994 private health insurance companies have been forced to offer a standard policy to all clients older than 65 years and who have been insured by the respective company for at least ten years. The benefits provided must correspond to those of the statutory funds and the premium may not exceed the average contribution charged by them. To date very little use has surprisingly been made of these contracts.

Healthcare providers

Healthcare services are provided by both public, private and charitable organisations. Inpatient care is the largest component of in-kind benefits paid by the health funds, followed by outpatient care and pharmaceuticals (Figure A1).

Figure A.1. **FINANCIAL FLOWS IN THE HEALTH SECTOR, 1994**
DM billion

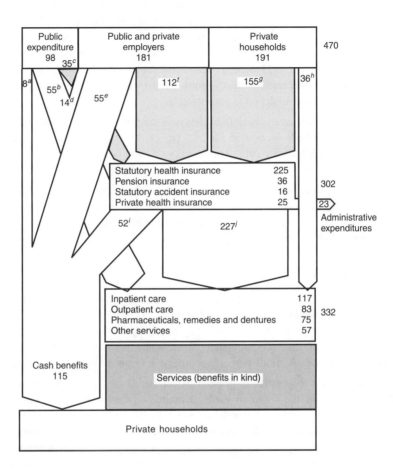

a.   Cash benefits, including statutory pensions for occupational disability.
b.   Services, current and investment subsidies.
c.   Subsidies and reimbursements to insurers.
d.   Services, particulary supplementary benefits and care allowances.
e.   Cash benefits, particularly sick-pay.
f+g. Premium payments to insurers.
h.   Heathcare-related payments.
i.   Cash benefits, including occupational disability pensions, sickness allowances, injury benefits.
j.   Services.

Source: Federal Statistical Office.

Hospitals and centres for preventative treatment and rehabilitation

While most hospitals (*Krankenhäuser*) are either public or run by charitable organisations, the preventative treatment and rehabilitation centres (*V&R Einrichtungen*) are largely private organisations. In 1994 there were roughly twice as many hospitals as treatment and rehabilitation centres although there has been a tendency for the latter to become more important. Hospitals accounted for about three times as many days of care as the treatment and rehabilitation centres, but in the latter the average length of stay is 31 days as opposed to 13 days in hospitals.

Medium-sized and small facilities dominate the size structure of hospitals: those with 100 to 200 beds accounted for 24.5 per cent of capacity in 1994 and hospitals with 50 to 100 beds for 13 per cent. The number of beds per capita varies significantly across the Länder.

The preventative and rehabilitation centres are predominantly financed by the public pension funds which have traditionally emphasised rehabilitation for those who could return to work after serious illness. The health funds only cover those persons not in the work force and are therefore only involved in financing these facilities to a minor extent.

The ambulatory sector

At the end of 1995 there were approximately 119 000 practising physicians in Germany and about 60 000 dentists. The vast majority of physicians practised in individual practices: only 26 500 were in group practices.[2] Patients are largely free to seek out the physician of their choice, apart from some restrictions on consulting specialists without a referral. A small percentage attend a large number of physicians.

The licence to practice is granted by the heads of the administrative districts within the Länder or by the regional medical boards (*Ärztekammer*). However, an additional licence must be obtained from the association of doctors (KV) in order to work under contract with the statutory health funds. They also specify where physicians may practise and in which specialities. In 1993, the right to set up a practice was severely restricted, but nearly 10 000 physicians rushed to set up independent practice under the old law. Doctors and dentists receive points for the services they render and the sum of the points at the end of each quarter determines the amount they receive from the regional association of doctors (KV). The value of the point is determined by dividing the budget available to the KV – paid to it by the statutory health insurance funds – by the total number of points submitted. The average value has been declining in recent years.

Pharmacies

Medicines may be dispensed only by pharmacies, which are subject to heavy regulation, ranging from the prices of prescription drugs to the criteria for pharmacy listing. Ownership is bound to one person – a qualified pharmacist – which effectively bans multiple owners and the development of pharmacy chain stores which could exercise purchasing power. However, unlike in many other EU countries there is no other restriction on establishing a pharmacy. In the old Länder the number of pharmacies has only increased by 3 per cent since 1985, but the number of pharmacists has increased by 37.5 per cent. Retail margins are specified by the Ministry of Economics and there is a unified price for drugs covering the whole country.

The pharmaceutical industry

The wholesaling side of the industry is already highly consolidated and the budget cap on expenditures has led to some vertical integration with manufacturers. Germany is a major manufacturer of pharmaceuticals although the market is quite fragmented with the top 50 companies accounting for just 18.5 per cent of total revenue. Nearly 90 per cent of the total revenue was from the 2 000 top selling products. 45 000 different drugs are registered in Germany, 8 000 of which account for most of the revenues earned on the domestic market.

Since 1993 there has been a budget cap on the cost of medicines which can be prescribed by the doctors of a regional association and the limit was exceeded in 1996 in some regions. If the cap is exceeded, the law makes provision for doctors as a group to make reimbursements to the health funds.

Although factory pricing is free, prices are subject to *de facto* control. The reform of 1989 introduced fixed maximum reimbursements for certain groups of drugs (reference prices) which in effect functions as a price ceiling. The reform of 1993 specified retail price reductions and a price moratorium for many items. A proposal to create a positive list of drugs for introduction in 1996 was not enacted and pharmaceuticals which have been authorised for marketing after December 1995 will not be subject to reference pricing controls for the period of the patent.

In 1996 the share of parallel imports amounted to 1.5 per cent of drug sales in pharmacies and for around 1.7 per cent of the pharmaceutical costs of the health funds. Prices for imports tend to be 10 per cent lower than the original price. Although pharmacies have not been obliged since 1996 to favour the imported drug, imports are still increasing. The use of generic drugs has increased by 10 percentage points since 1990 and now account for some 30 per cent of turnover and for some 58 per cent of the market for multisource drugs.

The new Länder

Since reunification, the structure of the west German health system has been extended to the new Länder which has required extensive restructuring. The ambulatory sector in the GDR was based around large outpatient clinics (polyclinics). In the absence of a long term commitment by the Länder, the clinics have been running down rapidly with specialists leaving to set up private practice; a network of practising physicians and dentists has been established surprisingly quickly. There has been significant financial help from government programmes in doing this and the debt level of many practices is said to be high. A major problem has arisen with the prescribing practices of doctors, who tend to favour high cost drugs. The hospital sector was burdened by a large number of long-term patients and by under-investment. Patients requiring long term nursing care have now been transferred from the acute care sector and there is a special programme of hospital investment amounting to some DM 21 billion shared equally between the federal government, the Länder and the health funds spread over the period 1995 to 2004.

All types of statutory health funds are now established in the new Länder (215 in all in 1994 including 6 AOK and 155 BKK), but the funds must be financed independently from those in the old Länder: there is no financial transfer at the level of the funds. However, with unemployment high and with extensive resort to early retirement the system is supported indirectly through the payments of health contributions by the Labour Office and the pension funds. Health costs are higher than in the west and with contribution income weaker, contribution rates are relatively high. A risk equalisation fund has also been established between funds in the new states with transfers amounting to some DM 4 billion in 1995. The two health systems – and in particular the health funds – are set to merge when the level of income in the new states exceeds 90 per cent of the western average.

Notes

1. See *Sachverständigenrat*, 1996 for a discussion of the problem.
2. In the new Länder the old polyclinics, which are an extended group practice, still exist although the number has been declining.

Chronology of main economic events

1996

January

Various fiscal policy measures come into force:

- The basic income tax allowance is increased along with child allowances and benefits.
- The tax depreciation allowance for the construction of rented housing is cut.
- Tax allowances for the promotion of owner occupied housing are restructured.
- The special levy for the subsidisation of coal mining (*Kohlepfennig*) is abolished and the financing of the coal subsidies is integrated into the federal budget.
- The pension contribution rate is increased from 18.6 to 19.2 per cent.

The government decides a fifty-point "Action Programme for Investment and Employment". Major policy objectives include a reduction of the solidarity tax surcharge and an enterprise tax reform in 1997, support for small and medium-sized companies (*Mittelstand*), reductions in social spending, reforms of vocational and tertiary education, and measures aimed at fostering competition, privatisation and improving the flexibility of the labour market.

The government agrees a pact to promote employment with the social partners. The non-binding statement of principles calls for moderate wage increases, improved labour market flexibility and lower social charges. A phased withdrawal of early retirement provisions is also agreed in principle.

February

After sharp declines in the repurchase rate the Bundesbank moves from floating rate tenders to fixed interest tenders (volume tender) at 3.3 per cent.

March

The Minister of Finance enacts expenditure controls for the federal budget (*Haushaltssperre*), according to which discretionary spending above a threshold requires the approval of the Minister of Finance.

April

The government announces a package of measures ("Programme to promote growth and employment") complementing the 50-point programme (see January 1996), aimed at reducing general government spending by almost DM 70 billion in 1997.

The Bundesbank lowers the discount rate from 3 to 2½ per cent and the Lombard rate from 5 to 4½ per cent.

A bill to control hospital budgets comes into force, back dated to the start of the year.

May

The official tax revenues estimates for 1996 and 1997 indicate a substantial downwards revision of revenues for the territorial authorities. For 1996 losses on account of lower growth rate assumptions amount to DM 22 billion in comparison with the estimates of October 1995. For 1997, lower revenues in comparison with the estimates of May 1995 amount to around DM 66 billion.

June

The Ministry of Finance and the Deutsche Bundesbank announce that from July onwards new short-term debt instruments with a maturity of six months will be issued at quarterly intervals. In 1996 and 1997 the overall stock of these instruments is not to exceed DM 20 billion. The government also announces increased issues in both the medium-term (two years) and long-term segments (thirty years) of public debt.

New legislation comes into force, back-dated to April, requiring that the wage base for calculating unemployment assistance is to be reduced by 3 per cent a year.

July

The second stage of the long-term care insurance comes into force covering in-patient care. The contribution rate for the long-term care insurance is increased from 1 per cent to 1.7 per cent.

Parliament passes the social assistance reform law. Main provisions are: statutory social assistance benefits are set to increase by 1 per cent in July 1996 and with the growth of net wages in 1997 and 1998; from August 1997 onwards social assistance will be reduced by at least 25 per cent if the recipient rejects acceptable work. Social assistance providers may instead support employment by granting wage subsidies.

The Council of the Deutsche Bundesbank confirms the monetary target for 1996 which aims at M3 growth of 4 to 7 per cent between the fourth quarters of 1995 and 1996.

August

A law comes into force (*Gesetz zur Förderung eines gleitenden Übergangs in den Ruhestand*) promoting part-time employment of formerly full-time employed elderly workers by grants from the federal labour office provided companies compensate for reduced work hours by employing the unemployed or newly graduated apprentices. The law provides for a phased increase of the minimum age for receiving a full pension on account of unemployment from 60 years to 63 years.

The Deutsche Bundesbank lowers the interest rate for fixed rate repurchase operations by 30 basis points to 3 per cent.

September

New regulations come into force designed to accelerate investment-related approval procedures of public administrations (*Genehmigungsverfahrensbeschleunigungsgesetz*).

October

A law comes into force liberalising employment conditions specified in the labour code (*Arbeitsrechtliches Beschäftigungsförderungsgesetz*). Legal conditions covering dismissals are relaxed, the minimum statutory rate for sickness pay is lowered, and the admissible duration of fixed-term contracts is extended.

November

Parliament passes the federal budget for 1997 which sets a deficit target of DM 53.4 billion.

Through a public offering of Deutsche Telekom shares totalling DM 20.1 billion, the government's stake is reduced to 74 per cent.

A law comes into force which allows for longer shop opening hours.

The official tax revenues estimates for 1996 and 1997 indicate revenue losses for the territorial authorities of some DM 5 billion in 1996 and DM 10 billion for 1997 in comparison with the estimates of May 1996.

December

The Bundesbank announces a target for money supply (M3) growth for both 1997 and 1998 of 5 per cent. For 1997 the M3 target range is set at 3½ to 6½ per cent between the fourth quarter of 1996 and the fourth quarter of 1997. The target range for 1998 is to be specified at the end of 1997.

Wage agreements for a two year period are reached in the metal and electrical industries, specifying a DM 200 lump sum payment for the first quarter 1997, and wage increases of 1.5 per cent in April 1997 and 2.5 per cent in April 1998. An agreement is made to retain sick pay at 100 per cent of gross wages irrespective of the statutory minimum level of 80 per cent, but overtime premia is excluded from the wage base and bonuses are cut.

1997

January

The 1997 tax reform law (*Jahressteuergesetz* 1997) comes into force. Major provisions are:

- The wealth tax is abolished.
- The inheritance and gift taxes are restructured.
- The real estate purchase tax is increased.
- Employment in private households is promoted by special tax allowances.
- Depreciation allowances are introduced for newly founded enterprises (*Ansparabschreibung*).

As legislated earlier, child allowances are also increased.

Contribution rates for the pension insurance are increased from 19.2 to 20.3 per cent of the wage base.

A commission of experts, appointed by the government, presents proposals for a reform of the personal and corporate income tax system which is later endorsed by the government. Statutory tax rates are to be cut, tax concessions reduced and the tax base broadened with the full reform taking effect in 1999.

A commission of experts, appointed by the government, proposes to reduce pension replacement rates from 70 per cent to 64 per cent by 2030 but rejects other measures such as greater resort to funding.

The law for the promotion of growth and employment (*Wachstums- und Beschäftigungsförderungsgesetz)* comes into force (some elements were already implemented earlier). An increase in the early retirement age for women and for the long-term insured to the standard retirement age of 65 will be phased in from 2000 onwards. Other important measures are: the accrual of pension rights which are not based on contributions are restricted, the level of pensions for immigrants is curbed, increased co-payments for spas are introduced, and the increase of unemployment benefits in 1997 is curbed.

A law comes into force (*Beitragsentlastungsgestz*) restricting some health care benefits and raising co-payments. The public health funds are required to lower contribution rates immediately to pass on these potential savings.

Minimum reserves are no longer required for repurchase operations with a maturity of up to one year in marketable securities.

April

Sections of the revision to the employment promotion law comes into force. A more flexible type of employment contract for hiring long-term unemployed is created, active labour market measures are more focused on long-term unemployed and unemployed with unfavourable characteristics, wage subsidies are curbed and job search controls for recipients of unemployment benefits strengthened.

May

The official tax revenues estimates for 1997 and 1998 indicate a substantial downwards revision of revenues for the territorial authorities. For 1997, losses on account of lower growth and employment, changes in tax legislation and other structural factors amount to DM 18 billion in comparison with the estimates of November 1996. For 1998 lower revenues in comparison to the estimates of May 1996 amount to DM 31.8 billion.

Proposals made to revalue gold and foreign exchange reserves of the Deutsche Bundesbank with the extraordinary profit to be paid to one of the off-budget debt funds.

June

The Minister of Finance introduces additional spending controls for the federal government.

The government tables a pension reform bill with the primary purpose of securing the long-term financing of the pension system. Among other elements, the law proposes a phased decrease of pensions from 70 per cent of average net wages (after 45 years of contributions) to 64 per cent by 2030, a tightening of the conditions for obtaining an invalidity pension, extended eligibility for pensions on account of child raising, and additional transfers from the federal budget.

In the chemical industry the tariff partners agree on an opening clause which allows companies to reduce wages by up to 10 per cent beneath the level specified in tariff agreements, provided this serves to secure employment or the competitiveness of the companies. Exercising the opening clause requires the approval of the tariff partners. The agreement also provides for workers to participate in profits of successful companies via bonuses.

The lower house (Bundestag) of parliament passes the government's tax reform providing for a lowering of statutory tax rates, cuts in tax concessions and a broadening of the tax base. The law needs the approval of the upper house. The Bundestag also passes a law extending aid to the new Länder until 2004. This law also needs the approval of the upper house.

Agreement reached with the Deutsche Bundesbank to revalue dollar foreign exchange reserves with the accounting profit to be paid to the Inherited Debt Fund in 1998. Gold reserves are to be revalued in 1999 in line with the rules of the new European Central Bank.

Plans are announced to accelerate privatisation in 1997 and in 1998. The government is to sell 25 per cent of its shareholding in Telekom to a state-owned bank for later sale to a strategic partner.

July

New regulations come into force concerning employment conditions for civil servants (*Beamte*). Among the provisions, the transferability between posts is enhanced and tenure in management positions restricted.

Two health reform laws come into force; increases in contribution rates to health funds are linked to increases in co-payments and clients are allowed to switch funds immediately. Budget limits on total expenditures by physicians and for pharmaceuticals are lifted with details to be negotiated between health funds and doctors.

STATISTICAL ANNEX AND STRUCTURAL INDICATORS

Table A. **Selected background statistics**

	1987	1988	1989	1990	1991	1992	1993	1994	1995	1996
A. Percentage change from previous year at constant prices[1]										
Private consumption	3.4	2.7	2.8	5.4	5.6	2.8	0.3	1.0	1.8	1.3
Gross fixed investment	1.8	4.4	6.3	8.5	6.0	3.5	-5.6	4.2	1.5	-0.8
Construction	0.0	3.1	4.4	4.9	2.7	9.7	0.9	7.7	1.2	-2.7
Public	-1.2	0.4	3.1	-0.8	0.3	11.1	-2.1	4.0	-4.4	-6.8
Residential	-1.2	3.7	4.9	8.5	4.3	9.4	3.8	12.4	3.0	-0.3
Business	2.5	3.6	4.4	2.8	1.6	9.4	-1.8	2.6	1.2	-4.5
Machinery and equipment	4.5	6.3	8.8	13.2	10.0	-3.5	-14.1	-1.2	2.0	2.4
GDP at market prices	1.5	3.7	3.6	5.7	5.0	2.2	-1.1	2.9	1.9	1.4
GDP implicit price deflator	1.9	1.5	2.4	3.2	3.9	5.5	3.8	2.2	2.2	1.0
Industrial production	0.4	3.6	4.7	5.2	3.0	-2.6	-7.3	3.6	2.0	0.2
Employment	0.7	0.8	1.5	3.0	2.5	-1.8	-1.7	-0.7	-0.3	-1.2
Compensation of employees (current prices)	4.2	4.0	4.5	7.8	8.0	8.0	2.1	2.4	3.0	1.0
Productivity (GDP/employment)	0.7	2.9	2.1	2.7	2.5	4.1	0.6	3.6	2.3	2.5
Unit labour costs (compensation of employees/GDP)	2.7	0.2	0.8	2.0	3.3	5.7	3.3	-0.4	1.1	-0.3
B. Percentage ratios										
Gross fixed investment										
As a per cent of GDP at constant prices	19.9	20.1	20.6	21.1	23.0	23.3	22.2	22.5	22.4	21.9
Stockbuilding										
As a per cent of GDP at constant prices	0.0	0.5	0.8	0.6	0.4	0.0	-0.2	0.8	1.0	0.8
Foreign balance										
As a per cent of GDP at constant prices	4.2	4.4	5.1	5.5	-0.1	-0.7	-0.4	-0.4	-0.5	0.1
Compensation of employees										
As a per cent of GDP at current prices	56.5	55.8	54.9	54.3	56.3	56.6	56.3	54.8	54.3	53.6
Direct taxes										
As a per cent of household income	8.9	8.7	8.9	8.0	8.3	8.7	8.5	8.5	9.1	8.2
Household saving										
As a per cent of disposable income	12.6	12.8	12.4	13.8	12.7	12.9	12.2	11.7	11.6	11.6
Unemployment										
As a per cent of civilian labour force	7.9	7.7	7.1	6.4	6.7	7.8	8.9	9.6	9.4	10.8
C. Other indicator[2]										
Current balance (billion $)	46.8	50.1	56.6	48.7	-18.1	-19.4	-14.1	-21.1	-23.6	-14.3

1. From 1992 all Germany.
2. From 1991 all Germany.
Source: Statistisches Bundesamt, *Volkswirtschaftliche Gesamtrechnungen, Reihe 1*; Deutsche Bundesbank, *Statistisches Beiheft den Monatsbericht, Reihe 4.*

Table B. Gross domestic product by origin[1]

DM billion

	1987	1988	1989	1990	1991	1992	1993	1994	1995	1996
Current prices										
Agriculture, forestry, fishing	30.2	33.7	37.2	36.7	41.0	40.6	36.5	36.1	35.8	37.2
Mining and quarrying, energy	68.7	67.8	69.3	70.2	90.0	90.3	90.6	89.6	89.2	82.4
Manufacturing	624.7	652.7	686.0	741.6	825.7	836.7	785.5	808.3	833.1	843.8
Construction	101.7	106.3	114.7	127.6	161.6	190.1	198.1	215.8	223.2	217.3
Trade, transport, communications	279.5	294.7	311.3	346.8	416.0	438.5	446.3	458.8	473.4	471.5
Government[2]	225.8	231.9	238.6	253.2	317.4	349.2	365.8	371.1	381.9	387.0
Non-profit organisations, households	49.3	51.7	53.9	58.3	69.6	78.3	83.6	88.8	94.7	99.7
Other services	610.6	657.3	713.5	791.6	932.4	1 052.0	1 151.7	1 251.9	1 326.1	1 402.1
Gross domestic product at market prices	1 990.5	2 096.0	2 224.4	2 426.0	2 853.6	3 075.6	3 158.1	3 320.4	3 457.4	3 541.0
At 1991 prices										
Agriculture, forestry, fishing	32.1	34.5	35.0	36.4	41.0	48.1	45.5	43.8	45.0	47.4
Mining and quarrying, energy	67.0	66.7	69.5	69.4	90.0	86.5	85.0	84.0	84.7	86.9
Manufacturing	677.0	698.6	722.6	762.3	825.7	805.8	744.9	763.6	768.6	768.3
Construction	124.6	127.1	132.5	136.8	161.6	172.3	170.6	180.2	180.8	175.0
Trade, transport, communications	301.2	315.8	330.0	355.8	416.0	424.7	424.8	430.5	439.1	443.5
Government[2]	259.0	261.7	262.6	266.9	317.4	322.1	324.9	327.6	328.2	327.9
Non-profit organisations, households	55.8	57.5	59.1	61.6	69.6	73.3	75.5	78.7	81.2	83.7
Other services	701.8	739.1	773.1	831.3	932.4	983.7	1 012.4	1 057.9	1 095.9	1 132.1
Gross domestic product at market prices	2 218.4	2 301.0	2 384.4	2 520.4	2 853.6	2 916.4	2 883.6	2 966.2	3 023.4	3 064.6

1. From 1991 all Germany.
2. Central and local government, municipalities and social security.
Source: Statistisches Bundesamt, *Volkswirtschaftliche Gesamtrechnungen, Fachserie 18, Reihe 1.*

Table C. Gross domestic product by demand components[1]

DM billion

	1987	1988	1989	1990	1991	1992	1993	1994	1995	1996
Current prices										
Private consumption	1 108.0	1 153.7	1 221.0	1 320.7	1 630.3	1 754.7	1 829.8	1 902.9	1 974.7	2 039.1
Public consumption	397.3	412.4	418.8	444.1	556.7	616.3	634.2	650.2	675.4	695.4
Gross fixed investment	385.8	409.9	448.5	507.8	656.0	709.4	689.2	729.4	750.7	743.6
Machinery and equipment	169.4	182.5	203.5	234.6	306.8	301.8	261.5	257.8	262.7	269.8
Public	7.1	7.2	8.1	8.8	13.5	14.4	13.1	11.5	11.0	11.3
Private	162.3	175.3	195.4	225.8	293.3	287.4	248.4	246.4	251.8	258.5
Construction	216.4	227.4	245.1	273.2	349.2	407.6	427.7	471.5	488.0	473.8
Public	40.9	41.7	44.3	46.8	61.5	72.8	73.9	78.2	75.8	70.0
Residential	102.6	108.6	117.9	135.9	168.2	195.4	212.5	245.4	259.7	259.2
Other private	72.9	77.1	82.8	90.6	119.5	139.4	141.4	147.9	152.5	144.5
Stockbuilding	-0.6	10.3	16.0	11.5	12.8	-3.5	-11.6	16.4	27.7	17.0
Total domestic demand	1 890.5	1 986.3	2 104.3	2 284.1	2 855.9	3 076.8	3 141.7	3 298.8	3 428.4	3 495.2
Exports of goods and services	576.6	619.8	701.4	778.9	727.1	732.1	698.0	758.6	817.2	859.7
Imports of goods and services	476.7	510.1	581.3	637.0	729.4	733.2	681.6	737.0	788.2	813.9
Gross domestic product at market prices	1 990.5	2 096.0	2 224.4	2 426.0	2 853.6	3 075.6	3 158.1	3 320.4	3 457.4	3 541.0
At 1991 prices										
Private consumption	1 230.6	1 264.3	1 300.2	1 370.0	1 630.3	1 676.0	1 680.3	1 697.9	1 728.8	1 751.4
Public consumption	452.7	462.3	454.9	465.0	556.7	580.7	580.4	588.2	600.0	614.2
Gross fixed investment	442.2	461.8	490.7	532.4	656.0	679.3	640.9	667.7	677.8	672.7
Machinery and equipment	184.0	195.7	212.8	240.9	306.8	296.2	254.5	251.6	256.6	262.7
Public	7.6	7.6	8.2	8.9	13.5	14.1	12.7	11.1	10.6	10.8
Private	176.4	188.1	204.6	232.0	293.3	282.1	241.8	240.4	246.0	251.8
Construction	258.2	266.1	277.9	291.4	349.2	383.1	386.4	416.2	421.2	410.0
Public	48.6	48.8	50.4	49.9	61.5	68.4	66.9	69.6	66.5	62.0
Residential	123.1	127.6	133.9	145.2	168.2	184.0	191.1	214.8	221.3	220.7
Other private	86.5	89.7	93.6	96.3	119.5	130.7	128.4	131.7	133.4	127.3
Stockbuilding	-0.6	12.1	18.1	15.0	12.8	0.0	-5.2	23.4	31.7	23.9
Total domestic demand	2 125.0	2 200.6	2 263.8	2 382.4	2 855.9	2 936.0	2 896.4	2 977.2	3 038.3	3 062.2
Exports of goods and services	611.7	645.3	710.9	789.1	727.1	724.6	689.1	744.3	788.5	826.9
Imports of goods and services	518.3	544.8	590.3	651.1	729.4	744.2	701.9	755.3	803.4	824.5
Gross domestic product at market prices	2 218.4	2 301.0	2 384.4	2 520.4	2 853.6	2 916.4	2 883.6	2 966.2	3 023.4	3 064.6

1. From 1991 all Germany.
Source: Statistisches Bundesamt, *Volkswirtschaftliche Gesamtrechnungen, Fachserie 18, Reihe 1.*

Table D. **Distribution of national income**[1]

DM billion, current prices

	1987	1988	1989	1990	1991	1992	1993	1994	1995	1996
Compensation of employees	1 124.7	1 169.4	1 221.9	1 317.1	1 611.8	1 741.2	1 777.7	1 821.0	1 875.7	1 895.2
less:										
Employers' social security contributions	211.9	220.5	229.1	247.5	298.1	323.5	327.0	349.9	362.3	371.2
Employees' social security contributions	129.3	135.6	142.1	152.4	193.3	212.4	220.6	235.3	246.0	255.9
Wage tax	162.4	165.5	179.2	173.7	220.6	251.7	252.3	263.3	294.0	273.2
Net wages and salaries[2]	621.1	647.8	671.6	743.6	899.7	953.6	977.8	972.6	973.4	994.9
Income from property and entrepreneurship	425.3	466.2	516.2	575.1	615.1	628.9	618.7	680.3	744.3	771.4
less:										
Direct taxes on business and property income	69.3	75.9	89.9	80.9	94.4	99.5	103.7	90.2	80.8	79.5
Net income from property and entrepreneurship	356.0	390.3	426.3	494.2	520.7	529.4	515.0	590.1	663.6	691.9
of which:										
Retained profits	35.6	64.8	54.9	74.4	16.7	–6.1	–27.2	–5.0	49.2	36.7
Accruing to Government	–30.7	–39.9	–29.0	–29.1	–38.4	–50.4	–55.6	–60.1	–88.0	–92.4
Distributed to households	351.1	365.4	400.4	448.8	542.4	585.9	597.8	655.1	702.4	747.6
Net national income at factor costs	1 550.0	1 635.5	1 738.1	1 892.2	2 226.8	2 370.1	2 396.4	2 501.3	2 620.0	2 666.6
Memorandum items:										
Household disposable income	1 267.6	1 323.2	1 394.3	1 532.7	1 871.3	2 013.4	2 084.8	2 154.8	2 233.2	2 306.6
Household saving ratio[3]	11.8	12.1	12.2	11.3	12.9	12.9	12.2	11.7	11.6	11.6

1. From 1991 all Germany.
2. Including voluntary fringe benefits.
3. Per cent of household disposable income.

Source: Statistisches Bundesamt, *Volkswirtschaftliche Gesamtrechnungen, Fachserie 18, Reihe 1.*

Table E.   **Receipts and expenditure of general government: national accounts basis**[1]

DM billion, current prices

	1987	1988	1989	1990	1991	1992	1993	1994	1995	1996
Current receipts										
Income from property and entrepreneurship	27.0	19.9	31.5	34.3	38.2	49.9	48.4	53.1	41.6	38.2
Indirect taxes	245.5	257.1	278.3	302.2	358.5	389.8	409.6	443.6	447.2	451.9
Direct taxes	243.9	255.4	281.8	271.0	330.8	364.9	363.4	367.7	391.4	369.1
Social security contributions	349.9	366.5	383.2	410.5	513.0	562.9	596.4	640.5	669.6	701.1
Other current transfers received	25.0	25.5	24.9	26.1	30.7	38.2	36.6	38.8	39.9	40.9
Total current receipts	891.3	924.5	999.6	1 044.0	1 271.1	1 405.7	1 454.2	1 543.6	1 589.7	1 601.2
Current expenditure										
Final consumption expenditure	397.3	412.4	418.8	444.1	556.7	616.3	634.2	650.2	675.4	695.4
Wages and salaries	211.5	216.9	222.8	236.3	297.2	327.0	342.0	346.2	355.9	360.4
Goods and services	185.8	195.5	195.5	207.8	259.5	289.3	292.3	304.1	319.5	335.0
Subsidies	44.8	47.7	46.8	48.8	65.0	59.8	62.0	67.8	75.4	76.5
Debt-interest payments	57.8	59.8	60.5	63.4	76.7	100.3	104.0	113.1	129.6	130.6
Current transfers paid	371.4	392.5	409.6	472.9	556.8	605.2	658.0	695.2	732.1	748.6
Total current expenditure	871.3	912.5	935.7	1 029.2	1 255.1	1 381.6	1 458.2	1 526.4	1 612.5	1 651.2
Savings	20.0	12.0	63.9	14.8	16.0	24.1	-4.0	17.2	-22.8	-50.0
Depreciation	14.1	14.7	15.6	16.7	19.9	21.8	23.5	24.6	25.6	26.3
Net capital transfers received	-24.0	-23.0	-24.3	-25.7	-55.7	-45.5	-42.2	-32.7	-38.7	-28.9
Gross fixed investment	48.0	48.9	52.4	55.5	75.0	87.2	87.0	89.7	86.7	81.3
Financial balance (net lending)	-37.9	-45.2	2.7	-49.7	-94.9	-86.8	-109.7	-80.6	-122.6	-134.0
As a per cent of GDP	-1.9	-2.2	0.1	-2.1	-3.3	-2.8	-3.5	-2.4	-3.5	-3.8

1.   From 1991 all Germany.
Source: Statistisches Bundesamt, *Volkswirtschaftliche Gesamtrechnungen, Fachserie 18, Reihe 1.*

Tableau F. **Balance of payments**[1]
DM billion

	1987	1988	1989	1990	1991	1992	1993	1994	1995	1996
A. Current account										
1. Foreign trade, net	117.7	128.0	134.6	105.4	21.9	33.7	60.3	71.8	85.3	98.6
Exports (f.o.b.)	527.4	567.7	641.0	662.0	665.8	671.2	632.2	694.7	749.5	784.3
Imports (c.i.f.)	409.6	439.6	506.5	556.7	643.9	637.5	571.9	622.9	664.2	685.7
2. Supplementary trade items	-3.7	-2.3	-3.5	-3.0	-2.0	-0.6	-2.1	0.1	-2.9	-1.0
Balance of trade	114.0	125.8	131.0	102.4	19.9	33.0	58.2	71.9	82.4	97.5
3. Services, net	-9.1	-14.2	-13.2	-17.6	-22.7	-35.9	-43.5	-53.3	-53.8	-55.1
Receipts	87.1	88.3	100.4	110.0	117.1	117.1	115.9	116.3	127.7	136.5
Expenditure	96.2	102.5	113.7	127.5	139.8	153.1	159.4	169.6	181.6	191.7
4. Factor income, net	10.9	11.4	25.8	32.0	34.3	26.8	20.4	10.0	-3.7	-8.5
Receipts	57.6	63.5	85.7	105.8	122.8	125.8	127.8	125.3	138.4	137.4
Expenditure	46.8	52.1	59.9	73.8	88.6	98.9	107.4	115.3	142.1	145.9
5. Transfer payments, net	-31.6	-35.0	-37.1	-38.2	-61.4	-54.2	-58.5	-62.8	-58.7	-54.8
of which:										
Remittances of foreign workers	-7.4	-7.5	-7.4	-7.1	-6.4	-6.8	-6.8	-7.5	-7.6	-7.4
Transfers to the European Community, net[2]	-11.1	-14.5	-14.8	-13.0	-21.3	-24.7	-21.7	-31.0	-29.3	-27.2
Balance on current account	84.2	88.0	106.5	78.7	-30.0	-30.2	-23.4	-34.2	-33.8	-20.9
B. Capital account										
6. Capital transfers	-0.2	0.0	0.1	-2.1	-1.0	0.9	0.8	0.3	-0.9	0.0
7. Financial transactions	-39.2	-125.6	-134.7	-90.5	20.2	91.5	14.0	64.9	74.0	18.2
German investment abroad (increase: –):	-86.7	-155.2	-248.6	-183.4	-106.0	-116.8	-295.9	-110.7	-173.8	-202.8
Direct investment	-17.4	-21.2	-28.5	-38.7	-39.3	-30.5	-25.3	-27.8	-55.2	-41.8
Portfolio investment	-25.0	-71.7	-50.1	-25.1	-29.9	-75.6	-52.8	-87.0	-31.1	-60.5
Credit transactions	-42.5	-60.6	-167.8	-117.5	-33.6	-8.1	-215.2	6.5	-83.4	-96.6
Long-term	-18.6	-2.5	-14.2	-43.0	-26.2	-14.1	-33.4	-26.3	-27.2	-22.7
Short-term	-24.0	-58.2	-153.6	-74.5	-7.4	5.9	-181.8	32.8	-56.2	-73.8
Other investment	-1.7	-1.7	-2.2	-2.1	-3.2	-2.6	-2.5	-2.4	-4.1	-3.9
Foreign investment in Germany (increase: +):	47.5	29.7	113.9	92.9	126.2	208.3	310.0	175.6	247.8	221.0
Direct investment	3.3	2.0	13.3	4.0	6.8	4.2	3.2	2.5	17.2	-4.9
Portfolio investment	32.3	7.4	45.7	19.4	71.2	122.5	235.7	46.9	87.6	138.4
Credit transactions	11.9	20.4	55.0	69.8	48.3	81.9	71.1	125.3	143.9	87.6
Long-term	2.9	1.7	14.3	20.7	-0.2	27.6	50.2	33.9	63.7	40.4
Short-term	9.0	18.7	40.7	49.2	48.4	54.3	20.9	91.5	80.2	47.2
Other investment	0.0	-0.0	-0.1	-0.4	-0.1	-0.2	-0.0	0.8	-1.0	-0.1
8. Unclassifiable transactions	-3.6	2.9	9.0	25.0	11.1	6.5	-27.2	-18.7	-21.6	1.1
C. Change in the Bundesbank's net external assets										
(transaction values) (increase: +)	41.2	-34.7	-19.0	11.0	0.3	68.7	-35.8	12.2	17.8	-1.6
9. Balancing item of the Bundesbank	-9.3	2.2	-2.6	-5.1	0.5	-6.3	1.5	-3.7	-2.7	0.1
D. Change in the Bundesbank's net external assets										
(balance sheet values) (increase: +)	31.9	-32.5	-21.6	5.9	0.8	62.4	-34.2	8.6	15.1	-1.5

1. From July 1990 including the external transactions of the former German Democratic Republic.
2. Excluding collection expenses, EAGGF (Guidance Funds) and Regional Fund.
Source : Deutsche Bundesbank, *Statistisches Beiheft zum Monatsbericht, Reihe 3.*

Tableau G. **Imports and exports of goods by regions**
DM billion

	1987	1988	1989	1990	1991	1992	1993	1994	1995	1996
Imports, f.o.b.										
OECD	324.8	350.3	403.4	440.8	507.6	503.1	433.6	468.0	504.6	516.5
EU	241.3	257.3	293.4	326.9	378.9	375.5	314.1	341.1	370.9	380.5
Austria	16.6	18.5	20.6	23.9	26.7	27.7	25.9	28.6	25.7	26.0
Belgium-Luxembourg	28.7	30.8	34.6	39.6	45.6	44.6	33.8	38.2	43.7	43.8
France	46.7	52.3	59.8	65.0	78.3	75.8	65.1	68.9	72.7	73.3
Italy	38.7	40.0	45.0	51.9	59.7	58.4	48.0	51.9	56.7	57.1
Netherlands	43.2	44.3	51.0	55.5	61.7	60.3	49.2	50.9	57.2	59.3
United Kingdom	28.6	29.7	34.0	36.5	42.3	42.6	35.4	38.9	43.2	47.3
Other European countries	27.7	29.2	32.7	36.6	39.7	40.8	39.2	42.9	46.1	47.9
Switzerland	18.3	19.1	20.5	22.9	24.7	24.9	23.3	25.7	27.2	26.7
Other OECD	55.8	63.9	77.3	77.3	89.0	86.8	80.4	83.9	87.6	88.0
Japan	25.9	29.6	33.3	33.2	40.7	38.4	34.9	34.6	36.0	33.4
United States	24.6	28.4	37.1	36.9	40.9	41.5	39.3	42.9	43.9	47.6
Central and Eastern European countries[1]	20.3	20.8	25.2	32.6	39.2	39.9	39.4	48.0	56.3	59.9
Non-oil developing countries	39.6	45.2	51.4	55.0	63.0	58.5	58.0	62.8	66.8	64.7
OPEC	10.5	9.9	11.4	13.2	13.8	14.0	12.8	11.9	10.3	11.7
China	3.4	4.2	5.8	7.7	11.3	11.1	13.4	14.9	15.8	17.4
Dynamic Asian economies	18.2	20.9	23.2	25.6	31.9	30.0	31.2	33.8	36.6	34.3
Total imports	398.8	430.6	497.1	549.2	634.7	626.7	563.3	612.2	654.5	672.6
Exports, f.o.b.										
OECD	435.6	474.4	534.3	539.1	541.9	542.1	489.8	536.3	577.0	596.4
EU	324.5	361.6	413.8	413.2	422.0	425.4	369.2	403.0	437.0	447.6
Austria	28.1	32.0	35.6	37.2	39.8	40.0	37.2	39.7	41.1	43.8
Belgium-Luxembourg	38.1	41.3	45.4	47.5	48.2	48.9	42.5	46.5	48.7	49.0
France	62.9	70.7	84.4	84.7	89.6	89.0	80.0	86.2	90.1	88.8
Italy	45.5	51.4	59.6	60.0	61.2	62.3	46.9	52.4	56.7	58.6
Netherlands	44.9	48.4	53.9	54.3	55.6	55.4	48.0	52.0	56.8	58.1
United Kingdom	46.3	52.7	59.1	54.6	50.5	50.9	50.0	55.4	62.1	63.4
Other European countries	43.1	44.4	49.1	51.6	50.9	48.6	48.0	49.9	55.8	56.5
Switzerland	31.6	34.4	38.3	38.4	37.5	35.2	33.4	36.6	39.3	37.1
Other OECD	68.0	67.8	71.4	74.2	69.0	68.1	72.5	83.5	84.2	92.3
Japan	10.3	12.9	15.0	17.2	16.3	14.5	15.2	17.3	18.4	20.7
United States	48.7	45.2	44.9	46.3	41.0	41.9	45.7	53.2	53.6	58.9
Central and Eastern European countries[1]	23.6	26.4	32.6	48.6	46.0	43.4	47.6	53.7	61.4	71.2
Non-oil developing countries	42.2	44.4	51.2	52.6	55.9	58.8	63.7	74.3	82.2	84.8
OPEC	14.0	15.3	16.2	18.3	21.4	23.0	18.5	17.8	17.0	17.0
China	4.9	4.9	4.6	4.6	4.0	5.7	9.5	10.1	10.7	10.8
Dynamic Asian economies	13.4	16.3	20.2	22.3	25.1	26.2	30.2	37.2	42.1	44.2
Total exports	520.7	565.2	638.6	661.8	667.1	671.0	632.4	696.0	749.5	783.1

1. Poland, ex-USSR, former Czechoslovakia and Hungary.
Source : Deutsche Bundesbank, Statistisches Beiheft zum Monatsbericht, Reihe 3.

Tableau H. Foreign trade by main commodity groups – customs basis[1]

DM billion

	1987	1988	1989	1990	1991	1992	1993	1994	1995	1996
Imports, c.i.f.										
SITC classification										
0. Food and live animals	40.1	41.4	43.8	46.4	53.4	54.7	46.8	52.4	52.4	53.9
1. Beverages and tobacco	4.5	4.4	4.7	5.4	6.6	6.7	6.0	6.5	6.2	6.4
2. Crude materials, except fuels	25.1	28.5	33.4	29.5	28.6	28.5	23.1	27.6	28.4	26.0
3. Mineral fuels, lubricants and related materials	39.5	33.5	38.3	45.5	53.6	47.5	44.9	43.2	40.6	52.8
4. Animal and vegetable oils, etc.	1.2	1.5	1.7	1.5	1.6	1.7	1.5	1.9	1.9	2.0
5. Chemicals	38.5	42.6	47.7	49.7	54.2	54.6	46.9	55.0	59.3	59.4
6. Manufactured goods classified chiefly by material	71.6	80.5	94.6	98.3	106.7	106.2	86.2	100.2	108.3	100.0
7. Machinery and transport equipment	114.3	128.1	154.4	178.1	225.6	220.5	187.5	208.9	217.9	229.9
8. Miscellaneous manufactured articles	61.5	65.7	73.3	83.1	102.7	103.3	94.2	99.2	94.6	99.6
9. Other	13.2	13.4	14.6	13.1	10.9	13.8	29.5	22.1	54.5	55.7
0-9. Total imports	409.6	439.6	506.5	550.6	643.9	637.5	566.6	617.0	664.1	685.7
Exports, f.o.b.										
SITC classification										
0. Food and live animals	21.1	23.6	26.0	25.1	29.2	29.7	27.8	29.3	29.3	31.5
1. Beverages and tobacco	3.1	3.2	3.6	3.7	4.2	4.7	4.5	5.3	4.9	5.3
2. Crude materials, except fuels	9.2	10.6	12.4	11.7	12.5	12.5	10.8	13.0	13.8	12.7
3. Mineral fuels, lubricants and related materials	7.1	6.9	7.9	8.2	8.3	8.2	7.5	7.8	6.7	9.7
4. Animal and vegetable oils, etc.	1.3	1.6	1.8	1.5	1.5	1.5	1.6	1.9	2.1	1.9
5. Chemicals	68.6	76.9	83.1	81.7	84.8	84.7	80.7	92.8	98.1	101.6
6. Manufactured goods classified chiefly by material	93.4	102.6	117.2	113.5	113.2	111.0	100.4	111.2	120.7	119.1
7. Machinery and transport equipment	254.6	272.8	311.7	317.2	325.9	333.1	303.5	338.4	360.8	383.1
8. Miscellaneous manufactured articles	56.8	62.4	69.7	71.7	74.4	75.5	68.7	72.3	72.6	76.8
9. Other	12.1	7.0	7.7	8.4	11.6	10.2	23.1	18.5	40.5	42.6
0-9. Total exports	527.4	567.7	641.0	642.8	665.8	671.2	628.6	690.5	749.4	784.3

1. From 1991 all Germany.
Source : Statistisches Bundesamt.

Tableau I. **Money and credit**[1]

End of period, DM billion

	1987	1988	1989	1990	1991	1992	1993	1994	1995	1996
Consolidated balance sheet of the banking system:										
I. Bank lending to domestic non-banks	2 214.1	2 346.8	2 483.9	2 888.6	3 160.6	3 497.5	3 839.8	4 149.0	4 446.5	4 781.7
Bundesbank	13.9	14.5	13.9	13.5	13.7	19.3	13.4	11.9	9.6	8.7
Credit institutions	2200.2	2332.3	2470.1	2875.1	3146.9	3478.3	3826.4	4137.1	4437.0	4773.0
To public sector	500.5	541.4	547.2	603.6	629.2	739.2	840.4	926.2	1067.5	1148.7
To private sector	1699.7	1790.9	1922.8	2271.5	2517.8	2739.0	2986.0	3210.9	3369.5	3624.3
Short-term	325.8	341.5	375.2	521.0	575.8	571.2	544.2	549.1	584.0	617.2
Medium- and long-term	1339.6	1412.3	1506.4	1697.4	1876.0	2077.2	2307.6	2458.7	2592.6	2801.3
Securities	34.3	37.1	41.2	53.1	65.9	90.6	134.2	203.2	192.9	205.9
II. Net foreign assets	270.8	255.9	288.4	325.4	334.4	338.1	414.0	287.5	280.6	328.5
Bundesbank	99.8	67.1	45.8	51.8	52.5	114.8	80.4	89.3	104.3	102.7
Credit institutions	171.1	188.8	242.6	273.6	281.9	223.3	333.6	198.2	176.3	225.8
III. Domestic monetary capital holdings	1339.5	1369.6	1482.9	1670.9	1852.8	1988.4	2146.1	2338.1	2561.2	2745.0
Time deposits (more than 4-year notification)[2]	406.2	452.6	491.3	524.9	560.1	564.3	603.1	669.5	726.1	796.6
Public sector	160.2	165.2	169.3	173.7	185.4	173.3	178.7	187.5	192.7	197.3
Private sector	246.1	287.5	322.0	351.1	374.7	391.0	424.4	482.0	533.4	599.3
Saving deposits and certificates	801.5	777.5	835.6	955.7	1080.8	1184.6	1280.9	1382.3	1526.3	1613.5
Share capital and reserves	131.7	139.4	156.0	190.3	211.9	239.5	262.1	286.3	308.8	334.9
IV. Public sector claims on the Bundesbank	4.7	3.5	6.9	19.1	12.7	0.4	13.5	3.0	2.2	6.7
V. Other items, net	-28.4	-40.0	-26.9	-20.9	-31.8	-128.1	-187.6	-158.5	-156.2	-176.9
VI. Money supply M3 (M3 = I + II – III – IV + V)	1112.4	1189.6	1255.6	1503.0	1597.7	1718.7	1906.7	1937.0	2007.4	2181.8
VII. Domestic non-banks' savings deposits[2]	466.8	493.5	479.1	515.4	513.1	522.2	587.4	654.3	749.7	865.8
VIII. Money supply M2 (M2 = VI – VII)	645.6	696.1	776.6	987.6	1 084.5	1 196.5	1 319.2	1 282.7	1 257.7	1 315.9
IX. Time deposits (less than 4-year notification)	260.5	269.1	325.8	403.3	480.5	527.0	592.9	518.6	441.6	399.0
X. Money supply (M1 = VIII – IX)	385.2	427.0	450.7	584.4	604.0	669.6	726.3	764.1	816.1	916.9
Sight deposits	261.1	284.4	303.8	425.8	432.3	469.1	514.3	538.2	578.6	670.1
Currency in circulation	124.1	142.6	146.9	158.6	171.8	200.5	212.0	225.9	237.5	246.8
Memorandum items:										
Central bank money[3]	188.7	207.2	216.6	246.1	266.3	305.0	294.3	280.9	271.9	286.2

1. From July 1990 the time series covesr the entire Deutsche Mark currency area.
2. At three months' notice. Until 1992 savings deposits at statutory notice.
3. Defined as currency in circulation plus minimum reserves on domestic bank liabilities at current reserve ratios. Data reported here are averages of daily figures for December.
Source : Deutsche Bundesbank, *Monatsbericht.*

Tableau J. **Population and employment**[1]

	1987	1988	1989	1990	1991	1992	1993	1994	1995	1996
					Thousands					
Population	61 077	61 449	62 063	63 253	79 984	80 595	81 180	81 423	81 662	::
Working-age population (15-64 years)	42 826	42 960	43 258	43 947	54 743	54 998	55 406	55 341	::	::
Labour force, total	29 386	29 608	29 799	30 369	39 165	38 836	38 634	38 666	38 443	38 386
Self-employed	3 016	3 001	3 011	3 026	3 424	3 485	3 533	3 586	3 622	3 651
Dependent employment, total	24 141	24 365	24 750	25 460	33 139	32 373	31 682	31 382	31 209	30 770
Nationals	22 564	22 755	23 072	23 685	::	::	::	::	::	::
Foreigners	1 577	1 610	1 678	1 775	::	::	::	::	::	::
Employment, total	27 157	27 366	27 761	28 486	36 563	35 858	35 215	34 968	34 831	34 421
					Per cent of civilian employment					
Agriculture, forestry, fishing	4.2	4.0	3.7	3.5	3.9	3.4	3.2	3.1	2.9	2.8
Industry	40.3	39.8	39.8	39.7	39.5	37.9	36.7	35.9	35.5	34.6
Commerce and communications	18.5	18.6	18.6	18.7	18.6	19.0	19.1	19.1	18.8	18.8
Other	37.1	37.6	37.9	38.1	38.0	39.7	41.0	42.0	42.7	43.8
					Thousands					
Unemployment	2 229	2 242	2 038	1 883	2 602	2 979	3 419	3 698	3 612	3 965
Short-time workers	278	208	108	56	1 761	653	948	372	199	277
Vacancies	171	189	251	314	363	356	279	285	321	327
					Per cent of civilian labour force					
Unemployment	7.9	7.7	7.1	6.4	6.7	7.8	8.9	9.6	9.4	10.8
Vacancies	0.6	0.6	0.9	1.1	0.9	0.9	0.7	0.7	0.8	0.9

1. From 1991 all Germany.
Source : Statistisches Bundesamt, Wirtschaft und Statistik and Volkswirtschaftliche Gesamtrechnungen, Fachserie 18 Reihe 1; and OECD, Labour Force Statistics.

Table K. **Wages and prices**

Indices 1991 = 100

	1987	1988	1989	1990	1991	1992	1993	1994	1995	1996
Wages and productivity, whole economy, western Germany										
Monthly contractual pay rates	85.5	87.8	90.2	94.1	100.0	106.3	110.4	112.3	116.5	118.8
Monthly gross wages and salaries										
per employee	85.1	87.6	90.2	94.5	100.0	105.8	108.8	110.9	114.3	116.5
Output per employee	90.4	93.1	95.0	97.6	100.0	100.8	100.4	103.9	106.2	108.7
Unit labour costs	94.1	94.2	94.9	96.8	100.0	105.0	108.4	108.0	109.0	108.8
Wages and productivity, manufacturing, western Germany										
Hourly contractual pay rates, blue collar	83.4	86.4	89.7	93.9	100.0	106.9	112.3	115.3	119.1	124.8
Hourly gross earnings, blue collar	82.8	86.2	89.6	94.3	100.0	105.4	110.7	114.2	118.7	..
Hours worked, blue collar[1]	97.2	97.1	98.7	100.2	100.0	97.5	87.9	84.1	100.0	95.2
Output per man-hour	86.4	90.1	93.4	96.8	100.0	100.8	103.1	111.2	..	..
Unit labour costs[1,2]	92.7	92.4	93.3	95.9	100.0	104.9	108.7	102.1	100.0	99.4
Prices[3]										
Agricultural producer prices, western Germany	97.4	97.6	106.1	100.6	100.0	97.7	90.0	91.9	92.6	91.8
Industrial producer prices	91.9	93.1	96.0	97.6	100.0	101.4	101.6	102.2	104.0	103.5
Costs of dwelling construction	83.1	84.9	88.0	93.7	100.0	106.4	111.7	114.3	117.1	117.0
GDP deflator	89.7	91.1	93.3	96.3	100.0	105.5	109.5	111.9	114.4	115.5
Private consumption deflator	90.0	91.2	93.9	96.4	100.0	104.7	108.9	112.1	114.2	116.4
Consumer prices[3]										
Including food	90.3	91.4	94.0	96.5	100.0	105.1	109.8	112.8	114.8	116.5
Excluding food	89.7	91.1	93.8	96.2	100.0	105.1	109.8	112.8	114.8	116.5
Foreign trade prices[3]										
Exports	94.3	96.3	98.9	99.0	100.0	100.7	100.7	101.6	103.3	103.5
Imports	96.0	97.2	101.5	99.2	100.0	97.6	96.1	96.9	97.3	97.8

1. From 1995 Germany, index 1995 = 100.
2. Including mining and quarrying.
3. From 1991 Germany.
Source: Statistisches Bundesamt.

Tableau L. **Structure of output and performance indicators**

A. Structure of output (constant prices)

	Share of GDP						Share of total employment					
	1991	1992	1993	1994	1995	1996	1991	1992	1993	1994	1995	1996
Agriculture, hunting, forestry and fishing	1.4	1.6	1.6	1.5	1.5	1.6	3.9	3.4	3.2	3.1	2.9	2.8
Energy, water supply, mining	3.2	3.0	2.9	2.8	2.8	2.8	1.9	1.7	1.7	1.6	1.5	1.4
Manufacturing	28.9	27.6	25.8	25.7	25.4	25.1	30.4	28.5	26.9	25.7	25.2	24.8
Construction	5.7	5.9	5.9	6.1	6.0	5.7	7.2	7.7	8.2	8.6	8.7	8.4
Trade, transport, communications	14.6	14.6	14.7	14.5	14.5	14.5	18.6	18.6	18.5	18.3	18.0	17.7
Services	29.3	30.3	31.9	32.4	33.2	34.8	17.9	18.8	19.5	20.3	21.0	21.6
Total traded goods and services	88.9	89.0	88.7	89.0	89.1	89.3	79.9	78.7	77.9	77.5	77.4	76.7
General government non-traded sector	10.6	11.0	11.3	11.0	10.9	10.7	15.9	16.1	16.0	15.8	15.6	15.5

B. Economic performance (constant prices)

	Productivity growth						Share of total investment					
	1991	1992	1993	1994	1995	1996	1991	1992	1993	1994	1995	1996
Agriculture, hunting, forestry and fishing	..	37.7	2.9	0.5	6.9	11.9	2.2	1.9	1.7	1.6	..	..
Energy, water supply, mining	..	6.2	5.8	4.9	5.5	8.8	4.7	5.6	6.0	6.4	6.6	..
Manufacturing	..	6.2	-0.5	8.1	2.9	3.1	20.2	18.7	16.1	14.4	15.4	..
Construction	..	2.1	-5.1	1.1	-0.9	1.2	1.8	2.0	2.1	1.9	1.9	..
Trade, transport, communications	..	1.9	1.0	2.4	3.5	2.6	15.5	15.6	15.6	14.6	..	..
Services	..	0.4	0.2	0.4	1.2	1.9	43.5	43.2	45.1	47.9	..	..
Total traded goods and services	..	4.6	0.7	3.8	2.7	3.4	87.8	87.0	86.6	86.8	..	..
General government non-traded sector	..	2.5	3.3	2.6	2.0	1.4	11.0	11.7	12.1	12.0	11.5	..

C. Others indicators (current prices)

	1987	1988	1989	1990	1991	1992	1993	1994	1995	1996
Total R&D expenditure as % of total GDP	2.90	2.90	2.90	2.75	2.61	2.48	2.43	2.33	2.28	2.26
R&D as % of GDP in business enterprise sector	2.60	2.60	2.60	2.48	2.29	2.16	2.08	1.97	1.92	..
Government-funded R&D as % of total	34.7	34.2	34.1	33.9	35.8	36.0	36.7	37.0	37.1	36.9

Source : Statistisches Bundesamt, *Volkswirtschaftliche Gesamtrechnungen, Fachserie 18 Reihe 1;* OECD, *Main Science and Technology Indicators.*

Tableau M. Labour market indicators

A. Trend

	Peak	Trough	1993	1994	1995	1996
Standardised unemployment rate	1983: 7.7	1980: 3.0	7.9	8.4	8.2	9.0
Unemployment rate[1]						
Total	1985: 9.3	1979: 3.8	9.8	10.6	10.4	11.5
Male	1985: 8.6	1979: 2.9	8.6	9.5	9.6	11.0
Female	1986: 10.6	1980: 5.2	11.3	12.0	11.4	12.1
Youth (15-19 year-old)	1983: 9.1	1980: 3.2	6.5	7.2	7.9	9.0
Share of long-term unemployment[2]	1988: 32.6	1980: 12.9	25.9	32.5	33.3	..
Registered vacancies (thousands)	1991: 331	1983: 76	279	285	321	327
Monthly hours of work, hrs min[3]	1980: 763	1988: 644	631	598	574	540

B. Structural and institutional features

	1989	1990	1991	1992	1993	1994	1995	1996
Labour force (% change)	0.6	1.9	..	-0.8	-0.5	0.1	-0.6	-0.1
Participation rate[4]								
Total	68.9	69.1	71.6	71.7	71.7	71.5	71.0	..
Males	81.4	80.8	81.8	81.4	81.2	80.8	80.3	..
Females	55.9	57.0	61.2	61.6	61.8	61.8	61.3	..
Employment/total population	44.7	45.0	45.7	44.5	43.4	42.9	42.7	..
Employers, self-employed and family workers (as % of total)	10.8	10.6	9.4	9.7	10.0	10.3	10.4	10.6
Wage-earners and salaried employees (as % of total)	89.2	89.4	90.6	90.3	90.0	89.7	89.3	89.3
Civilian employment by sector (% change)								
Agriculture	-4.6	-3.2	..	-14.9	-8.0	-4.3	-3.8	-5.9
Industry	1.2	2.8	..	-5.9	-4.8	-3.0	-1.4	-3.5
Services	2.0	3.5	..	1.9	0.6	1.0	0.5	0.4
of which: General government	0.6	0.7	..	-1.0	-2.3	-1.8	-1.8	-1.5
Total	1.5	3.0	..	-1.8	-1.7	-0.7	-0.3	-1.2
Civilian employment by sector (as % of total)								
Agriculture	3.7	3.5	3.9	3.4	3.2	3.1	2.9	2.8
Industry	39.8	39.7	39.5	37.9	36.7	35.9	35.5	34.6
Services	56.5	56.8	56.6	58.7	60.1	61.1	61.6	62.6
of which: General government	15.4	15.1	15.9	16.1	16.0	15.8	15.6	15.5
Short-time workers[5]	0.8	0.4	4.8	1.8	2.7	1.1	0.6	0.8
Non-wage labour costs[6]	16.5	16.4	17.0	17.0	17.3	18.3	18.5	18.9

1. Total unemployment as a per cent of total dependent employment.
2. People looking for a job one year or more as a percentage of total registered unemployment.
3. Data refer to the total number of hours worked in the month by wage-earners in the mining and manufacturing industries.
4. Labour force as a percentage of population from 15 to 64 years.
5. Short-time workers as percentage of total employment.
6. Employers' social security contributions as a percentage of total wage, from 1991 all Germany.

Source : Statistisches Bundesamt; Bundesanstalt für Arbeit, Amtliche Nachrichten, Jahreszahlen; OECD, National Accounts, Labour Force Statistics and Main Economic Indicators.

Table N. **Public sector**[1]

	1991	1992	1993	1994	1995	1996
Budgetary indicators: general government accounts (% of potential GDP)						
Cyclically adjusted primary current receipts (excluding interest)	45.1	46.2	44.9	45.5	45.0	44.0
Cyclically adjusted primary current disbursements (excluding interest)	42.2	43.0	42.4	42.2	42.4	42.2
Cyclically adjusted primary budget balance	-2.3	-1.7	-0.5	0.6	0.0	0.0
General government budget balance	-4.3	-4.3	-3.0	-2.1	-3.1	-3.1
Structure of expenditure and taxes (% of GDP)						
General government expenditure[1]	48.6	49.2	50.3	49.7	50.3	49.7
Consumption	19.5	20.0	20.1	19.6	19.5	19.6
Subsidies	2.3	2.0	2.0	2.0	2.2	2.2
Investment	2.6	2.8	2.8	2.7	2.5	2.3
General government revenue[2]	45.2	46.4	46.8	47.2	46.7	46.0
Direct taxes	11.5	11.8	11.4	11.0	11.2	10.3
Indirect taxes	12.6	12.7	13.0	13.4	12.9	12.8
Social security contributions	17.9	18.2	18.8	19.2	19.3	19.7
Other indicators[3]						
Income tax as a per cent of total tax	47.7	47.9	46.7	44.9	46.3	44.4
Income tax elasticity[4]	0.7	1.3	-0.1	0.3	1.8	-1.9
Tax rates (%)						
Average effective personal income tax rate	25.0	25.5	24.9	24.8	25.6	23.9
Average rate of employees' social security contribution paid[5]	18.2	18.3	18.3	19.4	..	..
Standard VAT rate	14.0	14.0	15.0	15.0	15.0	15.0

1. Defined as current disbursements plus gross investment plus net capital transfers paid.
2. Defined as tax and non-tax receipts plus consumption of fixed capital.
3. Households. Income tax elasticity is with respect to household disposable income.
4. In 1995 the increase in the tax elasticity is due to the introduction of the solidarity tax surcharge.
5. For an unmarried average production worker, per cent of gross earnings
Source: OECD, *National Accounts* and *The Tax/Benefit position of production workers* ; Deutsche Bundesbank, *Monatsbericht.*

Table O. **Financial markets**[1]

	1970	1975	1980	1985	1990	1993	1994	1995	1996
Structure of financial flows[2]									
Share of intermediated financing in total financing	88.9	73.2	88.6	59.4	57.4	51.5	58.3	84.9	76.4
Financial institutions' share of financial assets	45.2	50.3	44.1	44.3	43.4	47.9	50.5	53.3	54.4
Structure of private non-financial sector's portfolio:									
Deposits	55.4	61.2	44.9	43.6	36.4	56.6	7.2	34.8	42.9
Bonds and bills[3]	12.1	7.4	15.5	17.0	31.7	4.8	49.2	18.5	4.6
Equities	5.1	3.6	3.9	2.8	8.2	2.9	5.6	4.8	3.6
Non-financial corporate financial structure	100.0	100.0	100.0	100.0	100.0	100.0	100.0	100.0	100.0
Own-financing	56.7	67.0	58.1	67.3	60.8	58.0	60.1	66.8	68.7
Debt and equity	43.3	33.0	41.9	32.7	39.2	42.0	39.9	33.2	31.3
Long-term debt	22.9	30.6	19.0	20.5	19.9	42.5	28.9	14.0	14.5
Equity	2.2	3.2	2.3	2.5	4.8	2.4	4.3	4.9	5.9
Short-term debt	18.3	-0.8	20.6	9.7	14.6	-2.9	6.7	14.3	10.9
Internationalisation of markets									
Foreign business of the banking sector[4]									
Assets	6.5	7.1	7.4	8.8	11.8	12.7	11.4	11.6	12.0
Liabilities	4.1	4.0	6.1	5.7	6.5	7.6	8.5	9.2	9.3
International banking networks:									
Foreign banks in Germany[5]	..	..	..	127	177	194	197	198	195
German bank branches abroad (without subsidiaries)	..	44	88	118	177	228	241	255	264
Share of long-term capital transactions:									
Net purchases of domestic bonds by non-residents[6]	..	-6.8	0.5	29.8	8.1	53.6	7.7	37.8	39.7
Net purchases of foreign bonds by residents[6]	6.8	2.8	13.7	26.0	10.0	3.2	9.0	10.6	8.5
Efficiency of markets									
Divergence between Euro rates and domestic interest rates[7]	-0.98	-0.42	-0.42	-0.14	-0.02	-0.04	-0.02	-0.09	-0.07

1. From 1991 all Germany.
2. Credits from domestic and foreign banks as percentage of total funds raised on the credit market by domestic non financial sectors.
3. 1991-1994 including investment certificates.
4. As a percentage of deposit banks' balance sheets.
5. Number of branches and subsidiaries.
6. As a percentage of total purchases.
7. Three-month Euro-DM interest rate minus three-month interbank rate.

Source: Deutsche Bundesbank, *Monatsbericht*, *Monatsberichte* and *Statistisches Beiheft zum Monatsbericht*, *Zahlungsbilanzstatistik*.

BASIC STATISTICS:

INTERNATIONAL COMPARISONS

	Units	Reference period [1]	Australia	Austria
Population				
Total	Thousands	1995	18 054	8 047
Inhabitants per sq. km.	Number	1995	2	96
Net average annual increase over previous 10 years	%	1995	1.4	0.6
Employment				
Total civilian employment (TCE)[2]	Thousands	1994	7 943	3 737
of which: Agriculture	% of TCE	1994	5.1	7.2
Industry	% of TCE	1994	23.5	33.2
Services	% of TCE	1994	71.4	59.6
Gross domestic product (GDP)				
At current prices and current exchange rates	Bill. US$	1995	360.3	233.3
Per capita	US$	1995	19 957	28 997
At current prices using current PPPs[3]	Bill. US$	1995	349.4	167.2
Per capita	US$	1995	19 354	20 773
Average annual volume growth over previous 5 years	%	1995	3.3	2
Gross fixed capital formation (GFCF)	% of GDP	1995	20.1	24.7
of which: Machinery and equipment	% of GDP	1995	10.5 (94)	9 (94)
Residential construction	% of GDP	1995	5.6 (94)	6.4 (94)
Average annual volume growth over previous 5 years	%	1995	3	3
Gross saving ratio[4]	% of GDP	1995	16.9	24.9
General government				
Current expenditure on goods and services	% of GDP	1995	17.2	18.9
Current disbursements[5]	% of GDP	1994	36.2	47.8
Current receipts	% of GDP	1994	34.2	47.3
Net official development assistance	% of GNP	1994	0.33	0.33
Indicators of living standards				
Private consumption per capita using current PPPs[3]	US$	1995	12 090	11 477
Passenger cars, per 1 000 inhabitants	Number	1993	438	418
Telephones, per 1 000 inhabitants	Number	1993	482	451
Television sets, per 1 000 inhabitants	Number	1992	482	480
Doctors, per 1 000 inhabitants	Number	1994	2.2 (91)	2.4
Infant mortality per 1 000 live births	Number	1994	5.9	6.3
Wages and prices (average annual increase over previous 5 years)				
Wages (earnings or rates according to availability)	%	1995	2	5
Consumer prices	%	1995	2.5	3.2
Foreign trade				
Exports of goods, fob*	Mill. US$	1995	53 092	57 200
As % of GDP	%	1995	14.7	24.5
Average annual increase over previous 5 years	%	1995	6	6.9
Imports of goods, cif*	Mill. US$	1995	57 406	65 293
As % of GDP	%	1995	15.9	28
Average annual increase over previous 5 years	%	1995	8.1	5.9
Total official reserves[6]	Mill. SDRs	1995	8 003	12 600
As ratio of average monthly imports of goods	Ratio	1995	1.7	2.3

* At current prices and exchange rates.
1. Unless otherwise stated.
2. According to the definitions used in OECD *Labour Force Statistics.*
3. PPPs = Purchasing Power Parities.
4. Gross saving = Gross national disposable income minus private and government consumption.
5. Current disbursements = Current expenditure on goods and services plus current transfers and payments of property income.
6. Gold included in reserves is valued at 35 SDRs per ounce. End of year.

EMPLOYMENT OPPORTUNITIES

Economics Department, OECD

The Economics Department of the OECD offers challenging and rewarding opportunities to economists interested in applied policy analysis in an international environment. The Department's concerns extend across the entire field of economic policy analysis, both macro-economic and microeconomic. Its main task is to provide, for discussion by committees of senior officials from Member countries, documents and papers dealing with current policy concerns. Within this programme of work, three major responsibilities are:

- to prepare regular surveys of the economies of individual Member countries;
- to issue full twice-yearly reviews of the economic situation and prospects of the OECD countries in the context of world economic trends;
- to analyse specific policy issues in a medium-term context for the OECD as a whole, and to a lesser extent for the non-OECD countries.

The documents prepared for these purposes, together with much of the Department's other economic work, appear in published form in the *OECD Economic Outlook, OECD Economic Surveys, OECD Economic Studies* and the Department's *Working Papers* series.

The Department maintains a world econometric model, INTERLINK, which plays an important role in the preparation of the policy analyses and twice-yearly projections. The availability of extensive cross-country data bases and good computer resources facilitates comparative empirical analysis, much of which is incorporated into the model.

The Department is made up of about 80 professional economists from a variety of backgrounds and Member countries. Most projects are carried out by small teams and last from four to eighteen months. Within the Department, ideas and points of view are widely discussed; there is a lively professional interchange, and all professional staff have the opportunity to contribute actively to the programme of work.

Skills the Economics Department is looking for:

a) Solid competence in using the tools of both microeconomic and macroeconomic theory to answer policy questions. Experience indicates that this normally requires the equivalent of a Ph.D. in economics or substantial relevant professional experience to compensate for a lower degree.

b) Solid knowledge of economic statistics and quantitative methods; this includes how to identify data, estimate structural relationships, apply basic techniques of time series analysis, and test hypotheses. It is essential to be able to interpret results sensibly in an economic policy context.

c) A keen interest in and extensive knowledge of policy issues, economic developments and their political/social contexts.

d) Interest and experience in analysing questions posed by policy-makers and presenting the results to them effectively and judiciously. Thus, work experience in government agencies or policy research institutions is an advantage.

e) The ability to write clearly, effectively, and to the point. The OECD is a bilingual organisation with French and English as the official languages. Candidates must have excellent knowledge of one of these languages, and some knowledge of the other. Knowledge of other languages might also be an advantage for certain posts.

f) For some posts, expertise in a particular area may be important, but a successful candidate is expected to be able to work on a broader range of topics relevant to the work of the Department. Thus, except in rare cases, the Department does not recruit narrow specialists.

g) The Department works on a tight time schedule with strict deadlines. Moreover, much of the work in the Department is carried out in small groups. Thus, the ability to work with other economists from a variety of cultural and professional backgrounds, to supervise junior staff, and to produce work on time is important.

General information

The salary for recruits depends on educational and professional background. Positions carry a basic salary from FF 305 700 or FF 377 208 for Administrators (economists) and from FF 438 348 for Principal Administrators (senior economists). This may be supplemented by expatriation and/or family allowances, depending on nationality, residence and family situation. Initial appointments are for a fixed term of two to three years.

Vacancies are open to candidates from OECD Member countries. The Organisation seeks to maintain an appropriate balance between female and male staff and among nationals from Member countries.

For further information on employment opportunities in the Economics Department, contact:

Administrative Unit
Economics Department
OECD
2, rue André-Pascal
75775 PARIS CEDEX 16
FRANCE

E-Mail: compte.esadmin@oecd.org

Applications citing ''ECSUR'', together with a detailed *curriculum vitae* in English or French, should be sent to the Head of Personnel at the above address.

MAIN SALES OUTLETS OF OECD PUBLICATIONS
PRINCIPAUX POINTS DE VENTE DES PUBLICATIONS DE L'OCDE

AUSTRALIA – AUSTRALIE
D.A. Information Services
648 Whitehorse Road, P.O.B 163
Mitcham, Victoria 3132   Tel. (03) 9210.7777
                         Fax: (03) 9210.7788

AUSTRIA – AUTRICHE
Gerold & Co.
Graben 31
Wien I   Tel. (0222) 533.50.14
                    Fax: (0222) 512.47.31.29

BELGIUM – BELGIQUE
Jean De Lannoy
Avenue du Roi, Koningslaan 202
B-1060 Bruxelles Tel. (02) 538.51.69/538.08.41
                         Fax: (02) 538.08.41

CANADA
Renouf Publishing Company Ltd.
5369 Canotek Road
Unit 1
Ottawa, Ont. K1J 9J3   Tel. (613) 745.2665
                         Fax: (613) 745.7660
Stores:
71 1/2 Sparks Street
Ottawa, Ont. K1P 5R1   Tel. (613) 238.8985
                         Fax: (613) 238.6041

12 Adelaide Street West
Toronto, QN M5H 1L6   Tel. (416) 363.3171
                         Fax: (416) 363.5963

Les Éditions La Liberté Inc.
3020 Chemin Sainte-Foy
Sainte-Foy, PQ G1X 3V6 Tel. (418) 658.3763
                         Fax: (418) 658.3763

Federal Publications Inc.
165 University Avenue, Suite 701
Toronto, ON M5H 3B8   Tel. (416) 860.1611
                         Fax: (416) 860.1608

Les Publications Fédérales
1185 Université
Montréal, QC H3B 3A7 Tel. (514) 954.1633
                         Fax: (514) 954.1635

CHINA – CHINE
Book Dept., China National Publications
Import and Export Corporation (CNPIEC)
16 Gongti E. Road, Chaoyang District
Beijing 100020   Tel. (10) 6506-6688 Ext. 8402
                             (10) 6506-3101

CHINESE TAIPEI – TAIPEI CHINOIS
Good Faith Worldwide Int'l. Co. Ltd.
9th Floor, No. 118, Sec. 2
Chung Hsiao E. Road
Taipei   Tel. (02) 391.7396/391.7397
                         Fax: (02) 394.9176

**CZECH REPUBLIC –
RÉPUBLIQUE TCHÈQUE**
National Information Centre
NIS – prodejna
Konviktská 5
Praha 1 – 113 57   Tel. (02) 24.23.09.07
                    Fax: (02) 24.22.94.33
E-mail: nkposp@dec.niz.cz
Internet: http://www.nis.cz

DENMARK – DANEMARK
Munksgaard Book and Subscription Service
35, Nørre Søgade, P.O. Box 2148
DK-1016 København K   Tel. (33) 12.85.70
                         Fax: (33) 12.93.87

J. H. Schultz Information A/S,
Herstedvang 12,
DK – 2620 Albertslung   Tel. 43 63 23 00
                         Fax: 43 63 19 69
Internet: s-info@inet.uni-c.dk

EGYPT – ÉGYPTE
The Middle East Observer
41 Sherif Street
Cairo   Tel. (2) 392.6919
                         Fax: (2) 360.6804

FINLAND – FINLANDE
Akateeminen Kirjakauppa
Keskuskatu 1, P.O. Box 128
00100 Helsinki

Subscription Services/Agence d'abonnements :
P.O. Box 23
00100 Helsinki   Tel. (358) 9.121.4403
                         Fax: (358) 9.121.4450

*FRANCE
OECD/OCDE
Mail Orders/Commandes par correspondance :
2, rue André-Pascal
75775 Paris Cedex 16 Tel. 33 (0)1.45.24.82.00
                    Fax: 33 (0)1.49.10.42.76
                    Telex: 640048 OCDE
Internet: Compte.PUBSINQ@oecd.org

Orders via Minitel, France only/
Commandes par Minitel, France
exclusivement : 36 15 OCDE

OECD Bookshop/Librairie de l'OCDE :
33, rue Octave-Feuillet
75016 Paris   Tel. 33 (0)1.45.24.81.81
                         33 (0)1.45.24.81.67

Dawson
B.P. 40
91121 Palaiseau Cedex   Tel. 01.89.10.47.00
                         Fax: 01.64.54.83.26

Documentation Française
29, quai Voltaire
75007 Paris   Tel. 01.40.15.70.00

Economica
49, rue Héricart
75015 Paris   Tel. 01.45.78.12.92
                         Fax: 01.45.75.05.67

Gibert Jeune (Droit-Économie)
6, place Saint-Michel
75006 Paris   Tel. 01.43.25.91.19

Librairie du Commerce International
10, avenue d'Iéna
75016 Paris   Tel. 01.40.73.34.60

Librairie Dunod
Université Paris-Dauphine
Place du Maréchal-de-Lattre-de-Tassigny
75016 Paris   Tel. 01.44.05.40.13

Librairie Lavoisier
11, rue Lavoisier
75008 Paris   Tel. 01.42.65.39.95

Librairie des Sciences Politiques
30, rue Saint-Guillaume
75007 Paris   Tel. 01.45.48.36.02

P.U.F.
49, boulevard Saint-Michel
75005 Paris   Tel. 01.43.25.83.40

Librairie de l'Université
12a, rue Nazareth
13100 Aix-en-Provence   Tel. 04.42.26.18.08

Documentation Française
165, rue Garibaldi
69003 Lyon   Tel. 04.78.63.32.23

Librairie Decitre
29, place Bellecour
69002 Lyon   Tel. 04.72.40.54.54

Librairie Sauramps
Le Triangle
34967 Montpellier Cedex 2 Tel. 04.67.58.85.15
                         Fax: 04.67.58.27.36

A la Sorbonne Actual
23, rue de l'Hôtel-des-Postes
06000 Nice   Tel. 04.93.13.77.75
                         Fax: 04.93.80.75.69

GERMANY – ALLEMAGNE
OECD Bonn Centre
August-Bebel-Allee 6
D-53175 Bonn   Tel. (0228) 959.120
                         Fax: (0228) 959.12.17

GREECE – GRÈCE
Librairie Kauffmann
Stadiou 28
10564 Athens   Tel. (01) 32.55.321
                         Fax: (01) 32.30.320

HONG-KONG
Swindon Book Co. Ltd.
Astoria Bldg. 3F
34 Ashley Road, Tsimshatsui
Kowloon, Hong Kong   Tel. 2376.2062
                         Fax: 2376.0685

HUNGARY – HONGRIE
Euro Info Service
Margitsziget, Európa Ház
1138 Budapest   Tel. (1) 111.60.61
                         Fax: (1) 302.50.35
E-mail: euroinfo@mail.matav.hu
Internet: http://www.euroinfo.hu//index.html

ICELAND – ISLANDE
Mál og Menning
Laugavegi 18, Pósthólf 392
121 Reykjavik   Tel. (1) 552.4240
                         Fax: (1) 562.3523

INDIA – INDE
Oxford Book and Stationery Co.
Scindia House
New Delhi 110001   Tel. (11) 331.5896/5308
                         Fax: (11) 332.2639
E-mail: oxford.publ@axcess.net.in

17 Park Street
Calcutta 700016   Tel. 240832

INDONESIA – INDONÉSIE
Pdii-Lipi
P.O. Box 4298
Jakarta 12042   Tel. (21) 573.34.67
                         Fax: (21) 573.34.67

IRELAND – IRLANDE
Government Supplies Agency
Publications Section
4/5 Harcourt Road
Dublin 2   Tel. 661.31.11
                         Fax: 475.27.60

ISRAEL – ISRAËL
Praedicta
5 Shatner Street
P.O. Box 34030
Jerusalem 91430   Tel. (2) 652.84.90/1/2
                         Fax: (2) 652.84.93

R.O.Y. International
P.O. Box 13056
Tel Aviv 61130   Tel. (3) 546 1423
                         Fax: (3) 546 1442
E-mail: royil@netvision.net.il

Palestinian Authority/Middle East:
INDEX Information Services
P.O.B. 19502
Jerusalem   Tel. (2) 627.16.34
                         Fax: (2) 627.12.19

ITALY – ITALIE
Libreria Commissionaria Sansoni
Via Duca di Calabria, 1/1
50125 Firenze   Tel. (055) 64.54.15
                         Fax: (055) 64.12.57
E-mail: licosa@ftbcc.it

Via Bartolini 29
20155 Milano   Tel. (02) 36.50.83

Editrice e Libreria Herder
Piazza Montecitorio 120
00186 Roma   Tel. 679.46.28
                         Fax: 678.47.51

Libreria Hoepli
Via Hoepli 5
20121 Milano   Tel. (02) 86.54.46
                           Fax: (02) 805.28.86

Libreria Scientifica
Dott. Lucio de Biasio 'Aeiou'
Via Coronelli, 6
20146 Milano   Tel. (02) 48.95.45.52
                           Fax: (02) 48.95.45.48

JAPAN – JAPON
OECD Tokyo Centre
Landic Akasaka Building
2-3-4 Akasaka, Minato-ku
Tokyo 107   Tel. (81.3) 3586.2016
                           Fax: (81.3) 3584.7929

KOREA – CORÉE
Kyobo Book Centre Co. Ltd.
P.O. Box 1658, Kwang Hwa Moon
Seoul   Tel. 730.78.91
                           Fax: 735.00.30

MALAYSIA – MALAISIE
University of Malaya Bookshop
University of Malaya
P.O. Box 1127, Jalan Pantai Baru
59700 Kuala Lumpur
Malaysia   Tel. 756.5000/756.5425
                           Fax: 756.3246

MEXICO – MEXIQUE
OECD Mexico Centre
Edificio INFOTEC
Av. San Fernando no. 37
Col. Toriello Guerra
Tlalpan C.P. 14050
Mexico D.F.   Tel. (525) 528.10.38
                           Fax: (525) 606.13.07
E-mail: ocde@rtn.net.mx

NETHERLANDS – PAYS-BAS
SDU Uitgeverij Plantijnstraat
Externe Fondsen
Postbus 20014
2500 EA's-Gravenhage   Tel. (070) 37.89.880
Voor bestellingen: Fax: (070) 34.75.778

Subscription Agency/Agence d'abonnements :
SWETS & ZEITLINGER BV
Heereweg 347B
P.O. Box 830
2160 SZ Lisse   Tel. 252.435.111
                           Fax: 252.415.888

**NEW ZEALAND –
NOUVELLE-ZÉLANDE**
GPLegislation Services
P.O. Box 12418
Thorndon, Wellington   Tel. (04) 496.5655
                           Fax: (04) 496.5698

NORWAY – NORVÈGE
NIC INFO A/S
Ostensjoveien 18
P.O. Box 6512 Etterstad
0606 Oslo   Tel. (22) 97.45.00
                           Fax: (22) 97.45.45

PAKISTAN
Mirza Book Agency
65 Shahrah Quaid-E-Azam
Lahore 54000   Tel. (42) 735.36.01
                           Fax: (42) 576.37.14

PHILIPPINE – PHILIPPINES
International Booksource Center Inc.
Rm 179/920 Cityland 10 Condo Tower 2
HV dela Costa Ext cor Valero St.
Makati Metro Manila   Tel. (632) 817 9676
                      Fax: (632) 817 1741

POLAND – POLOGNE
Ars Polona
00-950 Warszawa
Krakowskie Prezdmiescie 7 Tel. (22) 264760
                           Fax: (22) 265334

PORTUGAL
Livraria Portugal
Rua do Carmo 70-74
Apart. 2681
1200 Lisboa   Tel. (01) 347.49.82/5
                           Fax: (01) 347.02.64

SINGAPORE – SINGAPOUR
Ashgate Publishing
Asia Pacific Pte. Ltd
Golden Wheel Building, 04-03
41, Kallang Pudding Road
Singapore 349316   Tel. 741.5166
                           Fax: 742.9356

SPAIN – ESPAGNE
Mundi-Prensa Libros S.A.
Castelló 37, Apartado 1223
Madrid 28001   Tel. (91) 431.33.99
                           Fax: (91) 575.39.98
E-mail: mundiprensa@tsai.es
Internet: http://www.mundiprensa.es

Mundi-Prensa Barcelona
Consell de Cent No. 391
08009 – Barcelona   Tel. (93) 488.34.92
                           Fax: (93) 487.76.59

Libreria de la Generalitat
Palau Moja
Rambla dels Estudis, 118
08002 – Barcelona
                (Suscripciones) Tel. (93) 318.80.12
                (Publicaciones) Tel. (93) 302.67.23
                           Fax: (93) 412.18.54

SRI LANKA
Centre for Policy Research
c/o Colombo Agencies Ltd.
No. 300-304, Galle Road
Colombo 3   Tel. (1) 574240, 573551-2
                  Fax: (1) 575394, 510711

SWEDEN – SUÈDE
CE Fritzes AB
S–106 47 Stockholm   Tel. (08) 690.90.90
                           Fax: (08) 20.50.21

For electronic publications only/
Publications électroniques seulement
STATISTICS SWEDEN
Informationsservice
S-115 81 Stockholm   Tel. 8 783 5066
                           Fax: 8 783 4045

Subscription Agency/Agence d'abonnements :
Wennergren-Williams Info AB
P.O. Box 1305
171 25 Solna   Tel. (08) 705.97.50
                           Fax: (08) 27.00.71

Liber distribution
Internatinal organizations
Fagerstagatan 21
S-163 52 Spanga

SWITZERLAND – SUISSE
Maditec S.A. (Books and Periodicals/Livres
et périodiques)
Chemin des Palettes 4
Case postale 266
1020 Renens VD 1   Tel. (021) 635.08.65
                           Fax: (021) 635.07.80

Librairie Payot S.A.
4, place Pépinet
CP 3212
1002 Lausanne   Tel. (021) 320.25.11
                           Fax: (021) 320.25.14

Librairie Unilivres
6, rue de Candolle
1205 Genève   Tel. (022) 320.26.23
                           Fax: (022) 329.73.18

Subscription Agency/Agence d'abonnements :
Dynapresse Marketing S.A.
38, avenue Vibert
1227 Carouge   Tel. (022) 308.08.70
                           Fax: (022) 308.07.99

See also – Voir aussi :
OECD Bonn Centre
August-Bebel-Allee 6
D-53175 Bonn (Germany) Tel. (0228) 959.120
                       Fax: (0228) 959.12.17

THAILAND – THAÏLANDE
Suksit Siam Co. Ltd.
113, 115 Fuang Nakhon Rd.
Opp. Wat Rajbopith
Bangkok 10200   Tel. (662) 225.9531/2
                           Fax: (662) 222.5188

**TRINIDAD & TOBAGO, CARIBBEAN
TRINITÉ-ET-TOBAGO, CARAÏBES**
Systematics Studies Limited
9 Watts Street
Curepe
Trinidad & Tobago, W.I. Tel. (1809) 645.3475
                        Fax: (1809) 662.5654
E-mail: tobe@trinidad.net

TUNISIA – TUNISIE
Grande Librairie Spécialisée
Fendri Ali
Avenue Haffouz Imm El-Intilaka
Bloc B 1 Sfax 3000   Tel. (216-4) 296 855
                           Fax: (216-4) 298.270

TURKEY – TURQUIE
Kültür Yayinlari Is-Türk Ltd.
Atatürk Bulvari No. 191/Kat 13
06684 Kavaklidere/Ankara
                        Tel. (312) 428.11.40 Ext. 2458
                        Fax : (312) 417.24.90

Dolmabahce Cad. No. 29
Besiktas/Istanbul   Tel. (212) 260 7188

UNITED KINGDOM – ROYAUME-UNI
The Stationery Office Ltd.
Postal orders only:
P.O. Box 276, London SW8 5DT
Gen. enquiries   Tel. (171) 873 0011
                           Fax: (171) 873 8463

The Stationery Office Ltd.
Postal orders only:
49 High Holborn, London WC1V 6HB
Branches at: Belfast, Birmingham, Bristol,
Edinburgh, Manchester

UNITED STATES – ÉTATS-UNIS
OECD Washington Center
2001 L Street N.W., Suite 650
Washington, D.C. 20036-4922
                           Tel. (202) 785.6323
                           Fax: (202) 785.0350
Internet: washcont@oecd.org

Subscriptions to OECD periodicals may also
be placed through main subscription agencies.

Les abonnements aux publications périodiques
de l'OCDE peuvent être souscrits auprès des
principales agences d'abonnement.

Orders and inquiries from countries where Dis-
tributors have not yet been appointed should be
sent to: OECD Publications, 2, rue André-Pascal, 75775 Paris Cedex 16, France.

Les commandes provenant de pays où l'OCDE
n'a pas encore désigné de distributeur peuvent
être adressées aux Éditions de l'OCDE, 2, rue
André-Pascal, 75775 Paris Cedex 16, France.

12-1996

OECD PUBLICATIONS, 2, rue André-Pascal, 75775 PARIS CEDEX 16
PRINTED IN FRANCE
(10 97 15 1 P) ISBN 92-64-15433-7 – No. 49369 1997
ISSN 0376-6438